W9-ACN-468

THE NEW
CORPORATE GOVERNANCE
IN THEORY AND PRACTICE

THE NEW
CORPORATE GOVERNANCE
IN THEORY AND PRACTICE

Stephen M. Bainbridge

OXFORD
UNIVERSITY PRESS

OXFORD
UNIVERSITY PRESS

Oxford University Press, Inc., publishes works that further Oxford University's objective of excellence in research, scholarship, and education.

Oxford New York
Auckland Cape Town Dar es Salaam Hong Kong Karachi Kuala Lumpur Madrid Melbourne
Mexico City Nairobi New Delhi Shanghai Taipei Toronto

With offices in
Argentina Austria Brazil Chile Czech Republic France Greece Guatemala Hungary Italy
Japan Poland Portugal Singapore South Korea Switzerland Thailand Turkey Ukraine
Vietnam

Copyright © 2008 by Oxford University Press, Inc.

Published by Oxford University Press, Inc.,
198 Madison Avenue, New York, New York 10016

Oxford is a registered trademark of Oxford University Press
Oxford University Press is a registered trademark of Oxford University Press, Inc.

Library of Congress Cataloging-in-Publication Data

Bainbridge, Stephen M.
   The new corporate governance in theory and practice/Stephen Bainbridge
   p. cm.
        Includes bibliographical references and index.
        ISBN 978-0-19-533750-1 (alk. paper)
1. Corporate governance—Law and legislation—United States.
2. Corporate governance—United States. I. Title.
   KF1422.B35 2008
   346. 73'0664—dc22

                                                                        2008010853

1 2 3 4 5 6 7 8 9

Printed in the United States of America on acid-free paper

Note to Readers
This publication is designed to provide accurate and authoritative information in regard to the subject matter covered. It is based upon sources believed to be accurate and reliable and is intended to be current as of the time it was written. It is sold with the understanding that the publisher is not engaged in rendering legal, accounting, or other professional services. If legal advice or other expert assistance is required, the services of a competent professional person should be sought. Also, to confirm that the information has not been affected or changed by recent developments, traditional legal research techniques should be used, including checking primary sources where appropriate.

*(Based on the Declaration of Principles jointly adopted by a Committee of the
American Bar Association and a Committee of Publishers and Associations.)*

> You may order this or any other Oxford University Press publication by
> visiting the Oxford University Press website at www.oup.com

CONTENTS

PREFACE

L egal scholarship tends to be critical of the status quo. Few self-respecting legal academics will end an article or book without some sort of reform proposal. This is perfectly understandable, of course. Academic rewards skew towards the new and novel. Mea culpa. A rather different concern, however, motivated the body of work that culminated in this book;[1] namely, to understand the existing statutory framework of corporate governance in U.S. law.

"The business and affairs of every corporation organized under this chapter shall be managed by or under the direction of a board of directors, except as may be otherwise provided in this chapter or in its certificate of incorporation," commands § 141(a) of the Delaware General Corporation Law. The drafters of the Model Business Corporation Act tell us that the corporation code of every state but one (Missouri, whose code is oddly silent) have some such formulation.[2] I call this the director primacy model of corporate governance.

Why is director primacy almost universally enshrined in corporate statutes? Why not shareholder primacy, in which management power is

---

[1] *See* Stephen M. Bainbridge, *Unocal at 20: Director Primacy in Corporate Takeovers*, 31 Del. J. Corp. L. 769 (2006); Stephen M. Bainbridge, *Director Primacy and Shareholder Disempowerment*, 119 Harv. L. Rev. 1735 (2006); Stephen M. Bainbridge, *The Case for Limited Shareholder Voting Rights*, 53 UCLA L. Rev. 601 (2006); Stephen M. Bainbridge, *The Business Judgment Rule as Abstention Doctrine*, 57 Vand. L. Rev. 83 (2004); Stephen M. Bainbridge, *Director Primacy: The Means and Ends of Corporate Governance*, 97 Nw. U. L. Rev. 547 (2003); Stephen M. Bainbridge, *The Board of Directors as Nexus of Contracts*, 88 Iowa L. Rev. 1 (2002); Stephen M. Bainbridge, *Director Primacy in Corporate Takeovers: Preliminary Reflections*, 55 Stan. L. Rev. 791 (2002); Stephen M. Bainbridge, *Director v. Shareholder Primacy in the Convergence Debate*, 16 Transnat'l Lawyer 45 (2002); Stephen M. Bainbridge, *Why a Board? Group Decision Making in Corporate Governance*, 55 Vand. L. Rev. 1 (2002).

[2] Model Bus. Corp. Act. Ann. § 8.11 stat. comp.

vested in the shareholders, who own the corporation? (Later we'll question the relevance of ownership in this context, but for now we follow conventional wisdom.) Alternatively, why not managerialism, in which management authority is vested in the Chief Executive Officer (CEO) or an executive committee of top management?

I set out not to reform the statutory allocation of power, but simply to understand it. My premise is that corporate law tends towards efficiency. A state generates revenue from franchise and other taxes imposed on firms that incorporate in the state. The more firms that choose to incorporate in a given state, the more revenue the state generates. Delaware, the runaway winner in this competition, generates so much revenue from incorporations that its resident taxpayers reportedly save thousands of dollars a year.

In order to attract capital, managers must offer investors attractive terms. Among those terms are the corporate governance rules imposed on investors by the law of the state of incorporation. Accordingly, managers have an incentive to incorporate in states offering terms preferred by investors. In turn, states have an incentive to attract incorporations by offering such terms. State competition for charters therefore results in a race to the top, driving corporate law towards efficient outcomes.

The foregoing claims are strongly contested in the literature, of course, and even those of us who generally accept the race to the top argument acknowledge the need for caveats and amendments when the question is examined in detail. We'll look at the relevant arguments and evidence in more detail below. For present purposes, however, I ask the reader simply to assume for the sake of argument that the race to the top is generally valid. If so, we need an account of why states "raced" to a governance structure topped by a board of directors.

The public corporation is a large, complex, and geographically dispersed entity with multiple stakeholders. Participatory democracy would be untenable in such an organization. We're dealing with vast numbers of people with radically asymmetric information and fundamentally competing interests. Under such conditions, collective action problems will prove intractable, even if the mechanics of allowing thousands of stakeholders to meaningfully participate in decision making could be solved.

Instead, it will be more efficient for decision-making authority to be assigned to some central person or group. This explains why corporate decision making is representative rather than participatory, relying on fiat rather than consensus. Hence, for example, the account to this point explains why shareholders have exceedingly limited control rights in the public corporation. (As for why other constituencies are entirely excluded from *de jure* control rights: we will take up that question in detail below.)

But why a board of directors rather than an individual autocrat? In Chapter 2, we'll see that groups tend to outperform individuals at tasks entailing the exercise of critical evaluative judgment, which is precisely the job of the top decision maker in any complex organization. Equally, if not more important, however, assigning decision-making authority to a group proves a useful adaptive response to the principal-agent problem inherent in the corporate separation of ownership and control. Director primacy is thus essential to the functioning of the modern public corporation.

My prior work in this area convinced a growing number of scholars and commentators that "corporate governance is best characterized as based on 'director primacy.'"[3] Likewise, other commentators opine that

- "Although theorists have long debated how to best describe the public company, a new theory of the firm has emerged that appears more complete than its predecessors: Professor Stephen M. Bainbridge's model of director primacy."[4]
- "Bainbridge has developed a coherent and comprehensive theory of Director Primacy. Simply put, 'Bainbridge-style' Director Primacy places the board of directors at the center of the firm. It is both a normative and predictive theory: Directors should manage and

---

[3] Larry Ribstein, *Why Corporations?*, 1 Berkeley Bus. L.J. 183, 196 (2004).

[4] Seth W. Ashby, *Strengthening the Public Company Board of Directors: Limited Shareholder Access to the Corporate Ballot vs. Required Majority Board Independence*, 2005 U. Ill. L. Rev. 521, 533 (2005). *See also, e.g.,* Iman Anabtawi, *Some Skepticism About Increasing Shareholder Power*, 53 UCLA L. Rev. 561, 562 (2006) ("In Stephen Bainbridge's director-primacy theory, for example, the board of directors is a mechanism for solving the organizational design problem that arises when one views the firm as a nexus of contracts among various factors of production, each with differing interests and information."); Douglas G. Baird & Robert K. Rasmussen, *Private Debt and the Missing Lever of Corporate Governance*, 154 U. Pa. L. Rev. 1209, 1213 n.8 (2006) ("Stephen Bainbridge has put forth a normative conception of the corporation suggesting that nearly absolute authority is and should be vested in a corporation's board of directors."); James McConvill & Mirko Bagaric, *Towards Mandatory Shareholder Committees in Australian Companies*, 28 Melb. U. L. Rev. 125, 128 n.15 (2004) ("The concept of 'director primacy' was recently developed by Professor Stephen Bainbridge, of the University of California Law School.").

control the corporation; directors do manage and control the corporation."[5]

- "For the most part, director primacy is descriptively accurate and offers a compelling normative justification for why the board, and not the shareholders or the courts, should be the institution that decides what a corporation does."[6]

- "Although 'Delaware has not explicitly embraced director primacy,' the relevant statutory provisions and the [cases] have largely intimated that directors retain authority and need not passively allow either exogenous events or shareholder action to determine corporate decision-making."[7]

- "Delaware jurisprudence favors director primacy in terms of the definitive decisionmaking power, while simultaneously requiring directors to be ultimately concerned with the shareholders' interest. . . . [T]he Delaware jurisprudence, while not explicitly affirming 'director primacy,' does implicitly leave the directors to make decisions with shareholders expressing their views only in specific and limited situations."[8]

To be sure, director primacy has its critics. Some see it as normatively unattractive, while others see it as lacking descriptive power. This book is intended in large part to answer these critics, while also restating, revising, and expanding the director primacy model.

[5] Charles R.T. O'Kelley, *The Entrepreneur and the Theory of the Modern Corporation*, 31 J. Corp. L. 753, 774 (2006).

[6] Wayne O. Hanewicz, *Director Primacy, Omnicare, and the Function of Corporate Law*, 71 Tenn. L. Rev. 511, 514 (2004).

[7] Harry G. Hutchison, *Director Primacy and Corporate Governance: Shareholder Voting Rights Captured by the Accountability/Authority Paradigm*, 36 Loy. U. Chi. L.J. 1111, 1194 (2005).

[8] Kevin L. Turner, *Settling the Debate: A Response to Professor Bebchuk's Proposed Reform of Hostile Takeover Defenses*, 57 Ala. L. Rev. 907, 927–28 (2006).

ACKNOWLEDGEMENTS

I was lucky enough to learn corporate law from University of Virginia law professor Michael Dooley. His passion for the subject, his skill at teaching, and intellectual prowess inspired me to set aside plans for a career in patent law in favor of becoming a corporate law academic. Later, Dooley's brilliant article, *Two Models of Corporate Governance*,[9] provided the intellectual framework on which I constructed the theory of director primacy presented herein. (Mike, of course, is not to be blamed for any misuses to which I have put his work here or elsewhere.) I owe him a debt of gratitude that I hope this acknowledgement in some small sense begins to repay.

A number of friends in the corporate law academy provided extensive comments on the proposal for this manuscript—which proved invaluable in outlining and writing the text—including: Iman Anabtawi, Bill Klein, Larry Mitchell, Larry Ribstein, Gordon Smith, and an anonymous reviewer.

[9] Michael P. Dooley, *Two Models of Corporate Governance*, 47 Bus. Law. 461 (1992).

Introduction

Forty years ago, managerialism dominated corporate governance in the United States. In both theory and practice, a team of senior managers ran the corporation with little or no interference from other stakeholders. Shareholders were essentially powerless and typically quiescent. Boards of directors were little more than rubber stamps.

Today, American corporate governance looks very different. The Imperial CEO is a declining breed. Some classes of shareholders have become quite restive, indeed. Most important for our purposes, boards are increasingly active in monitoring top management rather than serving as mere pawns of the CEO.

Several important trends coalesced in recent decades to encourage more active and effective board oversight. Much director compensation now comes as stock rather than cash, which helps to align director and shareholder interests.[1] Courts have made clear that effective board processes and oversight are essential if board decisions are to receive the deference traditionally accorded to them under the business judgment rule, especially insofar as structural decisions are concerned (such as those relating to corporate takeovers).[2] Director conduct is further constrained, some say, by activist shareholders.[3] The Sarbanes-Oxley Act mandated enhanced director independence from management, as did changes in stock exchange listing standards.

---

[1] Charles M. Elson, *Director Compensation and the Management-Captured Board—The History of a Symptom and a Cure*, 50 SMU L. Rev. 127, 130–31 (1996).
[2] *See, e.g.*, Smith v. Van Gorkom, 488 A.2d 858 (Del. 1985).
[3] Daniel P. Forbes & Frances J. Milliken, *Cognition and Corporate Governance: Understanding Boards of Directors as Strategic Decision-Making Groups*, 24 Acad. Mgmt. Rev. 489 (1999).

Today, as a result of these forces, boards of directors typically are smaller than their antecedents, meet more often, are more independent from management, own more stock, and have better access to information. As *The Economist* reported in 2003, "boards are undoubtedly becoming less deferential. . . . Boards have also become smaller and more hard-working. . . . Probably the most important change, though, is the growing tendency for boards to meet in what Americans confusingly call 'executive session,' which excludes the CEO and all other executives."[4] In sum, boards are becoming change agents rather than rubber stamps.

In this book, I offer an interdisciplinary analysis of the emerging board-centered system of corporate governance. I draw on doctrinal legal analysis, behavioral economic insights into how individuals and groups make decisions, the work of new institutional economics on organizational structure, and management studies of corporate governance. Using those tools, I trace the process by which this new corporate governance system emerged. How did we move from the managerial revolution famously celebrated by Alfred Chandler to the director independence model recently codified in the Sarbanes-Oxley Act and other post-Enron corporate governance mandates? In addition, of course, the book will look at the future. Despite the extensive changes made to the legal structure of corporate governance post-Enron, many legal academics and shareholder activists want to see still more changes, mainly designed to empower shareholders relative to both boards and managers. In the latter portions of this book, I explore whether such changes are desirable. (In short, no.)

On the Necessity of Models

If analysis is to transcend mere description, we must situate it in a normative model. Inevitably, however, any such model is constrained by the limits of human cognition. Accordingly, we must make simplifying assumptions. Milton Friedman therefore argued that a model is properly judged by its predictive power with respect to the phenomena it purports to explain, not by whether it is a valid description of an objective reality. As such, "the relevant question to ask about the 'assumptions' of a theory is

---

[4] *Who Is in Charge?*, The Economist, Oct. 25, 2003.

not whether they are descriptively 'realistic,' for they never are, but whether they are sufficiently good approximations for the purpose in hand." [5]

The predictive power of any model of the corporation must be measured by the model's ability to predict the separation of ownership and control, the formal institutional governance structures following from their separation, and the legal rules responsive to their separation. Shareholders, who are said to "own" the firm, have virtually no power to control either its day-to-day operation or its long-term policies. Instead, the firm is controlled by its board of directors and subordinate managers, whose equity stake is often small.[6] As we shall see, most commentators see this separation as a problem to be solved. In contrast, I will argue that the separation of ownership and control is the unique genius of the modern American public corporation.

The Basic Dichotomy: Consensus Versus Authority

Any organization needs a governance system that facilitates efficient decision making. The two basic options are "consensus" and "authority."[7] The former is defined as "any reasonable and acceptable means of aggregating [the] individual interests" of the organization's constituents.[8] The latter is characterized by the existence of a central agency to which all relevant information is transmitted and that is empowered to make decisions binding on the whole.

Organizations tend to use consensus-based structures where each member of the organization has comparable information and interests. This is so because, under such conditions, and assuming there are no serious collective action problems to be overcome, decision-maker preferences can be aggregated at low cost. In contrast, authority-based decision-making structures arise where there are important information asymmetries among the organization's members or where those members have competing interests.

---

[5] Milton Friedman, *The Methodology of Positive Economics*, in Essays in Positive Economics 23, 27 (1985).
[6] Adolf A. Berle & Gardiner C. Means, *The Modern Corporation and Private Property* 84–89 (1932).
[7] Kenneth J. Arrow, *The Limits of Organization* 68–70 (1974).
[8] *Id.* at 69.

U.S. law provides business organizations with an array of off-the-rack governance systems ranging from the almost purely consensus-based partnership form to the almost purely authority-based corporate form. Consensus is facilitated in the partnership because each partner has equal rights to participate in management of the firm on a one-vote-per-partner basis.[9] Most decisions are made by majority vote, although a few particularly significant actions require unanimity. These rules work well in this context because all partners are entitled to share equally in profits and losses, giving them essentially identical interests (namely, higher profits), and are entitled to equal access to information, which helps to prevent serious information asymmetries from arising. In addition, the small size characteristic of most partnerships means that collective action problems generally are not serious in this setting.

At the other extreme, a publicly held corporation's decision-making structure is principally authority-based. Corporation statutes effectively separate ownership from control. Indeed, this *de jure* separation of ownership and control is one of the chief features distinguishing the corporation from other forms of business organizations.

The Separation of Ownership and Control

Corporation law virtually carves the separation of ownership and control into stone. Under all corporation statutes, the key players in the formal decision-making structure are the members of the board of directors who are empowered to make or delegate to employees most decisions affecting the business and affairs of the corporation. Shareholders have essentially no power to initiate corporate action and, indeed, are entitled to approve or disapprove only a very few board actions. The vote thus confers neither decision-making nor even oversight rights on shareholders in any meaningful sense. By virtue of the business judgment rule and the closely related rules governing shareholder litigation, moreover, indirect shareholder oversight of directors through litigation is also foreclosed.

Although the separation of ownership and control is one of the corporation's essential attributes, it is also one of the most controversial ones. This controversy began taking its modern shape in what still may be the

---

[9] As with most partnership rules, the off-the-rack rule is subject to contrary agreement among the parties. Unif. Partnership Act § 18(e) (1914).

most influential book ever written about corporations, Adolf Berle and Gardiner Means' *The Modern Corporation and Private Property*.[10] They identified three types of public corporations, classified according to the nature of share ownership within the firm:

- Majority control exists where the corporation has a dominant shareholder (or group of shareholders acting together) who owns more than 50 percent of the outstanding voting shares. Majority-controlled corporations exhibit a partial separation of ownership and control, since minority shareholders share in the corporation's ownership, but not in its control.
- Minority control exists where the corporation has a dominant shareholder (or group of shareholders acting together) who owns less than 50 percent of the outstanding voting shares, but is nevertheless able to exercise effective voting control. Minority-controlled corporations also exhibit partial separation of ownership and control.
- Managerial control exists when the corporation has no one shareholder (or group of shareholders acting together) who owns sufficient stock to give him working control of the firm. Manager-controlled corporations exhibit complete separation of ownership and control.

Manager-controlled corporations emerged, according to Berle and Means, because stock ownership was dispersed amongst many shareholders, no one of whom owned enough shares to affect materially the corporation's management. In turn, Berle and Means believed that dispersed ownership was inherent in the corporate system. Important technological changes during the decades preceding publication of their work, especially the development of modern mass production techniques, gave great advantages to firms large enough to achieve economics of scale, which gave rise to giant industrial corporations. These firms required enormous amounts of capital, far exceeding the resources of most individuals or families. They were financed by aggregating many small investments, which was accomplished by selling shares to many investors. Because small

---

[10] Berle & Means, *supra* note 6. In fact, however, Berle and Means were not the first to document the phenomenon of separation of ownership and control. Herbert Hovenkamp, *Enterprise and American Law: 1836–1937* 357 (1991). Alfred Marshall had made the same point in 1890, *id.*, as did William W. Cook in 1891. *Id.* at 16.

investors needed diversification, even very wealthy individuals limited the amount they would put at risk in any particular firm, fragmenting share ownership. The modern separation of ownership and control was the direct result of these forces, or so the story goes. Vesting decision-making power in the corporation's board of directors and managers allows shareholders to remain passive, while also preventing the chaos that would result from shareholder involvement in day-to-day decision making.

The Central Problem of Corporate Governance

Although the separation of ownership and control facilitated the growth of large industrial corporations, Berle and Means recognized that that separation also created the potential for shareholder and managerial interests to diverge. As the residual claimants on the corporation's assets and earnings, the shareholders are entitled to the corporation's profits. But it is the corporation's directors and managers, not the shareholders, who decide how to spend the firm's earnings. Accordingly, there is a risk that directors or managers will expend firm earnings on projects benefiting themselves, rather than shareholders. Suppose the board of directors of Acme, Inc., is musing over the following question: "I can either spend $100 million on a new corporate jet or I can distribute the $100 million to the shareholders by increasing the size of the dividend." Can anyone doubt that some boards will buy the jet?

The Survival Value of the Separation of Ownership and Control

Although the potential for opportunistic conduct by directors and managers is a legitimate and significant concern, it's important to remember that the separation of ownership and control has proven to have significant survival value. Professor Walter Werner aptly referred to the Berle and Means account as the "erosion doctrine." According to their version of history, Werner explained, there was a time when the corporation behaved as it was supposed to:

> The shareholders who owned the corporation controlled it. They elected a board of directors to whom they delegated management powers, but they retained residual control, uniting control and ownership. In the nation's early years the states created corporations

sparingly and regulated them strictly. The first corporations, run by their proprietors and constrained by law, exercised state-granted privileges to further the public interest. The states then curtailed regulation . . . , and this Eden ended. The corporation expanded into a huge concentrate of resources. Its operation vitally affected society, but it was run by managers who were accountable only to themselves and could blink at obligations to shareholders and society.[11]

The erosion doctrine, however, rested on a false account of the history of corporations. Werner explained that economic separation of ownership and control in fact was a feature of American corporations almost from the beginning of the nation: "Banks, and the other public-issue corporations of the [antebellum] period, contained the essential elements of big corporations today: a tripartite internal government structure, a share market that dispersed shareholdings and divided ownership and control, and tendencies to centralize management in full-time administrators and to diminish participation of outside directors in management."[12]

In contrast to Berle and Means' account, which rests on technological changes during the nineteenth century, Werner's account rests on the early development of secondary trading markets. Such markets existed in New York and Philadelphia by the beginning of the nineteenth century. The resulting liquidity of corporate stock made it an especially attractive investment, which in turn made selling stock to the public an attractive financing mechanism. Stocks were purchased by a diversified and dispersed clientele, including both institutions and individuals. The national taste for speculation also played a part in the early growth of the secondary trading markets and, in turn, to dispersal of stock ownership. As a result of these economic forces, ownership and control separated not at the end of the nineteenth century, but at its beginning.

A slightly different version of this story is told by Herbert Hovenkamp, who argues that separation of ownership and control is less a function of firm size than of firm complexity. Under this model, neither technological change nor corporate financing was the dispositive factor. Rather, ownership and control separated when, because of a high degree of

[11] Walter Werner, *Corporation Law in Search of Its Future*, 81 Colum. L. Rev. 1611, 1612 (1981).
[12] *Id.* at 1637.

vertical integration, firms became sufficiently complex to require professional managers.[13]

If either Werner or Hovenkamp's account is correct, there never was a time in which unity of control and ownership was a defining feature of public corporations. To the contrary, it appears that ownership and control separated at a very early date. In turn, this analysis suggests that the separation of ownership and control may be an essential economic characteristic of such corporations.

This revisionist history suggests that the separation of ownership and control must have considerable survival value. In a sense, the goal of this book is to identify the evidence for such value.

Theories of Corporate Governance

Given the centrality of the separation of ownership and control to the problems of corporate governance, any plausible model of the corporation must be able to explain why ownership and control separated, the institutional governance structures following from their separation, and the legal rules responsive to their separation. Over the years, legal scholars have developed numerous theories of the firm that purport to satisfy that standard.

Although these theories can be classified in various ways, and although some defy classification, two basic systems of classification capture most of the competing theories. One taxonomy categorizes theories of the firm according to whether they emphasize managerial or shareholder primacy. Theories at the shareholder primacy end of the spectrum traditionally claimed that shareholders own the corporation and, accordingly, that directors and officers are mere stewards of the shareholders' interests. A more recent variation of the shareholder primacy model, which arguably is the dominant model in today's scholarship, treats shareholders as merely one of many factors of production bound together in a complex web of explicit and implicit contracts. Influenced by agency cost economics, however, proponents of this variant continue to treat directors and officers as agents of the shareholders, with fiduciary obligations to maximize

---

[13] Herbert Hovenkamp, *Enterprise and American Law: 1836–1937* 357–60 (1991). Notice the close fit between this interpretation and the economic model advanced herein. Under both, the unique attribute of modern public corporations is a hierarchical decision-making structure adopted as an adaptive response to organizational complexity.

shareholder wealth. Shareholders therefore retain a privileged position among the corporation's various constituencies, enjoying a contract with the firm having ownership-like features, including the right to vote and the fiduciary obligations of directors and officers.

At the other end of the spectrum in this taxonomy lies managerialism. Managerialism conceives the corporation as a bureaucratic hierarchy dominated by professional managers. Directors are figureheads, while shareholders are nonentities. Managers are thus autonomous actors free to pursue whatever interests they choose. Instructively, the index to Peter Drucker's famous study of General Motors, which remains one of the classics of managerial scholarship, contains no references to GM's shareholders and only one to its board of directors.[14] There could not be a more effective illustration of the irrelevance of both directors and shareholders to managerialists.

The second taxonomy categorizes theories of the firm according to the interests the corporation serves (or is alleged to serve). At one end of the spectrum are those theorists who contend corporations should be run so as to maximize shareholder wealth. At the other end are stakeholderists, who argue that directors and managers should consider the interests of all corporate constituencies in making corporate decisions.[15] This taxonomy reflects the division in corporate law scholarship along public-private lines. Proponents of shareholder wealth maximization typically treat corporate governance as a species of private law, such that the separation of ownership and control does not in and of itself justify state intervention in corporate governance. In contrast, stakeholderists commonly treat corporate governance as a species of public law, such that the separation of ownership and control becomes principally a justification for regulating corporate governance so as to achieve social goals unrelated to corporate profitability.[16]

---

[14] Peter F. Drucker, *Concept of the Corporation* (rev. ed. 1972).

[15] As applied to corporation law and policy, the term "stakeholders" reportedly originated in a 1963 Stanford Research Institute memorandum as a descriptive term for "those groups without whose support the organization would cease to exist." R. Edward Freeman & David L. Reed, *Stockholders and Stakeholders: A New Perspective on Corporate Governance*, 25 Cal. Mgmt. Rev. 88, 89 (1983). I have a slight preference for the term "nonshareholder constituencies," which captures the idea of shareholders as having distinct interests from those of other stakeholders, but use the terms interchangeably.

[16] *See* William W. Bratton, *Berle and Means Reconsidered at the Century's End*, 26 J. Corp. L. 737, 760–61 (2001) (noting public/private divide); Lawrence E. Mitchell, *Private Law, Public Interest? The ALI Principles of Corporate Governance*, 61 Geo. Wash. L. Rev. 871,

As suggested by these taxonomies, theories of the firm potentially confront two basic questions: (1) As to the means of corporate govern-ance, who decides? In other words, when push comes to shove, who ulti-mately is in control? (2) As to the ends of corporate governance, whose interests prevail? When the ultimate decision maker is presented with a zero sum game, in which it must prefer the interests of one constituency over those of all others, which constituency wins?

Shareholder primacy models thus assume that shareholders both control the corporation, at least in some ultimate fashion, and are the appropriate beneficiaries of director fiduciary duties. Managerialist models assume that top management controls the corporation, but differ as to the interests managers should uphold. Stakeholderist models rarely focus on control issues, instead emphasizing the argument that share-holders should not be the sole beneficiaries of director and officer fiduciary duties.

Any model that can command the loyalty of one or more generations of scholars doubtless has more than a grain of truth. Yet, none of the standard models provides a fully satisfactory answer to these questions. Hence, there is a need for an alternative, such as director primacy.[17]

As to the question of control, director primacy asserts that neither end of the spectrum gets it right. Neither shareholders nor managers control corporations; instead, boards of directors have the ultimate right of fiat. As to the stakeholder versus shareholder question, director pri-macy claims that shareholders are the appropriate beneficiary of director

---

876 (1993) (noting debate as to "whether the modern corporation is essentially a matter of public or private concern").

[17] Another important alternative to the prevailing theories is offered by the team produc-tion model developed by Lynn Stout and Margaret Blair, the former of whom I'm lucky enough to have as a colleague at UCLA. As far as control is concerned, Blair and Stout take a director primacy–like view of corporate governance. Blair and Stout argue, for example, that directors "are not subject to direct control or supervision by anyone, including the firm's shareholders." Margaret M. Blair & Lynn A. Stout, *A Team Production Theory of Corporate Law*, 85 Va. L. Rev. 247 (1999). A critical difference between our respective models, however, is suggested by Blair and Stout's argument that directors are "hierarchs" who "work for team members (including employees) who 'hire' them to control shirking and rent-seeking among team members." *Id.* at 280 (emphasis removed). As explained in Chapter 1 below, director primacy claims this is exactly backwards—directors hire factors of production, not vice versa. Hence, director primacy rejects Blair and Stout's argument that directors serve as mediating hierarchs.

fiduciary duties. Hence, director accountability for maximizing share-holder wealth remains an important component of director primacy.[18]

A principal claim of this work is that prevailing models of corporate governance skew toward accountability concerns and thus pay insufficient attention to the power of fiat vested in the board by statute. Some commentators go so far as to claim that fiat does not exist. Still others acknowledge the board's discretionary powers, but treat those powers mainly as a source of agency costs to be constrained by market and/or legal forces. In doing so, however, the latter allow the tail to wag the dog. To be sure, ensuring that directors use their power in pursuit of share-holder wealth maximization is a critical problem. Accountability standing alone, however, is an inadequate normative account of corporate law. Fiat exists; fiat matters. A fully specified account of corporate law therefore must incorporate the value of authority—i.e., the need to develop a set of rules and procedures that provides the most efficient decision-making system.

A core normative claim of the director primacy model thus is that the virtues of fiat, in terms of corporate decision-making efficiency, can be ensured only by preserving the board's decision-making authority from being trumped by either shareholders or courts. Achieving an appropriate mix between authority and accountability is a daunting task, but a necessary one. Ultimately, authority and accountability cannot be reconciled.[19] At some point, greater accountability necessarily makes the decision-making process less efficient, while highly efficient decision-making structures necessarily entail limits on the reviewability of discretionary decisions.

The predictive power of director primacy is demonstrated in the host of legal doctrines and governance structures that resolve the tension between authority and accountability in the favor of the former. Because only shareholders are entitled to elect directors, for example, boards of public corporations are insulated from pressure by nonshareholder corporate constituencies, such as employees or creditors. At the same time, the diffuse nature of U.S. stockownership and regulatory impediments to investor activism insulate directors from shareholder pressure. As such, the

---

[18] The director primacy model builds on work done by Professor Michael Dooley, *see, e.g., Two Models of Corporate Governance,* 47 Bus. Law. 462 (1992), which in turn built on Arrow, *supra* note 7.

[19] Dooley, *supra* note 18, at 464–71.

board has virtually unconstrained freedom to exercise business judgment. Hence the term *director primacy*, which reflects the board's sovereignty.

Of course, when it comes to assessing proposed changes to such laws, the core director primacy claim only gets one so far. Consider the many proposals made in recent years to empower shareholders (see Chapter 5 for details). To say that such proposals would shift authority from directors to shareholders is more of a description than an argument.

Having made that concession, however, I want to recall Benjamin Cardozo's famous dictum that the legal duties of a fiduciary should not be undermined by "the 'disintegrating erosion' of particular exceptions." Just so, if one believes that authority has survival value, one should protect the board of directors' decision-making authority from the "disintegrating erosion" of reform.

This does not mean that one should always reject reforms that shift the balance toward accountability. It does, however, suggest one must pay attention to the cumulative impact of repeated reform proposals, lest one subject the board's authority to the legal equivalent of death by a thousand cuts. It also suggests that there ought to be at least a presumption in favor of authority. In light of the huge advantages authority offers the corporate form, the burden should be on those who wish to constrain the board's authority.

Having said that, however, I acknowledge that the argument to this point rarely will prove dispositive. Returning to the example of proposals for shareholder empowerment, it's not enough to point out that such proposals shift the balance toward accountability. One must go on to ask why such a shift is undesirable (or, preferably, to defend the presumption against such a shift). Hence, in Chapter 5, we consider such questions as whether the shareholders would use such powers, whether certain shareholders are more likely to do so than others, and whether those shareholders are likely to use their new powers to pursue private gains at the expense of other shareholders.

The Domain of Director Primacy

At the outset, I should acknowledge that there are important limits on the domain of cases within which the model is relevant. First, director primacy's claims fare poorly whenever there is a dominant shareholder. As such, the model's utility is vitiated with respect to close corporations, wholly-owned subsidiaries, and publicly held corporations with a controlling shareholder.

This is so, of course, because the shareholders' right to elect the board of directors can give the former *de facto* control even though the statute assigns *de jure* control to the latter. Consequently, we can speak of a "control block"; i.e., shares held by one or more shareholders whose stockownership gives them effective control. In their classic study, Berle and Means in fact found that relatively small blocks of stock could give their owners effective control of the enterprise.[20] In fact, at the time they wrote, only about half of the 200 largest U.S. corporations exhibited total separation of ownership and control.

Second, many publicly held corporations lacking a controlling shareholder are dominated by top management. Indeed, until quite recently, a significant percentage of publicly held corporations had boards in which insiders comprised a majority of the members. Even where a majority of the board is nominally independent, moreover, the board may be captured by management. As we'll see, board capture is less of a concern today than it was even as recently as a decade ago, but it admittedly remains an important limiting factor on the domain of director primacy.

Finally, it's important to recognize that the analysis herein focuses exclusively on corporate governance in the United States. In *Strong Managers, Weak Owners*, Mark Roe posed the foundational question of whether Berle and Means were correct in assuming that the separation of ownership and control is an inherent aspect of large public corporations. Roe contended that dispersed ownership was not the inevitable consequence of impersonal economic forces, but rather the result of a series of political decisions motivated by a fear of concentrated economic power.[21] If the legal rules flowing from those decisions had not existed, Roe opined, ownership might not have fragmented and thus might not have separated from control. The implication of his thesis, of course, is that while economic forces shaped modern corporate governance, they did so within the parameters set by law. As such, the governance structure of U.S. public corporations may not be optimal in an absolute sense, but only relative to the set of possibilities defined by our legal system.

---

[20] Berle & Means, *supra* note 6, at 80–84.
[21] Mark J. Roe, *Strong Managers, Weak Owners: The Political Roots of American Corporate Finance* (1994).

Roe's evidence suggests that organizational forms tend to be all or nothing: passive and fragmented, as in the United States, or concentrated and active, as in Germany. The choice between organizational forms must be made by countries, rather than by companies. As such, the domain of director primacy claimed herein is limited to corporate governance in the United States.

Is a Unified Field Theory of Corporate Governance Possible?

Are the limits on the domain of director primacy a reason for rejecting the model? Christopher Bruner argues that "we have three prevailing theories [of corporate governance], each of which has 'dealt deadly blows to the other.'"[22] The three are: nexus of contracts (into which he places director primacy), Margaret Blair and Lynn Stout's team production model, and shareholder-centrism. Bruner claims that:

> Prevailing theories of corporate law have tended to advance strong claims regarding the corporate governance primacy and legitimacy of either the board or the shareholders, as the case may be. In this paper I challenge the descriptive power of these theories and advance an alternative, arguing that corporate law is, and will remain, deeply ambivalent—both doctrinally and morally—with respect to three fundamental and related issues: the locus of ultimate corporate governance authority, the intended beneficiaries of corporate production, and the relationship between corporate law and the achievement of the social good.

Let's examine two of Bruner's critiques that particularly relate to director primacy. First, Bruner asserts that director primacy and other nexus of contracts–based theories have "a difficult time accounting for the law of corporate takeovers, and [are absent] any clear mandate to maximize the wealth of shareholders under any but the most limited circumstances."[23] In fact, however, I addressed those issues in detail in an article entitled *Unocal at 20: Director Primacy in Corporate Takeovers*, which acknowledged that Delaware's takeover jurisprudence is almost universally condemned

---

[22] Christopher Bruner, *The Enduring Ambivalence of Corporate Law* 23 (Aug. 9, 2007), available at http://papers.ssrn.com/sol3/papers.cfm?abstract_id=1005729.
[23] *Id.* at 13.

in the academic corporate law literature. Building on my director primacy model of corporate governance and law, however, I offered a defense of that jurisprudence. Specifically, I argued that Delaware courts struck an appropriate balance between two competing but equally legitimate goals of corporate law: On the one hand, because the power to review differs only in degree and not in kind from the power to decide, the discretionary authority of the board of directors must be insulated from shareholder and judicial oversight in order to promote efficient corporate decision making. On the other hand, because directors are obligated to maximize shareholder wealth, there must be mechanisms to ensure director accountability. The framework developed by the Delaware courts provides them with a mechanism for filtering out those cases in which directors have abused their authority from those in which directors have not.[24] A version of this argument also is offered in the present work in Chapter 3. Second, Bruner argues that:

> The very existence of any shareholder voting power inevitably proves problematic for those who identify the board as the very essence of the corporate enterprise itself. Bainbridge, for example, who depicts the board as a "sui generis body" and "a sort of Platonic guardian," justifies giving voting power to shareholders by reference to the disciplinary effects of the market for corporate control (made possible by the transferability of their interests), but then proves amenable to "sharply constrain[ing]" the market for control through takeover defenses in favor of the efficiency of board governance—an account that undercuts its own explanation for the existence of even minimal shareholder voting rights.[25]

In a world of pure director primacy, in which directors could be counted on to be faithful to the shareholder wealth maximization norm, shareholder voting rights likely would not exist. Hence, in *The Case for Limited Shareholder Voting Rights*, I argued that shareholder voting is properly understood not as an integral aspect of the corporate decision-making structure, but rather as an accountability device of last resort to be used sparingly, at best. Why sparingly? As we have just seen, corporate governance is made at the margins of an unending competition between two

---

[24] Stephen M. Bainbridge, *Unocal at 20: Director Primacy in Corporate Takeovers*, 31 Del. J. Corp. L. 769 (2006).
[25] Bruner, *supra* note 22, at 14.

competing values; namely, authority and accountability. Both are essential to effective corporate governance, but they are ultimately irreconcilable. Efforts to hold someone to account inevitably limit his or her discretion.[26] The inconsistency Bruner claims to see in my work arises inherently out of the tension between authority and accountability. Shareholder voting is an accountability mechanism, exercised mainly through the takeover market, but preservation of the board's authority requires that both the franchise and the market for corporate control have limits. Again, a version of this argument is developed in the present work in Chapter 5.

Bruner makes a good case that pure theories of corporate governance all have problems. I've believed for a long time that there is no unified field theory that explains all of corporate governance. In *Executive Compensation: Who Decides?*, for example, I wrote that:

> Physicists have long sought a unified field theory, which would provide a single set of simple laws that explain the four interactions or forces that affect matter—i.e., the strong, electromagnetic, weak, and gravitational forces. To date, they have failed, which provides a strong cautionary tale for anyone seeking a unified field theory of social interactions among fallible humans, whose behavior is far harder to predict than is that of, say, an electron.[27]

But so what? Elegant and parsimonious models are more important for economists than for lawyers. Instead, situation-specific mini-theories often are more useful for making legal decisions than a single unified theory. I thus don't claim that director primacy explains everything about corporate governance. The claim made herein is that director primacy has a larger domain of explanatory and justificatory power than any other theory on the market.

The Plan of the Work

The formal, statutory model of corporate governance contemplates a pyramidal hierarchy surmounted not by an individual but by a small

---

[26] Stephen M. Bainbridge, *The Case for Limited Shareholder Voting Rights*, 53 UCLA L. Rev. 601 (2006).

[27] Stephen M. Bainbridge, *Executive Compensation: Who Decides?*, 83 Tex. L. Rev. 1615, 1628 (2005).

collaborative body.[28] This model raises a number of questions we will explore in the chapters that follow: Why are corporate decisions made through the exercise of authority rather than by consensus? Why is corporate authority exercised hierarchically? Put another way, what survival advantage does a large corporation gain by being structured as a bureaucratic hierarchy? Why is the firm's ultimate decision maker a collective rather than an individual? Why do only shareholders, among all the corporation's constituencies, elect the board? Why do shareholders nevertheless have such limited control rights?

These are the critical features of corporate governance this book will explore. The director primacy model explains why these features came into existence, provides them with a normative justification, and allows us to make predictions about whether changes in the law or governance practices will prove efficacious.

In order to build that model, we need to understand the nature of the beast we are studying. Chapter 1 thus opens with a foundational question: What is the corporation? Is the corporation a person, a thing capable of being owned, or a legal fiction representing a nexus of contracts among various groups of stakeholders?

This question is critical because it goes to the issue of whether shareholders have the control rights that an owner of the business would normally expect. The corporation is properly understood not as a person, entity, or thing, but as a nexus of contracts. The contract between the shareholders and the firm is one in which the shareholders provide equity capital and the firm agrees to seek to maximize the value of the shareholders' residual claim on firm assets. As such, we should not expect shareholders to have the rights of ownership, although their contract with the firm (represented by the corporation statute) does have some ownership-like features.

Chapter 1 contrasts this contractual conception of the corporation to the entity-based theories that traditionally informed both managerialist and shareholder primacy theories of the corporation. Accordingly, this chapter lays the foundation for my argument that corporate governance is board-centered, which is to say that the board of directors is a unique

---

[28] Alfred D. Chandler, Jr., *The Visible Hand: The Managerial Revolution in American Business* 8 (1977) (over time, corporate hierarchies have proven to possess "a permanence beyond that of any individual or group of individuals who worked in them"); Drucker, *supra* note 14, at 141 ("the corporation must be organized on hierarchical lines").

organizational form that is designed to have superior decision-making authority vis-à-vis both managers and shareholders.

To say that the corporation is a nexus of contracts, of course, is to engage in reification. Nexuses do not contract; people contract. Chapter 1 therefore goes on to ask: Where is the nexus—the central contracting party—with whom all other corporate stakeholders contract?

The corporation statutes in every state make clear that the nexus is the board of directors. As the Delaware General Corporation Law, for example, puts it: the corporation's "business and affairs . . . shall be managed by or under the direction of the board of directors."[29]

We thus can begin to see the corporation as a vehicle by which the board of directors hires various factors of production. Hence, the board of directors is not a mere agent of the shareholders, but rather is a *sui generis* body serving as the nexus for the various contracts making up the corporation. The board's powers flow from that set of contracts in its totality and not just from shareholders.

But why do corporate governance statutes provide for the corporate hierarchy to be topped by a group acting by consensus (i.e., the board) rather than an individual autocrat? Chapter 2 demonstrates that decision making by groups rather than by individuals is superior with respect to most of the functions performed by the board by reviewing the extensive evidence on (a) what boards do—i.e., what is their proper corporate governance role—and (b) why group decision making is preferable with respect to such matters.

The analysis to this point focuses on the statutory framework of corporate governance. The statute establishes a hierarchy in which decision making is effected by authority rather consensus. At the very least, the obvious mechanical difficulties of achieving consensus among thousands of decision makers impede shareholders from taking an active role. Yet, even if those collective action problems could be overcome, active shareholder participation in corporate decision making still would be precluded by the intractable information asymmetries that exist between the firm and its shareholders (and among shareholders), as well as the shareholders' widely divergent interests.

In Chapter 3, I turn to the inherent tension between authority and accountability. Although authority is essential for organizational efficiency,

---

[29] Del. Code Ann., tit. 8, § 141(a).

it must be exercised responsibly. Because human cognitive powers are limited and subject to being overwhelmed by information flows, decision makers inevitably make errors. If the decision makers' authority is unreviewable, those errors will go uncorrected. A concern that is even more pertinent for our purposes, however, is that unaccountable authority may be exercised opportunistically. The central decision maker may divert organizational resources to its own benefit rather than the good of the organization and its constituents.

A complete theory of the firm requires one to balance the virtues of discretionary fiat on the part of the board of directors against the need to ensure that the power of fiat is used responsibly. Neither fiat nor accountability can be ignored, because both promote values essential to the survival of business organizations. Unfortunately, however, because the power to hold to account differs only in degree and not in kind from the power to decide, fiat and accountability also are antithetical.[30]

One of the most striking things about American corporate law, albeit one that often gets short shrift from commentators, is the extent to which that body of law consistently comes down on the side of protecting the board of directors' authority. Chapter 3 draws on the theoretical framework developed in the preceding chapters to develop a normative model explaining why it is appropriate for corporate law to be so blatantly biased in favor of authority rather than accountability. As such, it also lays out a model for how courts should adapt to the new corporate governance.

By now, the informed reader likely is objecting that all this is beside the point. Neither shareholders nor directors run the corporation; CEOs do. Managerialism may have fallen out of favor as a normative theory of corporate governance, but it remains the work-a-day world reality. Chapter 4 turns to a practical analysis of contemporary corporate governance to argue that the balance of power is shifting from imperial CEOs to boards. To be sure, while the corporation statute envisions a board-centered governance structure, the statutory theory has long failed to translate into real world practice. Adolf Berle compared corporate managers to "princes and ministers."[31] Ralph Nader went so far as to compare

---

[30] *See generally* Dooley, *supra* note 18, 464–71.
[31] A.A. Berle, Jr., *For Whom Corporate Managers Are Trustees*, 45 Harv. L. Rev. 1365, 1366 (1932).

directors to "cuckolds" who are "often the last to know when [their] dominant partner—management—has done something illicit."[32]

Starting in the 1970s, however, the ground began to shift under management's feet. A combination of legal changes and market developments empowered both boards and shareholders vis-à-vis management. For example, the rise of the hostile takeover bid as a viable market transaction meant that managers who let their company's stock price fall became vulnerable to displacement by a "corporate raider" (if I may use that term, which some regard as pejorative). In turn, as managers sought to resist tender offers and proxy contests, judicial review of such takeover defenses came to hinge in large part on whether independent and disinterested directors made the relevant decisions.

Other relevant legal and market forces will be explored in similar fashion. Among these are judicial review of both operational and structural decisions, stock exchange listing standards mandating an independent audit function, enhanced disclosure, and the many recent changes worked by Sarbanes-Oxley and related post-Enron developments.

Chapter 4 thus traces the transformation of corporate governance from managerialism to director primacy. Modern boards of directors typically are smaller than their antecedents, meet more often, are more independent from management, own more stock, and have better access to information. Granted, the transformation remains incomplete. There are still some imperial CEOs to be found. As a March 2005 US News story explained, and as a wealth of empirical data confirm, however, "boards with new backbone are dumping imperial CEOs."[33] The trend of corporate governance is bringing the statutory theory and real world practice increasingly into line.

If I am right that the future of corporate governance increasingly will be board-centered, how do we operationalize this trend in both law and practice? The statutory model of corporate governance is splendidly minimalist. Corporation codes provide only very limited guidance as to the proper roles of boards of directors. As corporations have gradually begun to move from managerialism to director primacy, however, best practices have started evolving.

Chapter 4 thus emphasizes the ways in which the theory developed in the chapters that precede it is being operationalized as best practices

---

[32] Ralph Nader et al., *Taming the Giant Corporation* 64 (1976).
[33] Matthew Benjamin, *Giving the Boot*, U.S. News & World Rep., March 28, 2005, at 48.

for boards of directors. This chapter is not intended to provide a cookbook approach to current best practice. Instead, it is designed simply to show that the board-centered theory of corporate governance set out in the corporation codes in fact can be—and is being—translated into real world practice.

Finally, Chapter 5 concludes with a look at the future of corporate governance. This board-centered model of corporate governance stands in sharp contrast to the prevailing shareholder primacy theory. Both the academic and popular business media repeatedly claim that investors are active in corporate governance and that the law should empower them to become even more active. Accordingly, we are told, ownership and control are uniting (or, as some say, reuniting) and this process needs to be accelerated by various legal reforms.

Because this model is already well entrenched and is becoming increasingly influential, it must be met head on. In Chapter 1, I set the stage for this discussion by disentangling two concepts that shareholder primacists typically conflate; namely, the means and ends of corporate governance. As already noted, corporate governance addresses two basic sets of questions: who decides and whose interests prevail?

Both the shareholder and director primacy models give the same answer to the latter question. The basic decision-making norm in corporate governance is shareholder wealth maximization. "A business corporation is organized and carried on primarily for the profit of the stockholders," as the Michigan Supreme Court famously opined.[34]

The two models depart with respect to the former issue. Properly understood, shareholder primacy contends not only that shareholders are the principals on whose behalf corporate governance is organized, but also that shareholders do (and should) exercise ultimate control of the corporate enterprise. In contrast, although director primacy accepts shareholder wealth maximization as the proper corporate decision-making norm, it rejects the notion that shareholders are entitled to either direct or indirect decision-making control.

In order to make the case for rejecting shareholder primacy, we need to consider two fundamental questions. First, why do shareholders—and only shareholders—have voting rights? Chapter 1 tackles that issue. Second, why are the voting rights of shareholders so limited? Although Chapter 1

---

[34] Dodge v. Ford Motor Co., 170 N.W. 668, 684 (Mich. 1919).

touches on that issue, I defer this latter question to Chapter 5 in order to contextualize the discussion of shareholder activism and the future of corporate governance.

Chapter 5 demonstrates that investor activism turns out to be rare and limited primarily to union and state or local public employee pensions. As a result, investor activism has not—and cannot—prove a panacea for the pathologies of corporate governance. Activist investors pursue agendas not shared by and often in conflict with those of passive investors. Activism by investors undermines the role of the board of directors as a central decision-making body, thereby making corporate governance less effective. Finally, relying on activist institutional investors will not solve the principal-agent problem inherent in corporate governance but rather will merely shift the locus of that problem.

In sum, there are significant economic advantages to vesting ultimate decision-making authority in a small group rather than either a single executive or a disperse body of shareholders. For much of the last century, persistent market failures allowed for managerial domination. In recent years, however, pressures for greater accountability have enabled the economic advantages of board-centered governance to overcome those market failures. In Chapter 5, I argue that the problem now is to solidify those gains and to continue empowering the board of directors.

CHAPTER 1

The Means and Ends of Corporate Governance

Words matter. Ideas have consequences. The way we think about something inevitably affects what we think ought to be done about it. Unfortunately, the object of this study—the "corporation"—can be a surprisingly indeterminate concept, whose nature depends very much on the eye of the beholder. Even so, however, it remains essential to develop a plausible model of the corporation. Reality is so complex and in such rapid flux that it can only be understood through the use of simplifying models.

The director primacy model proposed herein is grounded in the prevailing law and economics conception of the firm; namely, the so-called nexus of contracts model. This chapter therefore opens with a summary (as brief as possible) of the standard contractarian account. I am not going to offer a detailed defense of the contractarian model against its external critics herein. I have done so elsewhere, as have numerous others.[1]

---

[1] Stephen M. Bainbridge, *Community and Statism: A Conservative Contractarian Critique of Progressive Corporate Law Scholarship*, 82 Cornell L. Rev. 856, 860 (1997). For criticisms of the contractarian model, *see, e.g.*, Victor Brudney, *Corporate Governance, Agency Costs, and the Rhetoric of Contract*, 85 Colum. L. Rev. 1403 (1985); Robert C. Clark, *Contracts, Elites, and Traditions in the Making of Corporate Law*, 89 Colum. L. Rev. 1703 (1989); Melvin Aron Eisenberg, *The Structure of Corporation Law*, 89 Colum. L. Rev. 1461 (1989). For defenses of contractarian theory, *see* Henry N. Butler & Larry E. Ribstein, *Opting Out of Fiduciary Duties: A Response to the Anti-Contractarians*, 65 Wash. L. Rev. 1 (1990); Frank H. Easterbrook & Daniel R. Fischel, *The Corporate Contract*, 89 Colum. L. Rev. 1416 (1989); Fred S. McChesney, *Economics, Law, and Science in the Corporate Field: A Comment on Eisenberg*, 89 Colum. L. Rev. 1530 (1989).

Instead, in this book, I am looking inward to work out an often-overlooked implication of contractarianism.

At the outset, it should be acknowledged that the phrase "nexus of contracts" is somewhat unfortunate. For lawyers, the term carries with it all of the baggage learned in Contracts class during the first year of law school. Among that baggage are two particularly problematic features. First, the term contract may suggest a focus on legal notions such as consideration and mutuality. Second, the paradigm contract used in law school typically is a transaction on a spot market that is thick and relatively untroubled by asymmetric information. Neither of these features are present in the corporate form, of course.

As used by contractarians, however, the term "contract" is not limited to those relationships that constitute legal contracts. Instead, contractarians use the word contract to refer to any process by which property rights to assets are created, modified, or transferred. Perhaps even more important, contractarians are concerned with long-term relationships characterized by asymmetric information, bilateral monopoly, and opportunism. The relationship between shareholders and creditors of a corporation is contractual in this sense, even though there is no single document we could identify as a legally binding contract through which they are in privity.

The nexus of contracts model thus is properly viewed as a metaphor rather than as a positive account of economic reality. Contractarianism is analogous to Newtonian physics, which no longer claims to be an accurate representation of the laws of physics, but yet provides a simple model that adequately explains a large and important set of physical phenomena.

After developing this contractarian understanding of the corporation, in which it is viewed as a nexus of explicit and implicit contracts among various stakeholders, this chapter argues that it is more useful to think of the corporation as having a nexus of contracts than to think of it as being a nexus of contracts. After all, nexuses don't contract, people do. Specifically, the board of directors—at least as a matter of statutory theory, if not always in practice—serves as the corporate nexus. We thus can think of the board as a sui generis body that hires all of the factors of production necessary for the corporation to conduct its business and affairs.

The chapter concludes with an assessment of the ends of corporate governance. Why does corporate law privilege shareholders by making them the sole beneficiaries of director fiduciary duties? Put another way, why is shareholder wealth maximization the end of corporate governance?

The Corporation as Person

In the eyes of the law, the corporation is an entity wholly separate from the people who own it and work for it. Accordingly, the law generally treats the corporation as though it were a legal person, having most of the rights and obligations of natural persons, and having an identity distinct from its constituents. Corporate law statutes, for example, typically give a corporation "the same powers as an individual to do all things necessary or convenient to carry out its business and affairs."[2]

Corporate constituents thus contract not with each other, but with the corporation. For example, a bond indenture is a contract between the corporation and its creditors,[3] an employment agreement is a contract between the corporation and its workers, and a collective bargaining agreement is a contract between the corporation and the union representing its workers. If such a contract is breached on the corporate side, the corporation will be the entity that is sued in most cases, rather than the individuals who decided not to perform. If that entity loses, damages typically will be paid out of its assets and earnings rather than out of those individuals' pockets.

The corporation's legal personality is a tremendously useful concept. Consider a large forestry company, owning land in many states. If the company were required to list all of its owners—i.e., every shareholder—on every deed recorded in every county in which it owned property, and also had to amend those filings every time a shareholder sold stock, there would be an intolerable burden not only on the firm but also on government agencies that deal with the firm.

An even more useful feature of the corporation's legal personality, however, is that it allows partitioning of business assets from the personal assets of shareholders, managers, and other corporate constituents.[4]

---

[2] Model Bus. Corp. Act § 3.02.

[3] *See, e.g.*, John Wiley & Sons, Inc. v. Livingston, 376 U.S. 543, 546 (1964) (asking "whether the arbitration provisions of the collective bargaining agreement survived the Wiley-Interscience merger, so as to be operative against" the successor corporation); Lorenz v. CSX Corp., 1 F.3d 1406, 1417 (3rd Cir. 1993) ("It is well-established that a corporation does not have a fiduciary relationship with its debt security holders, as with its shareholders. The relationship between a corporation and its debentureholders is contractual in nature."); Simons v. Cogan, 549 A.2d 300, 303–4 (Del. 1988) (holding that "a convertible debenture represents a contractual entitlement to the repayment of a debt").

[4] *See* Henry Hansmann & Reinier Kraakman, *The Essential Role of Organizational Law*, 110 Yale L. J. 387 (2000), on which the following discussion draws.

His partitioning has two important aspects. On the one hand, asset partitioning creates a distinct pool of assets belonging to the firm on which the firm's creditors have a claim that is prior to the claims of personal creditors of the corporation's constituencies. By eliminating the risk that the firm will be affected by the financial difficulties of its constituencies, asset partitioning reduces the risks borne by creditors of the firm and thus enables the firm to raise capital at a lower cost. On the other hand, asset partitioning also protects the personal assets of the corporation's constituencies from the vicissitudes of corporate life. The doctrine of limited liability means that creditors of the firm may not reach the personal assets of shareholders or other corporate constituents.

Despite its utility, however, personhood is an inapt model for understanding the corporation. Although some theorists have made highfalutin arguments to the contrary, the corporation self-evidently lacks the basic characteristics of personhood. As Baron Thurlow famously asked, "Did you ever expect a corporation to have a conscience, when it has no soul to be damned, and no body to be kicked?"[5] Instead, the corporation is properly understood to be a legal fiction characterized by six attributes: formal creation as prescribed by state law; an artificial personality; separation of ownership and control; freely alienable ownership interests; indefinite duration; and limited liability.

The Corporation as Entity

Another widely-held model of the corporation claims that stock ownership is no different than any other species of private property. Nobel economics laureate Milton Friedman's famous essay on corporate social responsibility remains a classic statement of this conception of the corporation:

> In a free enterprise, private-property system, a corporate executive is an employé of the owners of the business. He has [a] direct responsibility to his employers. That responsibility is to conduct the business in accordance with their desires, which generally will be to make as much money as possible while conforming to the basic rules of society....

---

[5] Some authorities claim that Thurlow actually said: "Corporations have neither bodies to be punished, nor souls to be condemned; they therefore do as they like."

Insofar as his actions in accord with his "social responsibility" reduce returns to stockholders, he is spending their money.[6]

Friedman is treating stockownership as a species of private property, which in turn implies a conception of the corporation as a thing capable of being owned. In other words, he is treating the corporation as a real entity with a corporeal existence distinct from that of its owners.

If the corporation is a thing capable of being owned, who owns it? Melvin Eisenberg argues that the shareholders of a corporation possess most of the incidents of ownership, which he identified as including "the rights to possess, use, and manage, and the rights to income and capital."[7] Accordingly, he claims, the shareholders own the corporation.

In fact, however, shareholders have no right to use or possess corporate property. As one court explained, "even a sole shareholder has no independent right which is violated by trespass upon or conversion of the corporation's property."[8] Likewise, management rights are assigned by statute solely to the board of directors and those officers to whom the board properly delegates such authority. Accordingly, to the extent that possessory and control rights are the indicia of a property right, the board is a better candidate for identification as the corporation's owner than are the shareholders. As an early New York opinion put it, "the directors in the performance of their duty possess [the corporation's property], and act in every way as if they owned it."[9]

Because private property is such a profound part of the American ethos, the normative implications of the conception of the corporation as property long dominated corporate governance discourse. Yet, in addition to this conception's doctrinal inaccuracy, it was further flawed because it required one to reify the corporation; i.e., to treat the corporation as something separate from its various constituents.[10] While reification provides a necessary semantic shorthand, it creates a sort of false consciousness when taken to extremes. The corporation is not a thing. The corporation

---

[6] Milton Friedman, *The Social Responsibility of Business Is to Increase Its Profits*, N.Y. Times, Sept. 13, 1970, at 32.

[7] Melvin A. Eisenberg, *The Conception that the Corporation is a Nexus of Contracts, and the Dual Nature of the Firm*, 24 J. Corp. L. 819, 825 (1999).

[8] W. Clay Jackson Enterprises, Inc. v. Greyhound Leasing and Financial Corp., 463 F. Supp. 666, 670 (D. P.R. 1979).

[9] Manson v. Curtis, 119 N.E. 559, 562 (N.Y. 1918).

[10] *See, e.g.*, William A. Klein & John C. Coffee, Jr., *Business Organization and Finance: Legal and Economic Principles* 108–9 (7th ed. 2000).

is a legal fiction representing the unique vehicle by which large groups of individuals, each offering a different factor of production, privately order their relationships so as to collectively produce marketable goods or services. To facilitate this process of private ordering, the state's corporation code offers a basic set of default rules that the parties are free generally to accept, reject, or modify as they see fit.

The Corporation as Nexus of Contracts

In an important but underappreciated article, my friend and colleague Bill Klein emphasized that understanding a business organization required one to examine the bargains reached by the enterprise's various stakeholders over four key deal points: risk of loss, return, control, and duration.[11] Similarly, Oliver Hart observed that "contractual relations with employees, suppliers, customers, creditors, and others are an essential aspect of the firm."[12] Thus, the problem with treating the corporation as either a person or a real entity is that it ignores the basic fact that corporations act only through individuals.

Contractarian theories of the corporation reject reification of the corporation except as a semantic shorthand. Instead of viewing the corporation either as a person or an entity, contractarian scholars view it as an aggregate of various inputs acting together to produce goods or services.[13] Employees provide labor. Creditors provide debt capital. Shareholders initially provide equity capital and subsequently bear the risk of losses and monitor the performance of management. Management monitors the performance of employees and coordinates the activities of all the firm's inputs. Accordingly, the firm is not a thing, but rather a nexus of explicit and implicit contracts establishing rights and obligations among the various inputs making up the firm.

---

[11] *See* William A. Klein, *The Modern Business Organization: Bargaining under Constraints*, 91 Yale L.J. 1521 (1982).

[12] Oliver Hart, *An Economist's Perspective on the Theory of the Firm*, 89 Colum. L. Rev. 1757, 1764 (1989).

[13] The nexus of contracts model's origins fairly can be traced to Nobel Prize laureate Ronald Coase's justly famous article, *The Nature of the Firm*. R.H. Coase, *The Nature of the Firm*, 4 Economica (n.s.) 386 (1937). *See generally* Thomas S. Ulen, *The Coasean Firm in Law and Economics*, 18 J. Corp. L. 301, 318–28 (1993).

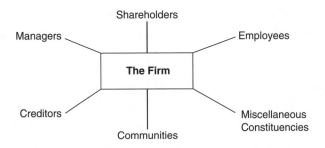

Figure 1 The firm as the nexus of contracts

The existence of a nexus with which corporate constituents contract is an essential component of any sensible model of corporate governance.[14] If there were no nexus, employment contracts would cascade—looking rather like a standard hierarchical organization chart—with each employee contracting with his superior. (Debt contracts would be even more complex.) Such a cascade would be costly to assemble, if not impossible, not least because it would be subject to opportunistic disassembly threats in which one or more of the contracting parties seeks to hold up the others.

Indeed, most corporate constituents lack any mechanism for communicating with other constituencies of the firm—let alone contract with one another. Instead, each constituency contracts with a central nexus. Accordingly, constituencies must be (and are) linked to the nexus and not each other.

Anti-contractarian scholar Melvin Eisenberg acknowledged this point, observing that "a particular corporation consists of all and only those reciprocal arrangements that are linked not just to each other, but

---

[14] In G. Mitu Gulati et al., *Connected Contracts*, 47 UCLA L. Rev. 887, 947 (2000), my friends Mitu Gulati, Bill Klein, and Eric Zolt challenged the nexus of contracts model. Although their new model remains contractarian in nature, it lacks a critical feature of the standard contractarian account—namely, a nexus. "In [their] model there is no primacy, no core, no hierarchy, no prominent participant, no firm, no fiduciary duty." *Id.* at 894–95. Instead, there is simply a set of contracts among the enterprise's various constituencies. Their challenge is significant for my purposes, because a nexus competent to exercise fiat is central to the director primacy model. Accordingly, I responded at length to their arguments in Stephen M. Bainbridge, *The Board of Directors as Nexus of Contracts*, 88 Iowa L. Rev. 1 (2002).

to something."[15] Eisenberg erroneously, however, sees this as an example of intellectual incoherence on the part of contractarians. Eisenberg asks, for example, "how we know that an individual is the manager or common agent of a firm unless we have a prior conception of the firm?" As we'll see, we know because the director primacy conception of the firm starts with the board and then assumes that the board hires all other inputs of production. Yet, Eisenberg may object, many contracts are executed by non-managerial employees. True, but when one agent hires another, the latter becomes a sub-agent of the original principal. Just so, non-managerial employees are ultimately linked contractually (at least in the economic sense of the word) to the corporate nexus—i.e., the board of directors.

Judicial Acceptance

Contractarianism is not only increasingly dominant in the legal academy, but also is also steadily working its way into judicial decision making. No less an authority than former Delaware Chancellor William Allen acknowledges that contractarianism is the dominant paradigm in corporate law.[16] Former Delaware Supreme Court Chief Justice Veasey opines: "Although the contract analogy is imperfect, it comes reasonably close to a working hypothesis. I think courts might consider using as a point of departure—but not necessarily a controlling principle—what they perceive to be the investors' reasonable contractual expectations."[17]

The Hypothetical Bargain Methodology

In the nexus of contracts model, corporate law can be thought of as a standard form contract voluntarily adopted—perhaps with modifications—by the parties. The point of a standard form contract, of course, is to reduce bargaining costs. Parties for whom the default rules are a good fit can take the default rules off the rack, without having to bargain over them.

---

[15] Eisenberg, *supra* note 7, at 830.
[16] William T. Allen, *Contracts and Communities in Corporation Law*, 50 Wash. & Lee L. Rev. 1395, 1399 (1993).
[17] E. Norman Veasey, *An Economic Rationale for Judicial Decisionmaking in Corporate Law*, 53 Bus. Law. 681 (1998).

Parties for whom the default rules are inappropriate, in contrast, are free to bargain out of the default rules.[18]

If transaction costs are zero, the default rules—whether contained in a statute or a private standard form contract—do not matter very much.[19] In the face of positive transaction costs, however, the default rule begins to matter very much. Indeed, if transaction costs are very high, bargaining around the rule becomes wholly impractical, forcing the parties to live with an inefficient rule. In such settings, we cannot depend on private contracting to achieve efficient outcomes. Instead, statutes must function as a substitute for private bargaining.

The public corporation—with its thousands of shareholders, managers, employees, and creditors, each with different interests and asymmetrical information—is a very high transaction cost environment indeed. Identifying the corporate constituency for whom getting its way has the highest value thus becomes the critical question. In effect, we must perform a thought experiment: "If the parties could costlessly bargain over the question, which rule would they adopt?" In other words, we mentally play out the following scenario: Sit all interested parties down around a conference table before organizing the corporation. Ask the prospective shareholders, employees, contract creditors, tort victims, and the like to bargain over what rules they would want to govern their relationships. Adopt that bargain as the corporate law default rule. Doing so reduces transaction costs and therefore makes it more efficient to run a business. Of course, you cannot really do this; but you can draw on your experience and economic analysis to predict what the parties would do in such a situation.

---

[18] To be sure, many rules of corporate law are phrased as mandatory provisions the parties supposedly are unable to modify. In fact, however, mandatory corporate law rules generally are trivial, in the sense that they are subject to evasion through choice of form or jurisdiction, or are rules almost everyone would reach in the event of actual bargaining. Bernard S. Black, *Is Corporate Law Trivial?: A Political and Economic Analysis*, 84 Nw. U. L. Rev. 542 (1990).

[19] This is simply a straightforward application of the famous Coase Theorem, which asserts that, in the absence of transaction costs, the initial assignment of a property right will not determine its ultimate use. R. H. Coase, *The Problem of Social Cost*, 3 J.L. & Econ. 1 (1960). According to the Coase Theorem, rights will be acquired by those who value them most highly, which creates an incentive to discover and implement transaction cost minimizing governance forms. A basic premise of the law and economics account thus is that corporate law provides a firm's stakeholders with a set of default rules reflecting the bargain they would strike if they were able to do so.

Implications of the Contractarian Model

At first glance, the implications of a contractarian understanding of the corporate entity may not seem as staggering as they actually are. Consider, for example, the traditional corporate law principle of shareholder wealth maximization. According to a significant line of corporate precedents, the principal obligation of corporate directors is to increase the value of the residual claim—i.e., to increase shareholder wealth. In its traditional guise, this shareholder primacy norm derives from a conception of the corporation as a thing capable of being owned. The shareholders own the corporation, while directors are merely stewards of the shareholders' property.

The nexus of contracts model squarely rejects this conception of the corporation. Indeed, because shareholders are simply one of the inputs bound together by a web of voluntary agreements, ownership simply is not a meaningful concept in nexus of contracts theory. To be sure, shareholders own the residual claim on the corporation's assets and earnings. As we'll see, ownership of that claim is why shareholders are the beneficiaries of director fiduciary duties. Ownership of the residual claim, however, is not the same as ownership of the corporation itself. Someone owns each factor of production hired by the corporation, but no one owns the totality. Instead, the corporation is an aggregation of people bound together by a complex web of contractual relationships.[20]

---

[20] The strong claim in the text is subject to qualification by a variant of contractarian theory associated with economist Oliver Hart, who focuses on processes by which property rights to assets are created, modified, or transferred. *See, e.g.,* Oliver D. Hart, *Incomplete Contracts and the Theory of the Firm,* in *The Nature of the Firm: Origins, Evolution, and Development* 138 (Oliver E. Williamson & Sidney G. Winter eds. 1991). Hart's insight is significant because it reminds us that business organization law does have elements of property law, as well as contract law. Because contract rights are in personam, they apply to persons directly on whom they impose prescribed obligations. In contrast, property rights are in rem and tend to impose generalized duties on a large and indefinite number of persons. Thomas Merrill and Henry Smith argue that in personam relations are governed by flexible default rules designed to minimize the costs of delineating prescribed duties imposed on particular parties, while in rem relations are governed by bright-line rules that impose immutable and standardized obligations on a large and indefinite class. Thomas W. Merrill & Henry E. Smith, *The Property/Contract Interface,* 101 Colum. L. Rev. 773, 789 (2001). They further contend that the distinction between the two types of relations is grounded in information costs. *Id.* at 798–99. Although corporate law has contractual elements, some corporate law rules impose generalized duties on a large and indefinite class of persons. In thinking about which transactions are effected across markets versus those effected within firms, accordingly, it seems plausible that transactions are brought within firms when it makes sense to

As such, the shareholder wealth maximization norm—like all other rules of corporation law—is transformed from a right incident to private property into a mere bargained-for contract term. As with the rights of other corporate constituents, the rights of shareholders are established through bargaining, even though the form of the bargain typically is a take-it-or-leave-it standard form contract provided off-the-rack by the default rules of corporate law and the corporation's organic documents. The contractarian account of this norm thus rests not on an outmoded reification of the corporation, but on the presumption of validity a free market society accords voluntary contracts.

Taken to its logical extreme, this insight allows us to transform the traditional notion of shareholder primacy into one of director primacy. The latter perspective regards the corporation as a vehicle by which the board of directors hires capital by selling equity and debt securities to risk-bearers with varying tastes for risk. Put another way, jettisoning the notion that the corporation is a thing capable of being owned radically changes our understanding of the shareholders' relationship with the corporation. Rather than owning the corporation itself, the shareholders merely own the residual claim on the corporation's assets and earnings. As a result, shareholders are not inherently privileged relative to other corporate constituents. Indeed, as we'll see in Chapter 5, the most interesting thing about the shareholders' contract is not the rights it confers but the very substantial limitations it imposes on those rights.

Locating the Nexus

To say that the corporation is a nexus is to imply the existence of a core or kernel capable of contracting. The chief difficulty with the standard nexus of contracts model thus becomes apparent. Kernels do not make contracts; people make contracts. It does us no good to avoid reifying the corporation by reifying the nexus at the center of the corporation. Accordingly, I argue herein that the defining characteristic of a corporation is the existence of a central decision maker vested with the power of

impose immutable and standardized obligations on a large and indefinite class. For example, Henry Hansmann and Reinier Kraakman argue that it makes sense to use firms in situations in which it is desirable to obtain affirmative asset protection against creditors. Henry Hansmann & Reinier Kraakman, *The Essential Role of Organizational Law*, 110 Yale L.J. 387, 406–23 (2000).

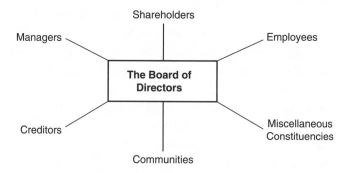

Figure 2 The board of directors as the nexus of contracts

fiat—i.e., a central coordinator that is a party to the set of contracts we call the firm and that has the power to effect adaptive responses to changed conditions by fiat.

If the corporation has such a nexus, where is it located? The Delaware code, like the corporate law of every other state, gives us a clear answer: the corporation's "business and affairs . . . shall be managed by or under the direction of the board of directors."[21] Put simply, the board is the corporate nexus of contracts.

To be sure, former Delaware Chancellor Allen once opined that "our corporation law confers power upon directors as the agents of the shareholders; it does not create Platonic masters."[22] In fact, however, under U.S. corporate law the board of directors is not a mere agent of the shareholders, but rather is a sui generis body whose powers are "original and undelegated."[23] Or, as an early California corporate law treatise put it: "The board of directors is the fountain of executive authority, and the shareholders, unless by unanimous vote, cannot control the powers of the board."[24]

Under all state corporation codes, the key players in the statutory decision-making structure are the corporation's directors. In all states, the corporation code provides for a system of nearly absolute delegation of power to the board of directors, which in turn is authorized to further

[21] Del. Code Ann., tit. 8, § 141(a).
[22] Blasius Industries, Inc. v. Atlas Corp., 564 A.2d 651, 663 (Del.Ch. 1988).
[23] Manson v. Curtis, 119 N.E. 559, 562 (N.Y. 1918).
[24] Henry Winthrop Ballantine, *California Corporation Laws* 145 (1932).

delegate power to subordinate firm agents.[25] The vast majority of corporate decisions accordingly are made by the board of directors alone (or by managers acting under delegated authority).[26] The statutory decision-making model thus is one in which the board acts and shareholders, at most, react. Put simply, control is vested in the board—not the shareholders.

The Shareholders' Deal

As we've just seen, in every state, corporation law offers up, as the default rule, a regime in which (1) the corporation is organized as a hierarchy surmounted by a board of directors empowered to effect adaptive change through fiat and (2) the shareholder wealth maximization norm provides the governing norm by which the board's decision making is to be guided. The basic thesis of the hypothetical bargain methodology is that by providing the rule to which the parties would agree if they could bargain (the so-called "majoritarian default"), society facilitates private ordering.[27] The logical question thus is whether the statutory framework is the majoritarian default and, if so, why.

There's good reason to think that the statutory rules are the majoritarian default rules. First, boards of directors charged with maximizing shareholder wealth have been around for a very long time, suggesting that something about them has considerable survival value.

Second, investors will not purchase, or at least will not pay as much for, securities of firms incorporated in states whose statutes either cater

---

[25] *See* Model Bus. Corp. Act Ann. § 8.01 at 8-10–8-11 (1995) (reviewing statutes).

[26] The word "decision" is used herein for semantic convenience to describe a process that often is much less discrete in practice. Most board of director activity "does not consist of taking affirmative action on individual matters; it is instead a continuing flow of supervisory process, punctuated only occasionally by a discrete transactional decision." Bayless Manning, *The Business Judgment Rule and the Director's Duty of Attention: Time for Reality*, 39 Bus. Law, 1477, 1494 (1984).

[27] In an important series of articles, however, Ian Ayres and his collaborators argued that majoritarian defaults are not always desirable, even if a potentially dominant one can be identified. *See, e.g.*, Ian Ayres, *Making a Difference: The Contractual Contributions of Easterbrook and Fischel*, 59 U. Chi. L. Rev. 1391 (1992); Ian Ayres and Robert Gertner, *Filling Gaps in Incomplete Contracts: An Economic Theory of Default Rules*, 99 Yale L.J. 87 (1989); Ian Ayres and Eric Talley, *Solomonic Bargaining: Dividing a Legal Entitlement to Facilitate Coasean Trade*, 104 Yale L.J. 1027 (1995). I have elsewhere argued that Ayres' critique of the majoritarian default has little traction insofar as corporation and other forms of business association law are concerned. Stephen M. Bainbridge, *Contractarianism in the Business Associations Classroom: Kovacik v. Reed and the Allocation of Capital Losses in Service Partnerships*, 34 Ga. L. Rev. 631 (2000).

too excessively to management or are otherwise inefficient. Lenders will not make loans to corporations incorporated in those states without compensation for the risks posed by such statutes. As a result, those firms' costs of capital will rise, while their earnings will fall. Among other things, such firms thereby become more vulnerable to hostile takeover and subsequent management purges. Corporate managers therefore have strong incentives to incorporate the business in a state offering rules preferred by investors. Competition for corporate charters thus should deter states from adopting statutes offering inefficient default rules.[28] The empirical research appears to bear out this view of state competition, suggesting that, while there are some important exceptions, efficient solutions to corporate law problems generally tend to win out over time.[29]

Given that the identification of the board of directors as the nexus of corporate contracts is universally enshrined in state corporation law in the United States, we may infer that director primacy is in fact the majoritarian default. Now we must ask why most people would choose director primacy rather than either shareholder or managerial primacy. It is to those questions that the next sections turn. We begin with the question of control; namely, why is the shareholders' bargain with the corporation codified in a default rule under which decision-making authority is vested

---

[28] See Ralph K. Winter, Jr., *State Law, Shareholder Protection, and the Theory of the Corporation*, 6 J. Legal Stud. 251 (1977) (the seminal response to Cary); *see also* William J. Carney, *The Political Economy of Competition for Corporate Charters*, 26 J. Legal Stud. 303 (1997); Frank H. Easterbrook, *Managers' Discretion and Investors' Welfare: Theories and Evidence*, 9 Del. J. Corp. L. 540, 654–71 (1984); Daniel R. Fischel, *The "Race to the Bottom" Revisited: Reflections on Recent Developments in Delaware's Corporation Law*, 76 Nw. U. L. Rev. 913 (1982); Roberta Romano, *The State Competition Debate in Corporate Law*, 8 Cardozo L. Rev. 709 (1987); cf. Jonathan R. Macey and Geoffrey P. Miller, *Toward an Interest Group Theory of Delaware Corporate Law*, 65 Tex. L. Rev. 469 (1987) (public choice-based theory of state competition). But *see* William L. Cary, *Federalism and Corporate Law: Reflections Upon Delaware*, 83 Yale L.J. 663 (1974) (classic statement of the race to the bottom hypothesis); *see also* Lucian Ayre Bebchuk, *Federalism and the Corporation: The Desirable Limits on State Competition in Corporate Law*, 105 Harv. L. Rev. 1437 (1992) (arguing that corporate law is a race to the bottom).

[29] See Roberta Romano, *The Genius of American Corporate Law* (1993) (setting forth both an empirical analysis and theoretical arguments challenging the race to the bottom hypothesis). As even many advocates of the race to the top hypothesis concede, however, state regulation of corporate takeovers appears to be an exception to the rule that efficient solutions tend to win out. *See, e.g.*, Roberta Romano, *Competition for Corporate Charters and the Lesson of Takeover Statutes*, 61 Fordham L. Rev. 843 (1993); Ralph K. Winter, *The "Race for the Top" Revisited: A Comment on Eisenberg*, 89 Colum. L. Rev. 1526 (1989); *see also* Lucian Ayre Bebchuk and Allen Ferrell, *Federalism and Corporate Law: The Race to Protect Managers from Takeovers*, 99 Colum. L. Rev. 1168 (1999) (contending that the race to the bottom in takeover regulation may be a general phenomenon).

in the board rather than shareholders (or some other constituency, for that matter). Once we've analyzed the bargain over the means of corporate governance, we'll turn our attention to the ends thereof. Why does the set of contracts making up the corporation assign the residual claim to shareholders and, accordingly, make shareholders—and shareholders alone—the beneficiaries of the board of directors and management's fiduciary duties?

The Bargaining Parties

In order for contractarian theory to be useful, it must be concerned not only with identifying the contracting parties, but also with how they contract. Put another way, we now must invoke the hypothetical bargain methodology to examine the corporation's critical governance features. In doing so, we are concerned with three principal sets of stakeholders: the board of directors, managers, and shareholders.

Many commentators, of course, will argue that this approach to corporate governance is too narrow. They contend that corporate governance should include concern for corporate social responsibility. Accordingly, they argue, one should include nonshareholder constituencies in the analysis. We'll consider those arguments later in this chapter. For present purposes, however, we will continue to treat the corporation as a vehicle by which directors hire capital, which leads to our focus here on bargaining between shareholders and the board of directors.

The Bargain over the Means of Corporate Governance

Kenneth Arrow identified two basic ways in which organizations make decisions: consensus and authority.[30] Consensus requires that each member of the organization have identical information and interests so that preferences can be aggregated at low cost. In contrast, authority-based decision-making structures arise where group members have different interests and information.

Despite their contractual nature, public corporations are not participatory democracies, but rather are hierarchies. Authority consistently trumps

---

[30] Kenneth J. Arrow, *The Limits of Organization* 63–79 (1974).

consensus in the corporation. Why? What survival advantages does a large corporation gain from authority-based decision-making structures?

These questions suggest an analysis proceeding in three steps. First, why do corporations not rely on consensus-based decision making? Second, why do corporations not permit multiple constituencies to elect directors? Finally, why are shareholders the favored constituency?

On the Necessity of Fiat

Armen Alchian and Harold Demsetz famously argued that the firm "has no power of fiat, no authority, no disciplinary action any different in the slightest degree from ordinary market contracting between any two people."[31] According to Alchian and Demsetz, an employer's control over its employees differs not at all from the power of a consumer over the grocer with whom the consumer does business.

If fiat is not an essential attribute of "firm-ishness," however, the firm would be nothing more than a quasi–market arena within which a set of contracts between various factors of production are constantly renegotiated. It is not. Power exists within firms, and it matters. The corporation has a nexus—and that nexus wields a power of fiat different from that of a consumer over a grocer. Indeed, fiat is the chief characteristic that distinguishes firms from markets.

As economist Ronald Coase explained long ago, firms emerge when it is efficient to substitute entrepreneurial fiat for the price mechanisms of the market. In markets, resources are allocated by the price system, while in firms resources are allocated by authoritative direction. "If a workman moves from department Y to department X, he does not go because of change in relative prices, but because he is ordered to do so."[32] Accordingly, economic activity will be conducted within a firm rather than across a market when command and control is cheaper than bargaining.

---

[31] Armen A. Alchian & Harold Demsetz, *Production, Information Costs, and Economic Organization*, 62 Am. Econ. Rev. 777, 777 (1972).

[32] R.H. Coase, *The Nature of the Firm*, 4 Economica (n.s.) 386, 387 (1937). Drawing a distinction between across-market transactions and intra-firm transactions serves a useful pedagogic purpose, but is not a wholly accurate description of the real world, in which there is a wide array of choices falling between purely contractual relationships and the classical economic firm. *See* Klein, *supra* note 11, at 1523 (discussing intermediary forms); *see also* Klein & Coffee, *supra* note 10, at 19 (suggesting that the dichotomy between firms and markets "could usefully be replaced" by the concept of "firmishness").

The relevant costs can be divided into three basic categories. First, there can be significant search and other transaction costs associated with bargaining. Adam Smith's account of pin manufacturing in eighteenth century England remains a classic example of the costs faced by entrepreneurs who rely on spot markets. Smith observed that making a pin involves eighteen distinct operations. An individual performing each of those operations on his own produced, at best, one pin a day. When a team was organized, in which each operation was conducted by a separate individual, a substantial synergistic effect resulted. Such a production team produced thousands of pins a day.[33]

In practice, this sort of team production requires personnel interactions too complex to be handled through a price mechanism. The firm therefore acts as a central coordinator. Some team member is charged with seeking out the necessary inputs and bringing them together for productive labor.

Second, organizing economic activity within a firm can help to prevent the opportunistic appropriation of quasi-rents. A transaction-specific asset is one whose value is appreciably lower in any other use than the transaction in question. Once a transaction-specific investment has been made, it generates quasi-rents; i.e., returns in excess of that necessary to maintain the asset in its current use. If those quasi-rents are appropriable by the party with control of the transaction-specific asset, a hold-up problem ensues. Vertical integration brings both parties within a single firm and, accordingly, is a common solution to the hold-up problem.[34]

Finally, command and control provides a mechanism for dealing with uncertainty and complexity. Uncertainty arises in business relationships because it is difficult to predict the future conditions the parties will face. Complexity arises when the parties attempt to contractually specify how they will respond to a given situation. As the relationship's term lengthens, it necessarily becomes more difficult to foresee the needs and threats of the future, which in turn presents an ever-growing myriad of contingencies to be dealt with. The more contingencies to be accounted

---

[33] Adam Smith, *An Inquiry into the Nature and Causes of the Wealth of Nations* (1776).

[34] *See, e.g.,* Benjamin R. Klein et al., *Vertical Integration, Appropriable Rents and the Competitive Contracting Process,* 21 J.L. & Econ. 297 (1978). Institutional economics also suggests that hierarchical ordering of production within a firm can reduce costs associated with informational asymmetries and bilateral monopolies. Oliver E. Williamson, Introduction, in *The Nature of the Firm: Origins, Evolution, and Development* 3, 4 (Oliver E. Williamson & Sidney G. Winter eds. 1991).

for, and the greater the degree of uncertainty that is present, the more difficult it becomes for the parties to draft completely specified contracts. Indeed, the phenomenon of bounded rationality implies that incomplete contracts are inevitable under conditions of uncertainty and complexity. In turn, incomplete contracts leave greater room for opportunistic behavior. All of which tends to encourage reliance on central coordination.[35]

Firms arise when it is possible to mitigate these costs by delegating to a team member the power to direct how the various inputs will be utilized by the firm. One team member is empowered to constantly and, more important, unilaterally rewrite certain terms of the contract between the firm and its various constituents. By creating a central decision maker—a nexus—with the power of fiat, the firm thus substitutes ex post governance for ex ante contract. Uncertainty and complexity are no longer as problematic, because the central decision maker can exercise its power of fiat to mandate a chosen adaptive response to new circumstances. Opportunism is deterred by the prospect of ex post sanctions, obviating the necessity of drafting a complete contract ex ante.

Granted, coordination can be achieved without fiat, as demonstrated by the more-or-less democratic decision-making processes of many partnerships and other small firms. In the public corporation, however, fiat is essential. As we saw above, all organizations must have some mechanism for aggregating the preferences of the organization's constituencies and converting them into collective decisions. As we also saw, such mechanisms fall out on a spectrum between "consensus" and "authority." Recall that authority-based decision-making structures—characterized by the existence of a central office empowered to make decisions binding on the firm as a whole—arise where the firm's constituencies have different interests and access to information.

---

[35] Oliver Williamson's transaction costs economics offers a more robust account of the costs associated with bargaining that can be reduced through hierarchical ordering of production within a firm, among which are informational asymmetries, bilateral monopolies, as well as incomplete contracting. Oliver E. Williamson, Introduction, in *The Nature of the Firm: Origins, Evolution, and Development* 3, 4 (Oliver E. Williamson & Sidney G. Winter eds. 1991). In particular, Williamson emphasizes that uncertainty and complexity do not provide a sufficient explanation for the emergence of ex post governance structures. Instead, one also must introduce some form of asset specificity, of which the most important for present purposes is the firm-specific human capital of the firm's agents. For a critique of the transaction cost literature in this area, *see* Harold Demsetz, *The Theory of the Firm Revisited*, 4 J.L. Econ. & Org. 141, 144–54 (1988).

Assume a corporation with 5,000 stakeholders entitled to participate in management decisions. Could such a firm function as a sort of participatory democracy, using some form of consensus-based decision making? Not if we hoped that each participant would make informed decisions. Our hypothetical stakeholders necessarily will have differing degrees of access to information. Employees serving in managerial and supervisory roles, for example, will tend to have broader perspectives, with more general business information, than do line workers. In contrast, the latter, will tend to have more specific information about particular aspects of the shop floor. Creditors, shareholders, and other stakeholders likewise will have important information of which employees are unaware and vice versa.

These information asymmetries will prove intractable. A rational decision maker expends effort to make informed decisions only if the expected benefits of doing so outweigh its costs. In a firm of the sort at bar, gathering information will be very costly. Efficient participatory democracy requires all decision makers to have roughly equal information, which requires that each decision maker have a communication channel to every other decision maker. As the number of decision makers increases, the number of communication channels within the firm increases as the square of the number of decision makers.[36]

The requisite communication channels will inevitably suffer certain disabling pathologies. First, the stakeholders could not credibly bind themselves to reveal information accurately and honestly or to follow prescribed decision-making rules. Second, bounded rationality makes it doubtful that anyone in a firm of any substantial size could process the vast number of resulting information flows. Although economic actors seek to maximize their expected utility, the limitations of human cognition often result in decisions that fail to maximize utility. Decision makers inherently have limited memories, computational skills, and other mental tools, which in turn limit their ability to gather and process information.[37] Third, the opportunity cost entailed in making informed decisions is also

---

[36] Oliver E. Williamson, *Markets and Hierarchies: Analysis and Antitrust Implications* 46 (1975).

[37] *See* Herbert A. Simon, *Rational Choice and the Structure of the Environment*, in *Models of Man* 261 (1957) (credited with coining the term bounded rationality); *see generally* Roy Radner, *Bounded Rationality, Indeterminacy, and the Theory of the Firm*, 106 Econ. J. 1360, 1362–68 (1996) (providing an especially detailed taxonomy of the various forms bounded rationality takes, with special emphasis on the theory's relevance to the organization for firms).

high and, even more important, readily apparent. In contrast, the expected benefits of becoming informed are quite low, as an individual decision maker's vote will not have a significant effect on the vote's outcome. Finally, the decision-making process inevitably will encounter serious collective action problems, such as free riding and holding out, not to mention the sheer mechanical difficulties inherent in conducting meetings with 5,000 participants. In sum, it seems safe to predict that our stakeholders will be rationally apathetic.

Note that this analysis helps to explain not only why corporations use authority rather than consensus at the top, but also helps us to understand why authority-based decision-making is pervasive within the corporation. The familiar corporate hierarchy emerged because it generally is an efficient mechanism for information development and transmittal. Bounded rationality places limits on the ability of individuals to gather and process information, which implies that an individual manager can gather information about the capacities of only a limited number of production units and that no supervisor should receive such information from more than a few subordinates. Branching hierarchies solve this problem by limiting the span of control over which any individual manager has supervision to a small number of subordinates. Specifically, branching hierarchies put people into small groups, each member of which reports information to the same supervisor. That supervisor is likewise a member of a small group that reports to a superior and so on up to the board of directors top, which supervises the CEO and the rest of the top management team. In most cases, such an organizational system gets reliable information to the right decision maker more efficiently than any other organizational system. Not surprisingly, some form of branching hierarchy therefore tends to be found in most public corporations: they could not make decisions without it.[38]

---

[38] For a detailed defense of this proposition, and corporate hierarchies generally, see Robert C. Clark, Corporate Law 801–16 (1986). For a description of circumstances under which hierarchy ceases to be an efficient information transmission mechanism, see Stephen M. Bainbridge, Privately Ordered Participatory Management, 23 Del. J. Corp. L. 979, 1011–14 (1998).

No implication is intended that information is always funneled to the top of the hierarchy or that all decisions are made there. To the contrary, all corporate hierarchies are characterized by a degree of decentralization of decision making, with numerous decision makers at various levels within the hierarchy being tasked with particular areas of responsibility. Indeed, firms most appropriately might be described as a set of many overlapping hierarchies. Roy Radner, Hierarchy: The Economics of Managing, 30 J.

Just as our stakeholders face serious and persistent information asymmetries, they also would have to deal with the problem of conflicting interests. Suppose, for the sake of argument, that all 5,000 of our stakeholders were also employees of the firm. Even in an employee-owned firm, there will be conflicting interests that preclude the use of consensus-based decision making. In some cases, employees will differ about the best way in which to achieve a common goal. In others, individual employees will be disparately affected by a proposed course of action. Although the problems created by divergent interests within the employee block may not be insurmountable, such differences at least raise the cost of using consensus-based decision-making structures in employee-owned firms.

Both the existence of such divergent interests within the employee group and the costs that result therefrom are confirmed by the empirical evidence. Labor-managed firms tend to remain small, to screen members carefully, to limit the franchise to relatively homogeneous groups, and to use agenda controls to prevent cycling and other public choice problems.[39] All of these characteristics are consistent with an attempt to minimize the likelihood and effect of divergent interests.

Now suppose our 5,000 stakeholders consisted of two sets of constituencies: labor and capital. Again complicate the analysis by separating capital and labor. Although employee and shareholder interests are often congruent, they can conflict. Consider, for example, the downsizing phenomenon. Corporate restructurings typically result in substantial reductions in force, reduced job security, longer work weeks, more stress, and diminished morale.[40] From the shareholders' perspective, however, the market typically rewards restructurings with substantial stock price increases. As the divergence of interest in this example suggests, conflicting interests loom large as a bar to the use of consensus in capitalist firms.

The necessity of a literal nexus—a center of power capable of exercising fiat—within the corporation thus follows as a matter of course from the asymmetries of information and interests among the corporation's various constituencies. Shareholders care about the value of the residual claim on the corporation. Customers care about the quality and quantity

Econ. Lit. 1382, 1412 (1992). The point is only that branching hierarchies are an efficient means of ensuring that information flows to the correct supervisor.
[39] Greg Dow & Louis Putterman, *Why Capital (Usually) Hires Labor: An Assessment of Proposed Explanations, in Employees and Corporate Governance* 17 (Margaret Blair & Mark Roe eds. 1999).
[40] Michael Useem, *Investor Capitalism* 164–65 (1996).

of the goods produced by the corporation. Workers care about salary and conditions of employment. And so on. In addition, of course, the collective action problems inherent in achieving consensus among thousands of decision makers further impede the use of consensus-based decision making in large corporations. Under these "conditions of widely dispersed information and the need for speed in decisions, authoritative control at the tactical level is essential for success."[41] This is so because it is "cheaper and more efficient to transmit all the pieces of information to a central place" and to have the central office "make the collective choice and transmit it rather than retransmit all the information on which the decision is based."[42]

In large corporations, authority-based decision-making structures are also desirable because of the potential they create for division and specialization of labor. Bounded rationality and complexity, as well as the practical costs of losing time when one shifts jobs, make it efficient for corporate constituents to specialize. Directors and managers specialize in the efficient coordination of other specialists. In order to reap the benefits of specialization, all other corporate constituents should prefer to specialize in functions unrelated to decision making, such as risk-bearing (shareholders) or labor (employees), delegating decision making to the board and senior management. This natural division of labor, however, requires that the chosen directors and officers be vested with discretion to make binding decisions. Separating ownership and control by vesting decision-making authority in a centralized nexus distinct from the shareholders and all other constituents is what makes the large public corporation feasible.

In sum, under conditions of asset specificity, bounded rationality, and opportunism, the ability to adapt becomes the central problem of organization.[43] In large public corporations, contrary to Alchian and Demsetz's claim, adaptation is effected by fiat. Obviously, fiat within firms has limits. Some choices are barred by contract, such as negative pledge covenants in bond indentures. Other choices may be barred by regulation or statute. Still other choices may be unattractive for business reasons, such as those with potentially adverse reputational consequences. Within such bounds, however, adaptation effected through fiat is the distinguishing characteristic of the firm.

---

[41] Arrow, *supra* note 30, at 69.

[42] *Id.* at 68–69.

[43] Oliver E. Williamson, *Transaction Cost Economics Meets Posnerian Law and Economics*, 149 J. Institutional & Theoretical Econ. 99, 102 (1993).

Fiat by Contract?

At first blush, there may appear to be an inconsistency between the command-and-control theory of the corporation just sketched and the contractarian model outlined above. Recall that Alchian and Demsetz rejected Coase's argument that fiat was the factor distinguishing firms from markets. As noted, they argued that a firm has no power of fiat. Instead, for example, an employer's power to direct its employees does not differ from a consumer's power to direct his grocer. Alchian and Demsetz's argument, however, simply doesn't reflect real world realities. Command and control is the norm in most corporations.[44]

In any case, there is no necessary contradiction between a theory of the corporation characterized by command-and-control decision making and the contractarian model. The set of contracts making up the firm consists in very large measure of implicit agreements, which by definition are both incomplete and unenforceable. Under conditions of uncertainty and complexity, the parties cannot execute a complete contract, so that many decisions must be left for later contractual rewrites imposed by fiat. It is precisely the non-enforceability of implicit corporate contracts that makes it possible for the central decision maker to rewrite them more or less freely. The parties to the corporate contract presumably accept this consequence of relying on implicit contracts because the resulting reduction in transaction costs benefits them all. Hence, the firm's constituents voluntarily enter into a relationship in which they accept the power of fiat, while reserving the right to disassociate from the firm.

The Inefficiency of Multiple Constituencies

The analysis to this point merely demonstrates that corporate decision making must be made on a representative, rather than on a participatory, basis. In other words, it explains why ownership and control separated and power was vested in the board rather than one or more of the

---

[44] *See* Joseph E. Stiglitz, *Incentives, Risk, and Information: Notes Toward a Theory of Hierarchy,* 6 Bell J. Econ. 552, 553 (1975) (stating: "The employer is allowed to assign the workers different tasks...."); *see also* John F. Witte, *Democracy, Authority, and Alienation in Work: Workers' Participation in an American Corporation* 38 (1980) (arguing that workers generally accept hierarchical authority and perceive obedience to authority as an integral part of their job: "for the majority, disobedience is unthinkable").

corporation's constituencies. As yet, nothing in the analysis dictates the U.S. model in which only shareholders elect directors. One could plausibly imagine a board of directors on which multiple constituencies are represented. Indeed, imagination is not required, because the supervisory board component of German codetermination provides a real world example of just such a board. Empirical evidence, however, suggests that codetermination does not lead to efficiency or productivity gains.[45]

Why not? In Arrow's terminology, the board of directors serves as a consensus-based decision-making body at the top of an authority-based structure. Recall that for consensus to function, however, two conditions must be met: equivalent interests and information. Neither condition can be met when both employee and shareholder representatives are on the board.

The two factors are closely related, of course. Indeed, it is the potential divergence of shareholder and employee interests that ensures employee representatives will be deprived of the information necessary for them to function. Because of the board's position at the apex of the corporate hierarchy, employee representatives are inevitably exposed to a far greater amount of information about the firm than is normally provided to employees. As the European experience with codetermination teaches, this can result in corporate information leaking to the work force as a whole or even to outsiders. In the Netherlands, for example, the obligation of works council representatives to respect the confidentiality of firm information "has not always been kept, causing serious concerns among management which is required . . . to provide extensive 'sensitive' information to the councils."[46]

---

[45] *See generally* Stephen M. Bainbridge, *Participatory Management Within a Theory of the Firm,* 21 J. Corp. L. 657 (1996) (summarizing studies). Codetermination statutes typically mandate, inter alia, a dual board structure. A supervisory board appoints and oversees a managing board, with the latter actively operating the firm. In theory, employees and shareholders are equally represented on the supervisory board. In practice, however, the board often is controlled either by the firm's managers or a dominant shareholder. One of the employee representatives must be from management, and shareholders are entitled to elect the chairman of the board, who has the power to break tie votes. If push comes to shove, which it reportedly rarely does, shareholders thus retain a slight but potentially critical edge. *See generally* Klaus J. Hopt, *Labor Representation on Corporate Boards: Impacts and Problems for Corporate Governance and Economic Integration in Europe,* 14 Int'l Rev. L. & Econ. 203 (1994).

[46] Tom R. Ottervanger & Ralph M. Pais, *Employee Participation in Corporate Decision Making: The Dutch Model,* 15 Int'l Law. 393, 399 (1981).

One sure result of lost confidentiality will be worker demands for higher wages. In unionized firms, management will be especially reluctant to inform union members on the board of information that might aid the union in collective bargaining. Perhaps the best anecdotal example of this problem is the famous observation made by Rick Dubinsky, head of United Airlines' pilots union: "We don't want to kill the golden goose. We just want to choke it by the neck until it gives us every last egg." That this anecdote can be generalized to non-unionized firms is confirmed by an empirical study finding that provision of financial and other business information to employees of non-unionized firms had a negative effect on firm profitability, which was attributed to the higher wages demanded by the informed employees.[47]

Given that providing board level information to employee representatives appears clearly contrary to shareholder interests, we would expect managers loyal to shareholder interests to withhold information from the board of directors in order to deny it to employee representatives, which would seriously undermine the board's ability to carry out its essential corporate governance roles. This prediction is borne out by the German experience with codetermination. German managers sometimes deprive the supervisory board of information, because they do not want the supervisory board's employee members to learn it. Alternatively, the board's real work may be done in committees or de facto rump caucuses from which employee representatives are excluded.[48] As a result, while codetermination raises the procedural costs of decision making, it may not have much effect on substantive outcomes.

Although Arrow's equality of information criterion is important, in this context the critical element is the divergence of shareholder and employee interests. The interests of shareholders will inevitably differ among themselves, as do those of employees, but individual constituents of the corporation nevertheless are more likely to share interests with members of the same constituency than with members of another constituency. Allowing board representation for employees thus tends only to compound

---

[47] Morris M. Kleiner & Marvin L. Bouillon, *Providing Business Information to Production Workers: Correlates of Compensation and Productivity*, 41 Ind. & Lab. Rel. Rev. 605, 614–15 (1988). *See also* Stuart Ogden, *The Limits to Employee Involvement: Profit Sharing and Disclosure of Information*, 29 J. Mgmt Stud. 229 (1992) (stating that U.K. employers are reluctant to provide disclosure of financial information for fear of stimulating workers to make demands respecting pay and working conditions).

[48] Hopt, *supra* note 45, at 206.

the problem that gives rise to an authority-based hierarchical decision-making structure by bringing the differing interests of employees and shareholders directly into the boardroom. The difficulty, of course, is not merely that the interests of employees and shareholders diverge, but also that different classes of employees have divergent interests. As we have seen, this seriously compounds the problem of aggregating constituency preferences.

The resulting conflicts of interest between shareholders and employees inevitably impede consensus-based decision making within the board of directors. Worker representatives on corporate boards tend to prefer greater labor advocacy than do traditional directors, no doubt in large part because workers evaluate their representatives on the basis of labor advocacy, which results in role conflicts.[49] This conflict is exacerbated in heavily unionized industries, as representatives of a single union might sit on the boards of multiple firms within the industry. In the extreme case, the demise of one firm might redound to the greater good of the greatest number by benefiting union members who work at competing corporations. This creates the potential for perverse incentives on the part of union representatives on the board.

The problem with codetermination thus is not only that the conflict of employee and shareholder interests impedes the achievement of consensus, but also that it may result in a substantial increase in agency costs. The most obvious concern is the possibility that employee representation will permit management to pursue its own self-interest at the expense of both shareholders and employees by playing worker and shareholder representatives off against each other. Legal and market accountability mechanisms constrain this tendency, but because they are not perfect there remains the possibility that self-interested managers may throw their support behind the side of the board whose interests happen to coincide with those of management in the issue at hand.

This conflict is well-known, of course, but there is a more subtle problem that is often overlooked. Corporate employees have an incentive to shirk so long as their compensation does not perfectly align their incentives with those of the firm's shareholders. In turn, knowing of this phenomenon, the firm's shareholders should expect management to reduce the compensation of the firm's employees by the amount necessary

[49] John L. Cotton, *Employee Involvement* 128 (1993).

to offset the expected degree of employee shirking. Because ex ante wage adjustments rarely are fully compensatory, due to bounded rationality and the resulting use of incomplete contracts, the firm's shareholders should expect management to monitor the employees and penalize ex post those who shirk.

Would it thus not seem odd that those who are to be monitored should be allowed to choose the monitors? Put another way, workers have an interest in supporting rules that free management from accountability to shareholders. This is so because managerial shirking of its responsibility to monitor employees redounds to the workers' benefit. Accordingly, employee representatives on the board of directors are less likely to insist on disciplining lax managers than are shareholder representatives. Hence, if employees are entitled to voting representation on the board of directors, monitoring by the board and its subordinate managers will be less effective, which will cause agency costs to rise.

The validity of this prediction also is confirmed by the German experience with codetermination. Conflicts of interest faced by employee representatives on the supervisory board remain a serious, but unresolved concern. Employee representation slows the finding of a consensus on the supervisory board and creates a built-in polarization problem. Hence, as already noted, it is standard practice for employee and shareholder representatives to have separate pre-meeting caucuses.

Although it is sometimes asserted that employee representation would benefit the board by promoting "discussion and consideration of alternative perspectives and arguments,"[50] the preceding analysis suggests that any such benefits would come at high cost. In addition, there is reason to doubt whether those benefits are very significant. Workers will be indifferent to most corporate decisions that do not bear directly on working conditions and benefits.[51] All of which tends to suggest that employee representatives add little except increased labor advocacy to the board.

---

[50] Robert Howse & Michael J. Trebilcock, *Protecting the Employment Bargain*, 43 U. Tor. L. Rev. 751, 769 (1993).

[51] *See* Michael P. Dooley, *European Proposals for Worker Information and Codetermination: An American Comment*, in *Harmonization of the Laws in the European Communities: Products Liability, Conflict of Laws, and Corporation Law* 126, 129 (Peter E. Herzog ed. 1983) ("As to the majority of managerial policies concerning, for example, dividend and investment policies, product development, and the like, the typical employee has as much interest and as much to offer as the typical purchaser of light bulbs.").

Allocating Control: Why Do Only Shareholders Vote?

The analysis thus far demonstrates that public corporation decision making must be conducted on a representative rather than participatory basis. It further demonstrates that only one constituency should be allowed to elect the board of directors. The remaining question is why shareholders are the chosen constituency, rather than, say, employees. Answering that question is the task of this section.

One plausible answer rests on the divergence of interests within constituency groups. Although investors have somewhat different preferences on issues such as dividends and the like, they are generally united by a desire to maximize share value. Board consensus therefore will be more easily achieved if directors are beholden solely to shareholder interests, rather than to the more diverse set of interests represented by employees and other stakeholders.

A related but perhaps more telling point is the problem of apportioning the vote. Financial capital is fungible, transferable, and quantifiable. Control rights based on financial capital are thus subject to low cost allocation and valuation. In contrast, the human capital of workers meets none of these criteria. While one-person/one-vote would be a low cost solution to the allocation problem, it appears highly inefficient given the unequal distribution of reasoning power and education. If the most competent people and/or those with the most at stake should have the most votes, some more costly allocation device will be necessary.

The standard law and economics explanation for vesting voting rights in shareholders, however, is that shareholders are the only corporate constituent with a residual, unfixed, ex post claim on corporate assets and earnings.[52] In contrast, the employees' claim is prior and largely fixed ex ante by contract, as are the claims of other stakeholders. This distinction has two implications of present import. First, as noted above, employee interests are too parochial to justify board representation. In contrast, shareholders have the strongest economic incentive to care about the size of the residual claim, which means that they have the greatest incentive to elect directors committed to maximizing firm profitability. Second, the nature of the employees' claim on the firm creates incentives for employees to shirk. Vesting control rights in the employees would

---

See, e.g., Frank H. Easterbrook and Daniel R. Fischel, *The Economic Structure of Corporate Law* 66–72 (1991).

increase their incentive to shirk. In turn, the prospect of employee shirking lowers the value of the shareholders' residual claim.

At this point, it is useful to invoke the hypothetical bargain methodology central to the contractarian approach to corporations. If the corporation's various constituencies could bargain over voting rights, to which constituency would they assign those rights? In light of their status as residual claimants and the adverse effects of employee representation, shareholders doubtless would bargain for control rights, so as to ensure a corporate decision-making system emphasizing monitoring mechanisms designed to prevent shirking by employees, and employees would be willing to concede such rights to shareholders.

Granted, as we'll see below, corporate law precludes the shareholders from exercising meaningful day-to-day or even year-to-year control over managerial decisions—and does so for very good reasons. Unlike the employees' claim, however, the shareholders' claim on the corporation is freely transferable. As such, if management fails to maximize the shareholders' residual claim, an outsider can profit by purchasing a majority of the shares and voting out the incumbent board of directors. Accordingly, vesting the right to vote solely in the hands of the firm's shareholders is what makes possible the market for corporate control and thus helps to minimize shirking. As the residual claimants, shareholders thus would bargain for sole voting control, in order to ensure that the value of their claim is maximized.[53] In turn, because all corporate constituents have an ex ante interest in minimizing shirking by managers and other agents, the firm's employees have an incentive to agree to such rules.

Put another way, the employees' lack of control rights can be seen as a way in which they bond their promise not to shirk. Their lack of control rights not only precludes them from double-dipping, but also facilitates managerial disciplining of employees who shirk. Accordingly, it is not surprising that the default rules of the standard form contract provided by all corporate statutes vest voting rights solely in the hands of common shareholders.

To be sure, the vote allows shareholders to allocate some risk to prior claimants. If a firm is in financial straits, directors and managers faithful

---

[53] To be sure, the existence of takeover defenses sharply constrains the exercise of shareholder control via the market for corporate control. The legitimacy of such defenses rests on considerations akin to those described in Chapter 3, and is developed more fully in Stephen M. Bainbridge, *Mergers and Acquisitions* 340–86 (2003).

to shareholder interests could protect the value of the shareholders' residual claim by, for example, financial and/or workforce restructurings that eliminate prior claimants. Why then do employees not get the vote in order to protect themselves against this risk? The answer is twofold. First, as we have seen, multiple constituencies are inefficient. Second, employees have significant protections that do not rely on voting.

Suppose a firm behaves opportunistically toward its employees. What protections do the employees have? Some are protected by job mobility. The value of continued dealings with an employer to an employee whose work involves solely general human capital does not depend on the value of the firm because neither the employee nor the firm have an incentive to preserve such an employment relationship. If the employee's general human capital suffices for him to do his job at Firm A, it presumably would suffice for him to do a similar job at Firm B. Such an employee resembles an independent contractor who can shift from firm to firm at low cost to either employee or employer. (This is not to say that exit is costless for either employees or firms. All employees are partially locked into their firms. Indeed, it must be so, or monitoring could not prevent shirking because disciplinary efforts would have no teeth. The question is one of relative costs.)

Mobility thus provides a defense against opportunistic conduct for such employees, because they can quit and be replaced without productive loss to either employee or employer. Put another way, because there are no appropriable quasi-rents in this category of employment relationships, rent seeking by management is not a concern.

Corporate employees who make firm-specific investments in human capital arguably need greater protection against employer opportunism, but such protections need not include board representation. Indeed, various specialized governance structures have arisen to protect such workers. Among these are severance pay, grievance procedures, promotion ladders, collective bargaining, and the like.

As private sector unions have declined, the federal government has intervened to provide through general welfare legislation many of the same protections for which unions might have bargained. The Family & Medical Leave Act grants unpaid leave for medical and other family problems. OSHA mandates safe working conditions. Plant closing laws require notice of layoffs. Civil rights laws protect against discrimination of various sorts. Even such matters as offensive horseplay have come within the purview of federal sexual harassment law.

In contrast, shareholders are poorly positioned to develop the kinds of specialized governance structures that protect employee interests. Unlike employees, whose relationship to the firm is subject to periodic renegotiation, shareholders have an indefinite relationship that is rarely renegotiated, if ever. The dispersed nature of stockownership also makes bilateral negotiation of specialized safeguards difficult. The board of directors thus is an essential governance mechanism for protecting shareholder interests.

Why Not Shareholder Primacy?

Our analysis to this point has explained why only shareholders, among the corporation's many stakeholders, are endowed with control rights through the voting process. Now we must turn to the second question with which we began; namely, why are those rights so sharply constrained?

Although they are often used interchangeably, the terms "shareholder primacy" and "shareholder wealth maximization" in fact express quite distinct concepts. The shareholder wealth maximization norm is a basic feature of U.S. corporate governance. In 1919, the Michigan Supreme Court gave the shareholder wealth maximization norm its classic statement: "A business corporation is organized and carried on primarily for the profit of the stockholders. The powers of the directors are to be employed for that end."[54] As we'll see below, despite occasional academic arguments to the contrary, the shareholder wealth maximization norm expounded by these courts indisputably is the law in the United States.

As it is typically used in both the academic and popular press, however, the term "shareholder primacy" encompasses the shareholder wealth maximization norm, but adds to it control claims. Shareholder primacy thus contends not only that shareholders are the principals on whose behalf corporate governance is organized, but also that shareholders do (and should) exercise ultimate control of the corporate enterprise.

In fact, however, shareholder control rights are so weak that they scarcely qualify as part of corporate governance. Under the Delaware code, for example, shareholder voting rights are essentially limited to the election of directors and approval of charter or bylaw amendments, mergers, sales

---

[54] Dodge v. Ford Motor Co., 170 N.W. 668, 684 (Mich. 1919).

of substantially all of the corporation's assets, and voluntary dissolution.[55] As a formal matter, only the election of directors and amending the bylaws do not require board approval before shareholder action is possible. In practice, of course, even the election of directors (absent a proxy contest) is predetermined by the existing board nominating the next year's board.[56]

These direct restrictions on shareholder power are supplemented by a host of other rules that indirectly prevent shareholders from exercising significant influence over corporate decision making. As we'll see in Chapter 5 in more detail, three sets of statutes are especially noteworthy. First, the disclosure requirements under Securities Exchange Act § 13(d) and the SEC rules thereunder, which require extensive disclosures from any person or group acting together which acquires beneficial ownership of more than 5 percent of the outstanding shares of any class of equity stock in a given issuer.[57] The disclosures required by § 13(d) impinge substantially on investor privacy and thus may discourage some investors from holding blocks greater than 4.9 percent of a company's stock. U.S. institutional investors frequently cite Section 13(d)'s application to groups and the consequent risk of liability for failing to provide adequate disclosures as an explanation for the general lack of shareholder activism on their part.[58] Second, the proxy regulatory regime discourages large shareholders from seeking to replace incumbent directors with their own nominees.[59] It also discourages shareholders from communicating with one another.[60] These concerns are significant because to the extent shareholders exercise any control over the corporation, they do so only through control of the board of directors. As such, it is the shareholders' ability to affect the election of directors that determines the degree of influence they will hold over the corporation. Finally, the insider trading and short

---

[55] See Michael P. Dooley, *Fundamentals of Corporation Law* 174–77 (1995) (summarizing state corporate law on shareholder voting entitlements).
[56] See generally Bayless Manning, *Book Review*, 67 Yale L.J. 1477, 1485–89 (1958) (describing incumbent control of the proxy voting machinery).
[57] 15 U.S.C. § 78m (2001).
[58] Bernard S. Black, *Shareholder Activism and Corporate Governance in the United States*, in *The New Palgrave Dictionary of Economics and the Law* 459, 461 (1998).
[59] See Stephen M. Bainbridge, *Redirecting State Takeover Laws at Proxy Contests*, 1992 Wis. L. Rev. 1071, 1075–84 (describing incentives against proxy contests).
[60] See Stephen Choi, *Proxy Issue Proposals: Impact of the 1992 SEC Proxy Reforms*, 16 J.L. Econ. & Org. 233 (2000) (explaining that liberalization of the proxy rules has not significantly affected shareholder communication practices).

swing profits rules. discourage both the formation of large stock blocks and communication and coordination among shareholders.[61]

Despite the limitations of shareholder voting rights, some scholars argue that the market for corporate control ensures a residual form of shareholder control, transforming "the limited de jure shareholder voice into a powerful de facto form of shareholder control."[62] To be sure, the market for corporate control depends on the existence of shareholder voting rights. Moreover, the market for corporate control doubtless is an important accountability mechanism. Market-based accountability and control—by which I mean the right to exercise decision-making fiat—are distinct concepts, however. Directors are held accountable to shareholders through a variety of market forces, such as the capital and reputational markets, but one cannot fairly say that those markets confer control rights on the shareholders. How then can one say that the market for corporate control does so? The right to fire is not the right to exercise fiat—it is only the right to discipline. In any event, takeover defenses—especially the combination of a poison pill and a classified board—go a long way toward restoring director primacy vis-à-vis the shareholders.

Other scholars have argued that institutional investor activism can give real teeth to shareholder control.[63] Acknowledging that the rational apathy phenomenon precludes small individual shareholders from playing an active role in corporate governance (even if the various legal impediments to shareholder activism were removed), these scholars focused their attention on institutional investors, such as pension and mutual funds. As we'll see in Chapter 5, however, to date institutional investor activism has been of only marginal import.

Many investors, especially institutions, rationally prefer liquidity to activism. For fully-diversified investors, even the total failure of a particular firm will not have a significant effect on their portfolios and may indeed

---

[61] See Stephen M. Bainbridge, *The Politics of Corporate Governance*, 18 Harv. J.L. & Pub. Pol'y 671, 712–13 (1995) (noting insider trading concerns raised by shareholder activism).

[62] John C. Coates IV, *Measuring the Domain of Mediating Hierarchy: How Contestable Are U.S. Public Corporations?*, 24 J. Corp. L. 837, 850 (1999).

[63] See, e.g., Mark J. Roe, *Strong Managers, Weak Owners: The Political Roots of American Corporate Finance* (1994); Bernard S. Black, *Shareholder Passivity Reexamined*, 89 Mich. L. Rev. 520 (1990). For more skeptical analyses, see Edward Rock, *The Logic and Uncertain Significance of Institutional Investor Activism*, 79 Geo. L.J. 445 (1991); Roberta Romano, *Public Pension Fund Activism in Corporate Governance Reconsidered*, 93 Colum. L. Rev. 795 (1993); Robert D. Rosenbaum, *Foundations of Sand: The Weak Premises Underlying the Current Push for Proxy Rule Changes*, 17 J. Corp. L. 163 (1991).

benefit them to the extent they also hold stock in competing firms. Such investors might prove less likely to become involved in corporate decision making than to simply use an activist's call for action as a signal to follow the so-called Wall Street Rule (its easier to switch than fight—a play on an old cigarette advertisement) and switch to a different investment before conditions further deteriorate.

We'll explore the reasons for shareholder passivity in more detail in Chapter 5. For now, however, suffice it to say that it is a logical extension of the analysis thus far. Even if one could overcome the seemingly intractable collective action problems plaguing shareholder decision making, active shareholder participation in corporate decision making would still be precluded by the shareholders' widely divergent interests and distinctly different levels of information. Although neoclassical economics assumes that shareholders come to the corporation with wealth maximization as their goal (and most presumably do so), once uncertainty is introduced it would be surprising if shareholder opinions did not differ on which course will maximize share value. To be sure, shareholder interests are less fragmented than those of the corporation's multiple constituencies taken as a whole, but as my colleague Iman Anabtawi nevertheless observes: "On close analysis, shareholder interests look highly fragmented."[64] She documents divergences among investors along multiple fault lines: short-term versus long-term, diversified versus undiversified, inside versus outside, social versus economic, and hedged versus unhedged. Shareholder investment time horizons are likely to vary from short-term speculation to long-term buy-and-hold strategies, for example, which in turn is likely to result in disagreements about corporate strategy. Even more prosaically, shareholders in different tax brackets are likely to disagree about such matters as dividend policy, as are shareholders who disagree about the merits of allowing management to invest the firm's free cash flow in new projects.

As to Arrow's information condition, shareholders lack incentives to gather the information necessary to actively participate in decision making. A rational shareholder will expend the effort necessary to make informed decisions only if the expected benefits of doing so outweigh its costs. Given the length and complexity of corporate disclosure documents, the opportunity cost entailed in making informed decisions is both high

---

[64] Iman Anabtawi, *Some Skepticism About Increasing Shareholder Power*, 53 UCLA L. Rev. 561 (2006).

and apparent. In contrast, the expected benefits of becoming informed are quite low, as most shareholders' holdings are too small to have significant effect on the vote's outcome. Corporate shareholders thus are rationally apathetic.

The efficient capital markets hypothesis provides yet another reason for shareholders to eschew active participation in the governance process. If the market is a reliable indicator of performance, as the efficient capital markets hypothesis claims, investors can easily check the performance of companies in which they hold shares and compare their current holdings with alternative investment positions. An occasional glance at the stock market listings in the newspaper is all that is required. Because it is so much easier to switch to a new investment than to fight incumbent managers, a rational shareholder will not even care why a firm's performance is faltering. With the expenditure of much less energy than is needed to read corporate disclosure statements, he will simply sell his holdings in the struggling firm and move on to other investments.

Consequently, it is hardly surprising that the modern public corporation's decision-making structure precisely fits Arrow's model of an authority-based decision-making system. Overcoming the collective action problems that prevent meaningful shareholder involvement would be difficult and costly, of course. Even if it were possible to do so, moreover, shareholders lack both the information and the incentives necessary to make sound decisions on either operational or policy questions.

The Bargain over the Ends of Corporate Governance

We began by posing two questions that any model of corporate governance must answer. First, who is in charge? Our answer is that the board of directors is in charge. Second, what normative principle properly guides the board's decision making? In the remaining sections of this chapter, I argue that shareholder wealth maximization is the proper answer to that question.

As we've seen, although they are often used interchangeably, the terms shareholder primacy and shareholder wealth maximization express distinct concepts. Shareholder primacy incorporates a decision-making model vesting ultimate control in the shareholders. In rejecting shareholder control, however, director primacy does not throw out the baby with the bath water.

Boards of directors sometimes face decisions wherein it is possible to make at least one corporate constituent better off without leaving any constituency worse off. In economic terms, such a decision is Pareto efficient—it moves the firm from a Pareto inferior position to the Pareto frontier. Other times, however, they face a decision that makes at least one constituency better off, but leaves at least one worse off. Imagine a decision with a pay-off for one constituency of $150 that leaves another constituency worse off by $100. As a whole, the organization is better off by $50. In economic terms, this decision is Kaldor-Hicks efficient.[65]

In this section, I argue that shareholders will bargain for a constraint on the directors' power of fiat under which the board agrees not to make Kaldor-Hicks efficient decisions that leave shareholders worse off. A commonly used justification for adopting Kaldor-Hicks efficiency as a decision-making norm is the claim that everything comes out in the wash. With respect to one decision, I may be in the constituency that loses, but with respect to another decision I may be in the constituency that gains. If the decision-making apparatus is systematically biased against a particular constituency, however, that justification fails. If shareholders suspected that their constituency were to be systematically saddled with losses, they would insist on contract terms precluding directors from making Kaldor-Hicks decisions that leave shareholders worse off. As explained below, shareholders in fact are the constituency most vulnerable to board misconduct and, by extension, to being on the losing end of Kaldor-Hicks efficient decisions. Hence, they predictably will bargain for something like the shareholder wealth maximization norm. They will provide equity capital to the firm only if the directors are charged with managing the corporation so as to maximize shareholder wealth.[66] As a bargained-for

---

[65] A Pareto superior transaction makes at least one person better off and no one worse off. *See generally* David M. Kreps, *A Course in Microeconomic Theory* 154–55 (describing Pareto efficiency). Kaldor-Hicks efficiency does not require that no one be made worse off by a reallocation of resources. Instead, it requires only that the resulting increase in wealth be sufficient to compensate the losers. Note that there does not need to be any actual compensation, compensation simply must be possible. Robert Cooter and Thomas Ulen, *Law and Economics* 41–42 (2d ed. 1997).

[66] In turn, it is for this reason that one cannot justify the shareholder wealth maximization norm by claiming that a rising tide lifts all boats. In many cases, this will be true. Nonshareholder constituencies have a claim on the corporation that is both fixed and prior to that of the shareholders. So long as general welfare laws prohibit the corporation from imposing negative externalities on those constituencies, the shareholder wealth maximization norm redounds to their benefit. In some cases, however, the rising tide argument is inapplicable because it fails to take into account the question of risk.

contract right of the shareholders, the norm thus plays a central role in the director primacy model.

The classic statement of the shareholder wealth maximization norm remains the Michigan Supreme Court's decision in *Dodge v. Ford Motor Co.*[67] Henry Ford embarked on a plan of retaining earnings, lowering prices, improving quality, and expanding production. The plaintiff-shareholders, the Dodge brothers, contended an improper altruism toward his workers and customers motivated Ford. The court agreed, strongly rebuking Ford:

> A business corporation is organized and carried on primarily for the profit of the stockholders. The powers of the directors are to be employed for that end. The discretion of directors is to be exercised in the choice of means to attain that end, and does not extend to a change in the end itself, to the reduction of profits, or to the non-distribution of profits among stockholders in order to devote them to other purposes.[68]

Consequently, "it is not within the lawful powers of a board of directors to shape and conduct the affairs of a corporation for the merely incidental benefit of shareholders and for the primary purpose of benefiting others."[69] *Dodge's* theory of shareholder wealth maximization has been widely accepted by courts over an extended period of time. Almost three-quarters of a century after *Dodge*, the Delaware chancery court similarly opined: "It is the obligation for directors to attempt, within the law, to maximize the long-run interests of the corporation's stockholders."[70]

Pursuing shareholder wealth maximization often requires one to make risky decisions, which disadvantages nonshareholder constituencies. The increased return associated with an increase in risk does not benefit nonshareholders, because their claim is fixed, whereas the simultaneous increase in the corporation's riskiness makes it less likely that nonshareholder claims will be satisfied. Hence, the rising tide argument cannot be a complete explanation for the shareholder wealth maximization norm.

[67] 170 N.W. 668 (Mich. 1919).

[68] *Id.* at 684.

[69] *Id.*

[70] Katz v. Oak Indus., Inc., 508 A.2d 873, 879 (Del. Ch. 1989). For an interesting interpretation of *Dodge*, which argues that the shareholder wealth maximization norm originated as a means for resolving disputes among majority and minority shareholders in closely held corporations, *see* D. Gordon Smith, *The Shareholder Primacy Norm*, 23 J. Corp. L. 277 (1998). For a more detailed defense of my interpretation of the case law, see Stephen M. Bainbridge, *Much Ado About Little? Directors' Fiduciary Duties in the Vicinity of Insolvency*, 1 J. Bus. & Tech. L. 335, 338–45 (2007).

Director Primacy Versus Team Production

Can the concept of director accountability for shareholder wealth maximization be squared with director primacy? Because ownership is not a meaningful concept in the contractarian model on which director primacy rests, there may appear to be an inconsistency between it and the traditional view espoused in cases like *Dodge*. Because director primacy treats the board of directors as a sort of Platonic guardian, whose power devolves from the set of contracts making up the corporation as a whole rather than solely from shareholders, it likely will appear to some readers to be more consistent with the stakeholderist model.

In fact, Blair and Stout have developed a so-called team production model of the corporation that accepts both the descriptive and normative claims of my director primacy model insofar as the allocation of control is concerned, but argues that the board of directors is properly understood as "mediating hierarchs" who "work for team members (including employees) who 'hire' them to control shirking and rent-seeking among team members."[71] Although Blair and Stout tend to downplay the normative implications of their model, they acknowledge that it "resonates" with the views of stakeholderists. They differ from stakeholderists mainly on positive grounds. Stakeholderists believe that corporate directors currently do not take sufficient account of nonshareholder constituency interests and that law reform is necessary. In contrast, Blair and Stout believe that corporate directors do take such interests into account and that the current law is adequate in this regard.

Why does director primacy reject the normative and descriptive claims of team production? Granted, team production is an important and highly useful concept in neoinstitutional economics. Blair and Stout, however, stretch the team production model to encompass the entire firm. Doing so is highly unconventional. Production teams are defined conventionally as "a collection of individuals who are interdependent in their tasks, who share responsibility for outcomes, [and] who see themselves and who are seen by others as an intact social entity embedded in

---

[71] Margaret M. Blair & Lynn A. Stout, *A Team Production Theory of Corporate Law*, 85 Va. L. Rev. 247, 280 (1999). *See also* Lynn A. Stout, *The Shareholder as Ulysses: Some Empirical Evidence on Why Investors in Public Corporations Tolerate Board Governance*, 152 U. Pa. L. Rev. 667, 669 (2003) (arguing that shareholders and other stakeholders benefit from the "system of public corporate governance that has been aptly described as 'director primacy' instead of 'shareholder primacy'").

one or more larger social systems. . . ."[72] This definition contemplates that production teams are embedded within a larger entity. As one commentator defines them, teams are "intact social systems that perform one or more tasks within an organizational context."[73] Characterizing an entire firm as a production team simply makes no sense.

More important, one can only stretch team production that far by mischaracterizing the basic nature of team production. Building on the work of economists Raghuram Rajan and Luigi Zingales, Blair and Stout define team production by reference to firm-specific investments.[74] Hence, for example, they describe the firm "as a nexus of firm-specific investments." In fact, however, firm-specific investments are not the defining characteristic of team production. Rather, the critical feature of team production is task nonseparability.

Oliver Williamson identifies two forms production teams take: primitive and relational. In both, team members perform nonseparable tasks.[75] The two forms are distinguished by the degree of firm-specific human capital possessed by such members. In primitive teams, workers have little such capital; in relational teams, they have substantial amounts. Because both primitive and relational team production requires task nonseparability, it is that characteristic that defines team production.

Most public corporations have both relational and primitive teams embedded throughout their organizational hierarchies. Self-directed work teams, for example, have become a common feature of manufacturing shop floors and even some service workplaces.[76] Even the board of directors can be regarded as a relational team. Hence, the modern public corporation arguably is better described as a hierarchy of teams rather than one of autonomous individuals. To call the entire firm a team, however, is neither accurate nor helpful.

As among shop floor workers organized into a self-directed work team, for example, team production is an appropriate model precisely

---

[72] Susan G. Cohen & Diane E. Bailey, *What Makes Teams Work: Group Effectiveness Research from the Shop Floor to the Executive Suite*, 23 J. Mgmt. 239, 241 (1997).

[73] Kenneth L. Bettenhausen, *Five Years of Groups Research: What Have We Learned and What Needs to Be Addressed?*, 17 J. Mgmt. 345, 346 (1991).

[74] *See* Blair & Stout, *supra* note 71, at 271–73 (discussing Raghuram G. Rajan & Luigi Zingales, *Power in the Theory of the Firm*, 113 Q. J. Econ. 387 (1998)). Of course, many corporate constituents invest little in firm-specific capital (human or otherwise), but this is mere quibbling.

[75] Oliver E. Williamson, *The Economic Institutions of Capitalism* 244–47 (1985).

[76] Bainbridge, *supra* note 38, at 1018–20.

because their collective output is not task-separable. In a large firm, however, the vast majority of tasks performed by the firm's various constituencies are task-separable. The contributions of employees of one division versus those of a second division can be separated. The contributions of employees and creditors can be separated. The contributions of supervisory employees can be separated from those of shop floor employees. And so on.

The canonical example of task nonseparability in a team production setting was developed by Alchian and Demsetz, who hypothesized a scenario in which two workers jointly lift heavy boxes into a truck. The marginal productivity of each worker is very difficult to measure and their joint output cannot be easily separated into individual components. In such situations, obtaining information about a team member's productivity and appropriately rewarding each team member are very difficult and costly. In the absence of such information, however, the disutility of labor gives each team member an incentive to shirk because the individual's reward is unlikely to be closely related to conscientiousness. Hence, the need for monitoring.[77] In order for an activity to be task-nonseparable, it must be impossible (or very costly) to measure individual marginal productivity. Is it useful to think of shareholders and creditors as part of a production team? If so, is it impossible to measure their marginal contributions to firm productivity? Firms can readily determine their respective equity and debt costs of capital, which seems a reasonable proxy for measuring the value of (and thus the contribution of) financial inputs. The effort firms devote to tweaking their capital structure when making financing decisions also suggests an ability to separate the relative contributions of creditors and equity investors. Accordingly, the concept of team production is simply inapt with respect to the large public corporations with which Blair and Stout are concerned.

In addition to questioning their choice of terminology, I am not persuaded by Blair and Stout's foundational hypothetical. Blair and Stout develop the mediating hierarchy model by telling the story of a start-up venture in which a number of individuals come together to undertake a team production project. The participating constituents know that incorporation, especially the selection of independent board members, will reduce their control over the firm and, consequently, expose their interests

---

[77] Alchian & Demsetz, *supra* note 31, at 779–80.

to shirking or self-dealing by other participants. The participants go forward, Blair and Stout suggest, because they know the board of directors will function as a mediating hierarch resolving horizontal disputes among team members about the allocation of the return on their production.[78]

On its face, Blair and Stout's scenario is not about established public corporations. Instead, their scenario seems heavily influenced by the high-tech start-ups of the late 1990s.[79] Yet, even in that setting, the model seems inapt. In the typical pattern, the entrepreneurial founders hire the first factors of production.[80] If the firm subsequently goes public, the founding entrepreneurs commonly are replaced by a more or less independent board. The board thus displaces the original promoters as the central party with whom all other corporate constituencies contract. In this sense, the board of directors—whether comprised of the founding entrepreneurs or subsequently appointed outsiders—hires factors of production, not the other way around.

Lest the foregoing seem like an argument for shareholder primacy, I think it is instructive to note that the corporation—unlike partnerships, for example—did not evolve from enterprises in which the owners of the residual claim managed the business. Instead, as a legal construct, the modern corporation evolved out of such antecedent forms as municipal

---

[78] *See* Blair & Stout, *supra* note 71, at 275–78. Blair and Stout argue that that "shareholders, employees, and perhaps other stakeholders such as creditors or the local community . . . enter into this mutual agreement in an effort to reduce wasteful shirking and rent-seeking by relegating to the internal hierarchy the right to determine the division of duties and resources in the joint enterprise." *Id.* at 278. Blair and Stout's model assumes that "the likely economic losses to a productive team from unconstrained shirking and rent-seeking are great enough to outweigh the likely economic losses from turning over decision-making power to a less-than-perfectly-faithful hierarch." *Id.* at 284. As yet, however, we lack empirical evidence that corporate constituents make such trade-offs and, if so, that the trade-off leans in the predicted direction.

[79] Given the vast media attention devoted to start-ups during the late 1990s, they admittedly made a seductive target for scholarly inquiry. Query, however, whether such firms tell us much about the governance of established public corporations. Ironically, the paradigmatic late 1990s start-up—dot-com firms—had notoriously severe corporate governance problems, which may have been a contributing factor in their ultimate economic problems. *See, e.g.,* Peter Buxbaum, *The Trouble with Dot-Com Boards,* Chief Executive, Oct. 1, 2000, at 50.

[80] Equity capital may be the principal exception. In many respects, it is more accurate to say that venture capitalists hire entrepreneurs than vice versa. At the very least, the two must collaborate closely. *See* Daniel M. Cable & Scott Shane, *A Prisoner's Dilemma Approach to Entrepreneur-Venture Capitalist Relationships,* 22 Acad. Mgmt. Rev. 142 (1997); D. Gordon Smith, *Team Production in Venture Capital Investing,* 24 J. Corp. L. 949, 960 (1999).

and ecclesiastical corporations.[81] The board of directors as an institution thus pre-dates the rise of shareholder capitalism. When the earliest industrial corporations began, moreover, they typically were large enterprises requiring centralized management.[82] Hence, as we've already seen, the separation of ownership and control was not a late development but rather a key institutional characteristic of the corporate form from its inception. At the risk of descending into chicken-and-egg pedantry, the historical record thus suggests that director primacy emerged long before shareholder primacy. Directors have always hired factors of production, not vice versa.

Finally, Blair and Stout's description of the role of the board is not supported by the evidence. In Blair and Stout's model, directors are hired by all constituencies and charged with balancing the competing interests of all team members "in a fashion that keeps everyone happy enough that the productive coalitions stays together."[83] In other words, the principal function of the mediating board is resolving disputes among other corporate constituents. This account of the board's role differs significantly from the standard account.

As discussed in more detail in Chapter 2, the literature typically identifies three functions performed by boards of public corporations: First, the board monitors and disciplines top management. Second, while boards typically are not involved in day-to-day operational decision making, most boards have managerial functions at the level of policy. Finally, the board provides access to a network of contacts that may be useful in gathering resources and/or obtaining business. In none of these capacities, however, does the board of directors directly referee between corporate constituencies.

To be sure, dispute resolution is an important function of any governance system. Ex post gap-filling and error correction are necessitated

---

[81] See John P. Davis, *Corporations: A Study of the Origin and Development of Great Business Corporations and of Their Relation to the Authority of the State II* 217 (1905) (stating: "In the beginning the germ of the future conception of a corporation made its way into the English law through the recognition of the 'communities' of cities and towns, and of the body of rights and duties appertaining to residence in them."); *see also id.* at 222 (noting the contributions of ecclesiastical corporations and guilds to the evolving corporate form).

[82] Ronald E. Seavoy, *The Origins of the American Business Corporation: 1784–1855* 4–5 (1982).

[83] Blair & Stout, *supra* note 71, at 281.

by the incomplete contracts inherent in corporate governance. Those functions inevitably entail dispute resolution. As we've seen, the firm addresses the problem of incomplete contracting by creating a central decision maker authorized to rewrite by fiat the implicit—and, in some cases, even the explicit—contracts of which the corporation is a nexus.

As the principal governance mechanism within the public corporation, the board of directors is that central decision maker and, accordingly, bears principal dispute resolution responsibility. Yet, in doing so, the board "is an instrument of the residual claimants."[84] Hence, if the board considers the interests of nonshareholder constituencies when making decisions, it does so only because shareholder wealth will be maximized in the long-run.

If directors suddenly began behaving as mediating hierarchs, rather than shareholder wealth maximizers, an adaptive response would be called forth. As we'll see below, shareholders would adjust their relationships with the firm, demanding a higher return to compensate them for the increase in risk brought to the value of their residual claim resulting from director freedom to make trade-offs between shareholder wealth and nonshareholder constituency interests. Ironically, this adaptation would raise the cost of capital and thus injure the interests of all corporate constituents whose claims vary in value with the fortunes of the firms.

Incorporating Shareholder Wealth Maximization into Director Primacy

While Blair and Stout's attempt to conflate director primacy and stakeholderism thus is unpersuasive, we still need to make the positive case that director primacy and shareholder wealth maximization are consistent.

---

[84] Oliver E. Williamson, *The Mechanisms of Governance* 175 (1996). Blair and Stout posit that the legal mechanisms purporting to ensure director accountability to shareholder interests—such as derivative litigation and voting rights—benefit all corporate constituents. Blair & Stout, *supra* note 71, at 289. *See also id.* at 313 (asserting that shareholders' self-interested exercise of voting rights can "serve the interest of other stakeholders in the firm as well"). Conceding that shareholder and nonshareholder interests are often congruent, it nevertheless remains the case that some situations present zero-sum games. Further conceding the weakness of those accountability mechanisms, shareholder standing to pursue litigation and/or the exercise of shareholder voting rights nevertheless give shareholders rights that potentially can be used to the disadvantage of other constituencies.

One reconciles the two by affirmatively answering the following question: Would a shareholder wealth maximization norm emerge from the hypothetical bargain as the majoritarian default?

It seems clear that directors and shareholders would strike a bargain in which directors pursue shareholder wealth maximization. Shareholders will insist on that norm when entering into their contract with the corporation or, at least, would be willing to pay more for stock protected by that norm. Return is positively correlated with risk. If directors expose shareholders to greater risk, shareholders will demand a higher rate of return. Greater risk thus translates directly into a higher corporate cost of capital. At the margins, a higher cost of capital increases the probability of firm failure or takeover.

Directors will seek to minimize the corporation's cost of capital because, first, there are reputational costs to firm failure. Second, to the extent the directors invest in firmspecific human capital, that investment will be lost if the directors lose their positions following a firm failure or takeover. Third, the growing emphasis on stock-based director compensation gives the board a direct financial interest in the firm's ongoing success. Fourth, director socialization inculcates effort and cooperation norms. Finally, there is the self-esteem—the pride in doing a job well—which some theorists regard as the basis for norm compliance. Taken together, these factors give directors strong incentives to minimize the firm's cost of capital.

Shareholders will view a director preference for other constituencies as a risk demanding compensatory returns.[85] First, absent the shareholder wealth maximization norm, the board would lack a determinate metric for assessing options. Because stakeholder decision-making models necessarily create a two masters problem, such models inevitably lead to indeterminate results. Suppose that the board of directors is considering closing an obsolete plant. The closing will harm the plant's workers and the local community, but will benefit shareholders, creditors, employees at a more modern plant to which the work previously performed at the old plant is transferred, and communities around the modern plant.

---

[85] I am using the term "risk" here in its colloquial rather than its technical sense. In the strict sense in which the term is used in conventional finance lingo, director misconduct of the type described here does not create risk, because such misconduct does not affect the variation of returns. Instead, director misconduct erodes the expected shareholder return.

Assume that the latter groups cannot gain except at the former groups' expense. By what standard should the board make the decision? Shareholder wealth maximization provides a clear answer—close the plant. Once the directors are allowed to deviate from shareholder wealth maximization, however, they must inevitably turn to indeterminate balancing standards.

Such standards deprive directors of the critical ability to determine ex ante whether their behavior comports with the law's demands, raising the transaction costs of corporate governance. The conflict of interest rules governing the legal profession provide a useful analogy. Despite many years of refinement, these rules are still widely viewed as inadequate, vague, and inconsistent—hardly the stuff of which certainty and predictability are made.[86]

Second, absent clear standards, directors will be tempted to pursue their own self-interest. One may celebrate the virtues of granting directors largely unfettered discretion to manage the business enterprise without having to ignore the agency costs associated with such discretion. Discretion should not be allowed to camouflage self-interest.

Directors who are responsible to everyone are accountable to no one. In the foregoing hypothetical, for example, if the board's interests favor keeping the plant open, we can expect the board to at least lean in that direction. The plant likely will stay open, with the decision being justified by reference to the impact of a closing on the plant's workers and the local community. In contrast, if directors' interests are served by closing the plant, the plant will likely close, with the decision being justified by concern for the firm's shareholders, creditors, and other benefited constituencies.

As compensation for bearing these risks, shareholders will demand a higher return on their investment. Whatever value unfettered discretion has for directors would be outweighed by the costs associated with the increased risk of error and opportunism that would follow from adoption of any decision-making principle other than shareholder wealth maximization. Accordingly, when directors use the corporation as a vehicle for hiring equity capital, they would include that norm as one of the terms of the deal. Society therefore appropriately adopts the shareholder wealth maximization norm as a governing principle—it is the majoritarian default that emerges from the hypothetical bargain.

---

[86] *See* Marc I. Steinberg & Timothy U. Sharpe, *Attorney Conflicts of Interest: The Need for a Coherent Framework*, 66 Notre Dame L. Rev. 1, 2 (1990).

This result does not change even if we introduce nonshareholder constituencies into the mix as a bargaining party. In the contractarian model, fiduciary duties are gap-fillers by which courts resolve disputes falling through the cracks of incomplete contracts. More specifically, fiduciary duties prevent corporate directors and officers from appropriating quasi-rents through opportunistic conduct unanticipated when the firm was formed. To be sure, investments in transaction-specific assets commonly are protected ex ante through specialized governance structures created by detailed contracts. As we have seen, however, under conditions of uncertainty and complexity, bounded rationality precludes complete contracting. Under such conditions, accordingly, fiduciary duties provide an alternative source of protection against opportunism.

The shareholder's investment in the firm is a transaction-specific asset, because the whole of the investment is both at risk and turned over to someone else's control.[87] In contrast, many corporate constituencies do not make firm-specific investments in either human capital or otherwise. Many corporate employees, for example, lack significant firm specific human capital.[88] As we have seen, for such employees, mobility may be a sufficient defense against opportunistic conduct, because they can quit and be replaced without productive loss to either employee or employer. In any case, because the relationship between such employees and the corporation does not create appropriable quasi-rents, opportunism by the board is not a concern.

Consequently, shareholders are more vulnerable to director misconduct than are most nonshareholder constituencies. To be sure, Blair and Stout assert that "when directors use their corporate position to steal money from the firm, every [constituency] suffers."[89] Consider, however, a classic case of self-dealing. Assume a solvent corporation able to pay its debts and other obligations (especially employee salaries) as they come due in the ordinary course of business. Further assume that the corporation has substantial free cash flow—i.e., cash flows in excess of the positive net present value investments available to the corporation. If the directors

---

[87] Oliver Williamson, *Corporate Governance*, 93 Yale L. J. 1197, 1225 (1984).

[88] Stephen M. Bainbridge, *Corporate Decisionmaking and the Moral Rights of Employees: Participatory Management and Natural Law*, 43 Vill. L. Rev. 741, 817–18 (1998). The claim is not that nonshareholder constituencies do not invest in firm-specific assets, such as firm-specific human capital. In fact, many do so. My point is only to remind the reader that many nonshareholder constituencies do not.

[89] Blair & Stout, *supra* note 71, at 299.

siphon some portion of the corporation's free cash flow into their own pockets, shareholders are clearly hurt, because the value of the residual claim has been impaired. Yet, in this case, there is no readily apparent injury to the value of the fixed claim of all other corporate constituents.

For the sake of argument, however, I assume herein that appropriation of quasi-rents is an equally severe problem for both shareholders and nonshareholder constituencies. Many employees do invest in firm-specific human capital. Creditors may also develop firmspecific expertise, particularly in long-term relationships with a significant number of repeat transactions.

Relative to many nonshareholder constituencies, shareholders are poorly positioned to extract contractual protections. Unlike bondholders, for example, whose term-limited relationship to the firm is subject to extensive negotiations and detailed contracts, shareholders have an indefinite relationship that is rarely the product of detailed negotiations. The dispersed nature of stockownership, moreover, makes bilateral negotiation of specialized safeguards especially difficult:

> Arrangements among a corporation, the underwriters of its debt, trustees under its indentures and sometimes ultimate investors are typically thoroughly negotiated and massively documented. The rights and obligations of the various parties are or should be spelled out in that documentation. The terms of the contractual relationship agreed to and not broad concepts such as fairness [therefore] define the corporation's obligation to its bondholders.[90]

Put another way, bond indentures necessarily are incomplete. Even so, they still provide bondholders with far greater contractual protections than shareholders receive from the corporate contract as represented by the firm's organic documents. Accordingly, we can confidently predict the majoritarian default that would emerge from the hypothetical bargain. Shareholders will want the protections provided by fiduciary duties, while bondholders will be satisfied with the ability to enforce their contractual rights, which is precisely what the law provides.

Like bondholders, employees regularly bargain with employers both individually and collectively. So do other stakeholders, such as local communities that bargain with existing or prospective employers, offering

---

[90] Katz v. Oak Indus. Inc., 508 A.2d 873, 879 (Del. Ch. 1986).

firms tax abatements and other inducements in return for which they could and should extract promises about the firm's conduct. In general, the interests of such constituents lend themselves to more concrete specification then do the open-ended claims of shareholders. Those nonshareholder constituencies that enter voluntary relationships with the corporation thus can protect themselves by adjusting the contract price to account for negative externalities imposed upon them by the firm.

Granted, the extent of negotiations between the corporation and nonshareholders is likely to vary widely. In many cases, such as hiring shop floor employees, the only negotiation will be a take-it-or-leave-it offer. But so what? Is a standard form contract any less of a contract just because it is offered on a take-it-or-leave-it basis? If the market is competitive, a party making a take-it-or-leave-it offer must set price and other terms that will lead to sales despite the absence of particularized negotiations. As long as the firm must attract inputs from nonshareholder constituencies in competitive markets, the firm similarly will have to offer those constituencies terms that compensate them for the risks they bear.

This point persistently eludes proponents of the stakeholder model, who ask: "Can it really be said that employees (or local communities or dependent suppliers) are really better able to negotiate the terms of their relationship to the corporation than are shareholders?"[91] While they presumably intend this to be a purely rhetorical question, it has an answer; i.e., an affirmative one.

As we have seen, shareholders have no meaningful voice in corporate decision making. In effect, shareholders have but a single mechanism by which they can "negotiate" with the board: withholding capital. If shareholder interests are inadequately protected, they can refuse to invest. The nexus of contracts model, however, demonstrates that equity capital is but one of the inputs that a firm needs to succeed. Nonshareholder corporate constituencies can thus "negotiate" with the board in precisely the same fashion as do shareholders: by withholding their inputs. If the firm disregards employee interests, it will have greater difficulty finding workers. Similarly, if the firm disregards creditor interests, it will have greater difficulty attracting debt financing, and so on.

In fact, withholding one's inputs may often be a more effective tool for nonshareholder constituencies than it is for shareholders. Some firms

[91] Ronald M. Green, *Shareholders as Stakeholders: Changing Metaphors of Corporate Governance*, 50 Wash. & Lee L. Rev. 1409, 1418 (1993).

go for years without seeking equity investments. If these firms' boards disregard shareholder interests, shareholders have little recourse other than to sell out at prices that will reflect the board's lack of concern for shareholder wealth. In contrast, few firms can survive for long without regular infusions of new employees and new debt financing. As a result, few boards can prosper for long while ignoring nonshareholder interests.

Unlike secured creditors or employees with firm-specific human capital, the shareholder's transaction-specific investment is not associated with particular assets. Also unlike other corporate constituents, shareholders have no right to periodic renegotiation of the firm's or their relationship with the firm. As a result, the shareholders' interest in the firm is more vulnerable to both uncertainty and opportunism than are the interests of other corporate constituents. Unlike those corporate constituents whose interests are adequately protected by contract, shareholders therefore require special protection. Hence, both the shareholder right to elect directors and the fiduciary obligation of those directors to maximize shareholder wealth emerge as the majoritarian default.

Let us assume, however, that nonshareholder constituencies are unable to protect themselves through contract. The right rule would still be director fiduciary duties incorporating the shareholder wealth maximization norm. Many nonshareholder constituencies have substantial power to protect themselves through the political process. Public choice theory teaches that well-defined interest groups are able to benefit themselves at the expense of larger, loosely defined groups by extracting legal rules from lawmakers that appear to be general welfare laws but in fact redound mainly to the interest group's advantage. Absent a few self-appointed spokesmen, most of whom are either gadflies or promoting some service they sell, shareholders—especially individuals—have no meaningful political voice. In contrast, many nonshareholder constituencies are represented by cohesive, politically powerful interest groups. Consider the enormous political power wielded by unions, who played a major role in passing state anti-takeover laws. Because those laws temporarily helped kill off hostile takeovers, the unions helped kill the goose that laid golden eggs for shareholders. From the unions' perspective, however, hostile takeovers were inflicting considerable harm on workers. The unions were probably wrong on that score, but the point is that the unions used their political power to transfer wealth from shareholders to nonshareholder constituencies.

Collective bargaining obviously does not protect non-unionized workers, but such protections are nevertheless provided by both legal and market forces. Various market mechanisms have evolved to protect employee investments in firm-specific human capital, such as ports of entry, seniority systems, and promotion ladders. As already noted, moreover, as private sector unions declined, the federal government has intervened to provide through general welfare legislation many of the same protections for which unions might have bargained.

Such targeted legislative approaches are a preferable solution to the externalities created by corporate conduct. General welfare laws designed to deter corporate misconduct through criminal and civil sanctions imposed on the corporation, its directors, and its senior officers are more efficient than stakeholderist tweaking of director fiduciary duties. By virtue of their inherent ambiguity, fiduciary duties are a blunt instrument. There can be no assurance that specific social ills will be addressed by the boards of the specific corporations that are creating the problematic externalities.

Note that while most of the foregoing analysis applies mainly to voluntary constituencies of the firm, this last argument applies equally well to involuntary constituencies (such as tort creditors). Corporate law is an inapt tool with which to protect involuntary constituencies (and voluntary constituencies, as well, for that matter), as tort, contract, and property law, as well as a host of general welfare laws, already provide them with a panoply of protections.[92]

In sum, in the director primacy model, the board negotiates contracts with various factors of production. The various inputs have distinct needs, but also distinct comparative advantages with respect to possible schemes of extra-judicial governance schema. Hence, for example, banks have great expertise in monitoring, so it makes sense that they have detailed contractual control rights triggered by financial defaults. To be sure, neither the contracting nor the political process is perfect, but each standing alone probably provides nonshareholder constituencies with more meaningful protections than would the stakeholder model of corporate law.

---

[92] See generally Jonathan R. Macey, An Economic Analysis of the Various Rationales for Making Shareholders the Exclusive Beneficiaries of Corporate Fiduciary Duties, 21 Stetson L. Rev. 23 (1991).

The "Problem" of Agency Costs

Although fiat is an essential attribute of the corporation, it must be exercised responsibly. In the corporate setting, the potential for opportunism arises because of the very separation of ownership and control that makes the corporate form feasible: "The separation of ownership from control produces a condition where the interests of owner and of ultimate manager may, and often do, diverge."[93] When the directors hire equity capital from shareholders, the directors undertake a contractual obligation to maximize the value of the shareholders' residual claim on the corporation's assets. As in most corporate law, this obligation is implied in the law, rather than expressed in formal contracts, of course; but as we've seen, there seems little doubt that shareholder wealth maximization is the majoritarian default that emerges when one brings the hypothetical bargain methodology to bear on the question. Because shareholders exercise so little direct control over the board of directors, however, shareholders have minimal ability to prevent directors from appropriating corporate assets that should have gone into the residue against which the shareholders have their claim.

Will the board of directors in fact use its control of the corporation to further the selfish interest of the board members rather than pursue the shareholders' bargained-for right of wealth maximization? To ask the question is to answer it. Given human nature, it would be very surprising if corporate law were not greatly concerned with constraining agency costs.[94] Indeed, some claim that "defining how agency costs can be controlled" is "the central problem of corporate law."[95]

---

[93] Adolf A. Berle & Gardiner C. Means, The Modern Corporation and Private Property 6 (1932).

[94] Agency costs are defined as the sum of the monitoring and bonding costs, plus any residual loss, incurred to prevent shirking by agents. In turn, shirking is defined to include any action by a member of a production team that diverges from the interests of the team as a whole. As such, shirking includes not only culpable cheating, but also negligence, oversight, incapacity, and even honest mistakes. In other words, shirking is simply the inevitable consequence of bounded rationality and opportunism within agency relationships. Eugene F. Fama & Michael C. Jensen, Separation of Ownership and Control, 26 J.L. & Econ. 301, 304 (1983); Michael C. Jensen & William H. Meckling, Theory of the Firm: Managerial Behavior, Agency Costs, and Ownership Structure, 3 J. Fin. Econ. 305, 308 (1976).

[95] Mark A. Sargent, Lawyers in the Perfect Storm, 43 Washburn L.J. 1, 1 (2003). See also Andrei Shleifer & Robert W. Vishny, A Survey of Corporate Governance, 52 J. Fin. 737, 740 (1997) (opining that the principal-agent problem between directors and shareholders is the central problem of corporate governance).

The principal-agent problem arises because, while the principal reaps part of the value of hard work by the agent, the agent receives all of the value of shirking. As a result, agents do not internalize all of the costs of shirking. Despite the resulting ex post incentives to shirk, agents also have ex ante incentives to agree to contract terms designed to prevent shirking. Bounded rationality and other transaction costs, however, preclude firms and agents from entering into the complete contract necessary to prevent shirking by the latter. Instead, there must be some system of ex post governance: some mechanism for detecting and punishing shirking. Accordingly, an essential economic function of management is monitoring the various inputs into the team effort: the manager meters the marginal productivity of each team member and then takes steps to reduce shirking. Note, again, how fiat emerges as an essential attribute of organization.

The existence of such fiat-based monitoring systems is especially obvious in M-form corporations, which is the dominant form of modern public corporations in the United States. The M-form corporation has two defining characteristics: many distinct operating units and management by a hierarchy of salaried executives. Just as a branching corporate hierarchy facilitates the flow of information within such firms, it also facilitates monitoring. It would be difficult, at best, for a plant manager with hundreds of employees to determine which deserve rewards and which deserve reprimands. Such a task obviously becomes impossible long before we reach the board of directors of a large public corporation. A branching hierarchy provides a ready solution. The board delegates responsibility to senior management and monitors their performance. The senior managers in the firm's central office delegate responsibility to managers of operating units. In turn, the managers of each operating unit are responsible for monitoring the productivity of their unit. The process continues down to the foreman on the shop floor. Creating such a branching hierarchy addresses the problems of uncertainty, bounded rationality, and shirking faced by monitors in all team situations by breaking the firm team into discrete segments, each of which is more readily monitored than the whole. At each hierarchical level, the responsible monitor is responsible for supervising only a few individuals, which usefully limits and focuses his task.

The central office is critical to understanding monitoring in M-form corporations. The monitoring mechanisms just described could be accomplished through a simple pyramidal hierarchy. The M-form corporation adds to that basic structure a rationalization of decision-making authority in which the central office has certain tasks and the operating units have others, which allows for more effective monitoring through specialization, sharper definition of purpose, and savings in informational costs.[96] The M-form corporation thus is a paradigm example of an authority-based decision-making structure.

The structure just described, however, raises the question: Who will monitor the monitors? In any team organization, one must have some ultimate monitor who has sufficient incentives to ensure firm productivity without himself having to be monitored. Otherwise, one ends up with a never-ending series of monitors monitoring lower level monitors. Alchian and Demsetz solved this dilemma by consolidating the roles of ultimate monitor and residual claimant: If the constituent entitled to the firm's residual income is given final monitoring authority, he is encouraged to detect and punish shirking by the firm's other inputs because his reward will vary exactly with his success as a monitor.[97]

Unfortunately, this elegant theory breaks down precisely where it would be most useful. Because of the separation of ownership and control, it simply does not describe the modern publicly-held corporation. As the corporation's residual claimants, the shareholders should act as the firm's ultimate monitors. But while the law provides shareholders with some enforcement and electoral rights, these are reserved for fairly extraordinary situations. In general, shareholders of public corporations have neither the legal right, the practical ability, nor the desire to exercise the kind of control necessary for meaningful monitoring of the corporation's agents.

How then are shareholders to be protected? Much of the remainder of this text is devoted to answering that question. To anticipate briefly, our answers to the foundational questions of who's in charge and by what principle are they to be guided turn out to pose a fundamental tension. On the one hand, directors must be held accountable for violating their obligation to maximize shareholder wealth. On the other hand, the substantial virtues of fiat can be ensured only by preserving the board's decision-making authority from being trumped by either shareholders or courts. Resolving that tension turns out to be the chief problem of corporate governance.

---

[96] Williamson, *supra* note 75, at 320.
[97] Alchian & Demsetz, *supra* note 31, at 781–83.

CHAPTER 2

Why a Board?

Chapter 1 explained that effective corporate governance requires (1) a separation of ownership and control and (2) a decision-making structure comprising a branching hierarchy in which decisions generally are made by fiat rather than through consensus. Despite the clear advantages to the public corporation of authority-based decision making and hierarchical governance, at the apex of that hierarchy is not a single autocrat, but rather a multi-member body that usually functions by consensus; namely, the board of directors. Acting alone, an individual director "has no power of his own to act on the corporation's behalf, but only as one of a body of directors acting as a board."[1] Moreover, as the commentary to Model Business Corporation Act (MBCA) § 8.20 puts it, "directors may act only at a meeting unless otherwise expressly authorized by statute."

Why does corporate law place this strong emphasis on collective action? Put another way, why do the default rules provided by statute vest the ultimate power of fiat in a collegial group rather than an individual autocrat?

Answering this question is critical to the success of my project, because that answer provides the first half of my reply to the principal

---

[1] Restatement (Second) of Agency § 14 C cmt. (1957).

charge leveled at the director primacy model by its critics; namely, the claim that "managerialism seems to have a far stronger empirical basis than the director-primacy model, and thus the director-primacy model is more vulnerable to criticism on the descriptive level than it is on the normative level."[2] In this chapter, I develop an argument based in economic analysis, empirical research, and cognitive psychology that provides a theoretical basis for believing that director primacy rather than managerialism is the appropriate majoritarian default. In Chapter 4, I will turn to the empirical question of whether managerialism in fact remains more powerful than director primacy "on the descriptive level." In doing so, the arguments set out herein will remain useful as tools for understanding certain emerging best practices that are shifting power from management to the board of directors.

Groups and Individuals

Much important economic activity takes place within institutions for which decisions typically are made by groups rather than single individuals. Within the public corporation, for example, we see group decision making at many levels of the corporate hierarchy. Indeed, with the emergence of quality circles and self-directed work teams, it arguably is more accurate to describe large corporations as hierarchies of teams rather than of individuals. At the apex of the corporate hierarchy stands yet another team—the board of directors.

Curiously, corporate law scholarship rarely focuses on the board as a team production problem.[3] In contrast, cognitive psychology has a long-standing tradition of studying individual versus group decision making. With the emergence of behavioral economics as a legitimate field of inquiry, moreover, experimental economists have begun looking at similar questions. Taken together with various strands of new institutional economics, these approaches shed considerable light on the role of the board of directors.

---

[2] D. A. Jeremy Telman, *The Business Judgment Rule, Disclosure, and Executive Compensation*, 81 Tul. L. Rev. 829, 858 (2007).

[3] Exceptions include Margaret M. Blair & Lynn A. Stout, *A Team Production Theory of Corporate Law*, 85 Va. L. Rev. 247 (1999); Donald C. Langevoort, *The Human Nature of Corporate Boards: Law, Norms and the Unintended Consequences of Independence and Accountability*, 89 Geo. L.J. 797 (2001).

In order to evaluate corporate law's preference for collective decision making, we need to know whether group decision making is superior to that of individuals. A wealth of experimental data suggests that groups often make better decisions than individuals. Even more strikingly, the conditions under which groups outperform individuals in laboratory settings have important similarities to board decision making. Prior corporate law scholarship has almost uniformly ignored this important body of research.[4] Yet, once this evidence is taken into account, the choice of a board of directors as the statutory default seems obvious.

The Board as Production Team

As we saw in Chapter 1, management and organization theorists devote considerable attention to the role of production teams within firms. Such a team is defined as "a collection of individuals who are interdependent in their tasks, who share responsibility for outcomes, [and] who see themselves and who are seen by others as an intact social entity embedded in one or more larger social systems. . . ."[5] Recall that Williamson identifies two forms such teams may take: primitive and relational. In both, team members perform nonseparable tasks. Both are distinguished by the degree of firm-specific human capital possessed by their members. In primitive teams, workers have little such capital; in relational teams, they have substantial amounts.[6] Most boards of directors probably qualify as relational teams in this schema.

What then does the board produce? Put another way, what are the institutional functions of the board?

First, while boards rarely are involved in day-to-day operational decision making, most boards have at least some managerial functions.

---

[4] An exception is Robert C. Clark, *Corporate Law* (1986), who acknowledged the potential utility of "empirical work of sociologists who have studied groups and organizations." *Id.* at 110. Other exceptions include Robert J. Haft, *Business Decisions by the New Board: Behavioral Science and Corporate Law*, 80 Mich. L. Rev. 1 (1981); Note, *The Propriety of Judicial Deference to Corporate Boards of Directors*, 96 Harv. L. Rev. 1894, 1896–97 (1983).

[5] Susan G. Cohen & Diane E. Bailey, *What Makes Teams Work: Group Effectiveness Research from the Shop Floor to the Executive Suite*, 23 J. Mgmt. 239, 241 (1997). *See also* Kenneth L. Bettenhausen, *Five Years of Groups Research: What Have We Learned and What Needs to Be Addressed?*, 17 J. Mgmt. 345, 346 (1991) (defining teams as "intact social systems that perform one or more tasks within an organizational context").

[6] Oliver E. Williamson, *The Economic Institutions of Capitalism* 246–47 (1985).

Broad policymaking is commonly a board prerogative, for example. Even more commonly, however, individual board members provide advice and guidance to top managers with respect to operational and/or policy decisions. Second, the board monitors and disciplines top management. One can imagine a structure of corporate authority identical to current norms except that the board acts as a mere advisory body to a single autocratic CEO. On the face of it, such a structure seemingly would preserve most of the informational and relational advantages of the current structure. Consequently, it is the board's power to hire and fire senior management that makes it something more than a mere advisory body. Finally, the board provides access to a network of contacts that may be useful in gathering resources and/or obtaining business. Outside directors affiliated with financial institutions, for example, apparently facilitate the firm's access to capital.[7]

The assignment of these tasks to a group rather than an individual has important costs. The effort of an individual can be measured. How hard does he or she work? An individual's output is also observable, at least by proxy. How well has the firm performed under his or her stewardship? In contrast, monitoring the work of a production team is more difficult. In team production, inputs (e.g., effort) are difficult to measure and, because team tasks typically are nonseparable, individual output is not readily observable. The monitoring mechanisms applicable to a single individual thus are largely irrelevant as applied to a team. Instead, agency costs are constrained in the team setting mainly by internal team governance structures.

In light of these monitoring problems, corporate law's preference for a collegial decision-making body rather than an individual autocrat seems puzzling. Yet, it gets worse. First, members of a production team often develop idiosyncratic working relationships with one another. In a sense, team members develop not only firm-specific human capital, but also team-specific human capital. Sanctions such as dismissal that

---

[7]   The analysis here tracks the taxonomy suggested by Johnson et al., who map "directors responsibilities into three broadly defined roles . . . labeled control, service, and resource dependence." Jonathan L. Johnson et al., *Boards of Directors: A Review and Research Agenda*, 22 J. Mgmt. 409, 411 (1996). Other taxonomies could be devised, of course. For example, law professor Lynne Dallas proposes a two-component taxonomy distinguishing between the board's monitoring and "relational" roles. Lynne L. Dallas, *Proposals for Reform of Corporate Boards of Directors: The Dual Board and Board Ombudsman*, 54 Wash. & Lee L. Rev. 91, 98–104 (1997).

disrupt these intra-team relationships thus may result in a substantial loss of efficiency.

Second, the phenomenon known as social loafing strongly supports a preference for individual rather than multiple decision makers. In a famous 1913 study, which measured how hard subjects pulled a rope, members of two-person teams pulled to only 93 percent of their individual capacity, members of trios pulled to only 85 percent, and members of groups of eight pulled to only 49 percent of capacity.[8] This phenomenon is attributable partially to the difficulty of coordinating group effort as the group's size increases. (Too many cooks spoil the soup.) Social loafing is also attributable, however, to the difficulty of motivating members of a group where identification and/or measurement of individual productivity is difficult—i.e., where the group functions as a production team. While board decision making differs rather dramatically from tug-of-war, members of a multi-member board likely engage in a certain amount of social loafing.

To be sure, unlike a team in a tug-of-war game, board members probably do not get into each other's way. Accordingly, it is unlikely that there will be physical coordination problems. Yet because social loafing is also attributable to the difficulty of motivating members of a team with non-separable outputs and non-observable inputs, it nevertheless can be expected with respect to the workings of a relational team like the board. This is so because group settings involving task nonseparability hinder evaluation of individual performance and limit the utility of individual feedback, thereby diminishing the reinforcing effects of praise and criticism. As one study of social loafing reported, "individual outputs were 'lost in the crowd,' and participants could receive neither credit nor blame for their performance."[9]

Accordingly, if board-based governance is a useful construct, there must be countervailing considerations that make group decision makers preferable to individuals. Further, it must be demonstrated that groups are likely to be more effective in carrying out the functions identified above than would be a single individual.

---

[8] D. Kravitz & B. Martin, *Ringelmann Rediscovered: The Original Article*, 50 J. Personality & Soc. Psych. 936 (1986).

[9] Kate Szymanski & Stephen G. Harkins, *Social Loafing and Self-Evaluation With a Social Standard*, 53 J. Personality & Soc. Psych. 891, 891 (1987).

The MBCA's drafters clearly believed that group decision making offers significant institutional advantages, as the commentary to § 8.20 affirmed that "consultation and exchange of views is an integral part of the functioning of the board." Indeed, "the very existence of the board as an institution is rooted in the wise belief that the effective oversight of an organization exceeds the capabilities of any individual and that collective knowledge and deliberation are better suited to this task."[10]

Groups v. Individuals: Experimental Evidence

Experimental psychologists and economists have found that group decision making, under certain circumstances, can be superior to decision making by individuals. Numerous studies have found that group decisions are not only superior to those of the average group member, but also to those made by the very best individual decision makers within the group. Because this literature has received little attention in legal scholarship, the following discussion recounts in some detail the findings of leading experiments conducted by several generations of researchers.

In the 1930s, Marjorie Shaw conducted a classic experiment in which four-person teams of undergraduates solved various problems with single, self-confirming solutions (so-called "Eureka" problems). One set of problems involved three variants on the classic missionaries and cannibals game.[11] The other set of problems required subjects to solve two word puzzles and another puzzle involving spatial relationships. As to both problem sets, the percentage of correct solutions coming from a sample of groups was significantly higher than that of a sample of individuals working alone.[12]

Some subsequent researchers claimed Shaw's data did not conclusively establish group superiority. In reviewing Shaw's data, they claimed

---

[10] Daniel P. Forbes & Frances J. Milliken, *Cognition and Corporate Governance: Understanding Boards of Directors as Strategic Decision-Making Groups*, 24 Acad. Mgmt. Rev. 489, 490 (1999).

[11] In the missionaries and cannibals game, subjects were given three disks representing missionaries and three disks representing cannibals. The missionaries and cannibals are on one side of a river. The decision maker must get all six to the other side of the river using a boat that can only carry two discs at a time. All missionaries and one cannibal can row. Cannibals must never outnumber missionaries in any location for obvious reasons, albeit politically incorrect ones.

[12] Marjorie E. Shaw, *Comparison of Individuals and Small Groups in the Rational Solution of Complex Problems*, 44 Am. J. Psych. 491 (1932).

that Shaw's groups rarely exceeded, and often fell short of, a theoretical baseline for predicting group performance. Consequently, they claimed, rather than being a more efficient way of making decisions, group decision making suffered from a phenomenon referred to as "process loss."[13]

In order for board-based governance to be preferred to that of a single autocrat, of course, group performance need only be superior to that of individuals, it need not be optimal relative to some theoretical model. The baselines used by Shaw's critics, moreover, are problematic with respect to choosing between individual and group decision making outside the laboratory. Two commonly used baselines are the performance of the best individual member of the group and statistical pooling of individual performances. Both require individual pre-tests unlikely to occur in the real world. Consequently, "such indicators should not be used to prescribe one process over another since they are posterior indicators of performance" that are not discernable by decision makers.[14] Perhaps a more substantial criticism, because many studies finding groups to be superior also used individual pre-tests, is that many studies dispute these findings, concluding that interacting groups outperform both baselines.

A much more recent study, with a radically different design, yielded comparable findings. In an article critical of their fellow economists for paying too little attention to group decision making, Alan Blinder and John Morgan report a pair of laboratory experiments that demonstrated that group decision making was superior to that of individuals. The first experiment involved a purely statistical problem that required even a smaller exercise of critical judgment than Shaw's Eureka problems. In this experiment—intended to replicate situations in which decision makers must choose between acting or waiting for new information—students were presented with computer-generated urns containing equal numbers of blue and red balls. They were told that at some point in the experiment the composition would shift either to 70 percent red and 30 percent blue or vice versa. Students were allowed to draw up to 40 balls from an urn, having been told that the change would occur after one of the first 10 draws. Students earned points for correctly guessing the direction in which the

---

[13] *See* Frederick C. Miner, Jr., *Group v. Individual Decision Making: An Investigation of Performance Measures, Decision Strategies, and Process Losses/Gains*, 33 Org. Beh. and Human Performance 112, 114 (1984) (summarizing argument).

[14] Miner, *supra* note 13, at 114.

composition had changed. In order to measure the speed of decision making as well as its accuracy, students were penalized for each draw made after the urn had changed composition. The subjects were given an incentive by having their compensation linked to their scores. Groups of five undergraduate students were pre-tested when they were asked to play the game as lone individuals. Then each set of five played the game as a group permitted to communicate freely. Three further rounds followed alternating individual and group play.[15]

In this experiment, Blinder and Morgan tested two hypotheses of interest for our purposes. First, they sought to determine whether groups would make decisions more slowly than individuals. Using the number of draws following the actual change in composition as the measurement of decision lag, they found that groups actually made decisions faster than individuals. The difference, however, was not statistically significant. Of course, the absence of a statistically significant difference between the speed of individual and group decision making is itself highly relevant, because it tends to disprove the common intuition that it takes groups longer to make decisions.

Second, Blinder and Morgan asked whether groups made better decisions. On average, group scores were 3.7 percent higher than individual scores, which was a statistically significant difference. Because scores reflected both speed and accuracy, Blinder and Morgan also looked at whether the groups or individuals were more likely to have correctly guessed the direction in which the urn's composition shifted. Groups got it right 89.3 percent of the time, whereas individuals did so only 84.3 percent of the time. This difference also was statistically significant.

Blinder and Morgan acknowledge the artificiality of this setting, but contend that it allowed them "to isolate the pure effect of individual versus group decision making."[16] Their claim raises the question of the extent to which one can rely on laboratory experiments, which is a pervasive problem in experimental economics and psychology. Indeed, some critics call into question the validity of the entire enterprise. Judge Richard Posner, for example, relied on this tactic in critiquing the somewhat

---

[15] Alan S. Blinder & John Morgan, *Are Two Heads Better than One? An Experimental Analysis of Group vs. Individual Decisionmaking*, NBER Working Paper No. 7909 (Sept. 2000).

[16] *Id.* at 6.

similar experiments used to demonstrate the famous endowment effect that has become a central feature of behavioral economics:

> Most individuals, including virtually all university students—the principal experimental subjects of behavioral economics, which relies much more heavily than standard economics does on experiments—are buyers but not sellers. When we do have something to sell, we usually sell through middlemen, such as real estate brokers, rather than directly to the ultimate consumer. Experimental situations in which the subjects are asked to trade with each other are artificial, and so we cannot have much confidence that the results generalize to real markets.[17]

Fair enough—the behavior of undergraduates swapping coffee mugs probably does not tell us very much about the behavior of experienced business people running a board of directors. Yet such criticisms are neither original to Posner nor even new. Both cognitive psychologists and experimental economists long have acknowledged the artificial nature of the groups, tasks, or settings in which their research is per force conducted. Some of the studies recounted herein address aspects of the problem by using MBA students or managerial personnel instead of undergraduates. In addition, some of the evidence recounted herein is taken from studies of real world groups, such as work teams within business firms. In any case, where empirical data are hard to come by, experimental data are surely better than nothing. Given the universality of boards of directors in public corporations, the wide variety of board roles and functions, and the difficulty of collecting useful empirical data on boards, the present context seems to be just such an area.

Returning to the data, Blinder and Morgan's second experiment required somewhat greater expertise and arguably somewhat greater exercise of critical judgment. Students with at least one undergraduate course in macroeconomics were presented with a computer generated model requiring them to make economic policy decisions. Specifically, students were required to set interest rates so as to meet both inflation

---

[17] Richard A. Posner, *Rational Choice, Behavioral Economics, and the Law*, 50 Stan. L. Rev. 1551, 1566 (1998). *See also* Jennifer Arlen, *Comment: The Future of Behavioral Economic Analysis of Law*, 51 Vand. L. Rev. 1765, 1769 (1998) ("we cannot be confident an observed bias really does affect actual decisions—as opposed to being simply an artifact of experimental design—until we can explain why the bias exists").

and unemployment targets. As with the urn experiment, individual and group play rounds alternated.

Again, there was no statistically significant difference in the speed with which groups and individuals made decisions. Again, group scores were higher than individual scores. Notably, when subjects acted alone, the "ersatz monetary policymakers moved interest rates in the wrong direction" more often than did groups.[18]

One significant finding is that the average individual performances of the five individuals making up the group had almost no explanatory power with respect to how well the group performed. Even more striking, the performance of the "best" member of the group did not predict group performance. As we shall see in the next section, these findings take on considerable importance in evaluating the merits of decision making by interacting groups.

In sum, Blinder and Morgan conclude that "two heads—or, in this case, five—are indeed better than one. Society is, in that case, wise to assign many important decisions to committees."[19] Still, Blinder and Morgan's research cannot conclusively establish that society is wise to assign corporate decision making to boards rather than individuals. Their experiments relied on dichotomous decision tasks, merely requiring subjects to make probabilistic estimates using simplistic decision-making processes.

One early literature review identified five categories of decision tasks experimenters had studied with the aim of evaluating individual versus group performance:

1. Learning and concept-attainment tasks, at which group performance was consistently superior to that of individuals
2. Concept mastery and creativity, at which groups tended to outperform individuals (although some studies found that groups did not outperform their best members)
3. Abstract problem solving, such as Shaw's experiment, in which the extent to which groups outperformed even their best members increased with the complexity of the problem.
4. Brainstorming over abstract problems, with no single correct answer, at which statistically created groups outperformed actual groups.

---

[18] Blinder & Morgan, *supra* note 15, at 33.
[19] *Id.* at 47.

5. Complex problems, such as the winter survival exercise described below, at which groups outperformed individuals but did not exceed baseline measurements of potential created by statistical pooling.[20]

Mapping these categories onto board decision making is difficult. Most board decision making does not involve problems with a single correct solution, let alone a self-confirming one. Instead, relevant experiments are those requiring the creative exercise of evaluative judgment with respect to complex problems having a range of solutions. Unfortunately, as suggested by the foregoing taxonomy, many experiments in this area focus on descriptive rather than evaluative judgments.

In contrast, management scholar Frederick Miner devised an experiment explicitly intended to compare the ability of groups to exercise evaluative judgment with that of individuals.[21] Miner's experiment required 69 self-selected groups, each composed of four undergraduate business students, to solve the so-called winter survival exercise. This exercise, which is variously attributed, has become something of a benchmark standard in the field. The subjects in a group are told that they are survivors of an airplane crash at a remote location. They first must decide whether to walk out or remain at the crash site. They then must rank the utility of 15 survival aids. In Miner's case, a group of four military winter survival experts were used to validate the exercise's purported correct solution.

Although Miner's experiment does not directly implicate corporate governance, it has certain instructive features. First, it used business students, who presumably resemble corporate directors more closely than other plausible experimental subjects. Second, the subjects knew one another before becoming members of the group and were allowed to form their own groups—both of which somewhat replicate the process by which boards form. Finally, and most importantly, the subjects shared a single goal (survival). Granted, the experiment thus did not require them to aggregate preferences as to which there might be value differences, but rather to pool their collective knowledge and use that knowledge

---

[20] Gayle W. Hill, *Group Versus Individual Performance: Are N + 1 Heads Better than One?*, 91 Psych. Bull. 517 (1982).

[21] *See* Miner, *supra* note 13. Miner's results were replicated by Roger J. Volkema & Ronald H. Gorman, *The Influence of Cognitive-Based Group Composition on Decision-Making Process and Outcome*, 35 J. Mgmt. Stud. 105, 114 (1998).

to evaluate alternatives in light of the shared goal. If we assume that directors generally share a primary goal of shareholder wealth maximization, however, this experimental condition also replicates corporate governance.

Turning to the results, Miner found that group rankings were more accurate than those of the average individual subject. Group rankings, however, tended to be less accurate than those of the best decision maker within each group. At first blush, Miner's results suggest a preference for individual decision making, but the ability to identify the "best" individual decision maker is solely an artifact of the experimental design. Individual evaluations could be scored by comparison to the correct solution and ranked by the experimenter. Yet, as discussed below, identifying a superior decision maker is far more problematic in the real world.

A subsequent study, which also conducted an experiment using the winter survival scenario, even more clearly favors the superiority of group decision making. Of the 16 groups studied: 11 produced better decisions, as groups, than any of their individual members in a pre-test; the performance of one group equaled that of its best member; and the remaining four groups did less well than their best individual. Comparable results were obtained by other researchers using similar experimental designs.[22]

In sum, groups appear to outperform their average-performing members consistently, even at relatively complex tasks requiring exercise of evaluative judgment. There is contested evidence as to whether groups outperform their best member, which the next section evaluates in more detail. Accordingly, it seems fair to conclude that group decision making often is preferable to that of individuals. In addition to the specific studies recounted above, which are corroborated by those described in following sections, a number of comprehensive literature reviews confirm that conclusion.[23] Corporate law's strong emphasis on collective decision making by the board thus seems to have a compelling efficiency rationale.

---

[22] Starr Roxanne Hiltz et al., *Experiments in Group Decision Making: Communication Process and Outcome in Face-to-Face Versus Computerized Conferences*, 13 Human Communication Research 225 (1986).

[23] James H. Davis, *Some Compelling Intuitions about Group Consensus Decisions, Theoretical and Empirical Research, and Interpersonal Aggregation Phenomena: Selected Examples, 1950–1990*, 52 Org. Beh. & Human Decision Processes 3 (1992); Haft, *supra* note 4; Hill, *supra* note 20.

Assuming group decision making is advantageous, however, why is that the case? Surprisingly, the behavioral literature on group decision making frequently offers quite rudimentary theories as to why groups outperform individuals. One contribution of my analysis is the use of new institutional economics to develop a theory of group superiority applicable to corporate law issues.

In the sections that follow, we consider three explanations for the superiority of groups. These explanations are complementary, not competing, and moreover, overlap to a considerable degree. Yet, it nonetheless seems helpful to break them out individually. Among other reasons, separate treatment helps identify the circumstances under which group decision making is most likely to be preferable to that of individuals.

Groups and Bounded Rationality

Decision making processes typically involve four major components: (1) observation, or the gathering of information; (2) memory, or the storage of information; (3) computation, or the manipulation of information; and (4) communication, or the transmission of information.[24] How do groups minimize transaction costs associated with these components vis-à-vis individual decision makers? Multiple sources of information may make it less costly to gather information, but it seems unlikely that directors qua directors do much to facilitate the observation process. Any such savings, moreover, likely are offset by increased communication costs. By decentralizing both access to information and decision-making power, group decision making requires additional resources.

If groups have an advantage relevant to the institution of the board of directors, it therefore seems most likely to arise with respect to either memory and/or computation. As to the former, groups develop a sort of collective memory that consists not only of the sum of individual memories, but also of an awareness of who knows what. Consequently, institutional memory is superior when the organization is structured as a set of teams rather than as a mere aggregate of individuals. There is some laboratory evidence, moreover, that the collective memory of groups leads to

---

[24] Roy Radner, *Bounded Rationality, Indeterminacy, and the Theory of the Firm*, 106 Econ. J. 1360, 1363 (1996).

higher-quality output. Group members, for example, seem to specialize in memorizing specific aspects of complex repetitive tasks.[25]

In a particularly striking demonstration of this phenomenon, the experimenters used a mock trial scenario to test group versus individual memory.[26] Subjects listened to a tape-recorded mock trial for assault and then were tested to determine how well they recalled facts presented. Group memory was superior to that of individuals as to accuracy, volume of information retained, ability to reproduce testimony verbatim, and even the order in which information was presented.

As to the relationship between group decision making and computation-based costs, the key question is whether board decision making is an efficient adaptive response to the problem of bounded rationality. Neoclassical rational choice theory assumes that individuals act so as to maximize their expected utility and acknowledges no cognitive limits on their power to do so. In contrast, both behavioral and new institutional economics posit that the limitations of human cognition often result in decisions that fail to maximize utility. Hence, the phenomenon of bounded rationality, which we've seen asserts that all humans have inherently limited memories, computational skills, and other mental tools.

Bounded rationality becomes a particularly significant constraint on decision making under conditions of complexity and uncertainty. Under such conditions, boundedly rational decision makers are unable to devise either a fully specified solution to the problem at hand or to fully assess the probable outcomes of their action. In effect, cognitive power is a scarce resource which the inexorable laws of economics tell us decision makers will (to the best of their ability) seek to allocate efficiently. Consistent with that prediction, there is evidence that actors attempt to minimize effort in the face of complexity and ambiguity.[27] Ironically, this is a rational adaptation to bounded rationality—in response to the limits on their cognitive powers, decision makers seek to reduce both the likelihood of error and the costs of decision making.

An actor can economize limited cognitive resources in two ways: first, by adopting institutional governance structures designed to promote

---

[25] Cohen & Bailey, *supra* note 5, at 259.

[26] David A. Vollrath et al., *Memory Performance by Decision-Making Groups and Individuals,* 43 Org. Beh. & Human Decision Processes 289 (1989).

[27] Russell B. Korobkin & Thomas S. Ulen, *Law and Behavioral Science: Removing the Rationality Assumption from Law and Economics,* 88 Cal. L. Rev. 1051, 1078 (2000) (citing studies).

more efficient decision making, and second, by invoking shortcuts, i.e., heuristic problem-solving decision-making processes. Here we focus on the former approach, positing that group decision making appears in the corporate context when a collective governance structure provides more efficient decision making than would a single individual. Put another way, group decision making may be an adaptive response to bounded rationality, creating a system for aggregating the inputs of multiple individuals with differing knowledge, interests, and skills. In the corporate context, the board of directors thus may have emerged as an institutional governance mechanism to constrain the deleterious effect of bounded rationality on the organizational decision-making process.

Does the process of social interaction at least help the cream to rise to the top, so that the group seizes upon the best ideas each member brings to the table? Or does group decision making have even more dramatic effects, such as generating synergies that allow groups to outperform even their best members?

Shaw explained the superiority of groups in her classic experiment on grounds that multi-member teams balance individual biases and detect errors by individuals. Proposed solutions put forward by one member of the group were three times more likely to be rejected by another group member than by the initial proponent of that solution. Among the proposals put forward, moreover, five times as many incorrect solutions were rejected as were correct ones. Accordingly, she concluded that "one point of group supremacy is the rejection of incorrect ideas that escape the notice of the individual when working alone."[28]

Shaw's analysis, of course, is more in the way of informed intuition than an explicit quantitative analysis of how social interaction affects group versus individual performance. Closer to the mark is an interesting 1963 study designed to test whether the apparent superiority of group decision making was, as then commonly hypothesized, an artifact of statistical pooling. One could create a statistical group by pooling the decisions of multiple individuals. If group interaction had no synergistic effects, the decisions of real groups should not differ significantly from those of such statistically created groups.

---

[28] Shaw, *supra* note 12, at 502. Vollrath et al., likewise found evidence that, as to memory tasks, groups corrected errors by individual members. Vollrath et al., *supra* note 26, at 299.

Ernest Hall and his co-authors showed their subjects a portion of the classic movie "Twelve Angry Men." Recall that the hold-out juror voting "not guilty" brings the other 11 jurors over to his point of view one-by-one. Acting alone, subjects were asked to predict the order in which the 11 in the majority would capitulate to the minority view. Statistical groups were then created by pooling the individual responses. Subjects were then brought together for group discussion, in which they were asked to reach a unanimous ranking. This is a nice problem for our purposes because it offers a complex issue as to which there is a preferred answer, but not one that is either self-confirming or even objectively correct. The actual groups produced a more accurate score than the average of pooled individual scores, with the difference being statistically significant. Hall therefore concluded that group interaction fostered critical evaluation of individual judgments.[29]

As an alternative to the pooling hypothesis, some researchers assert that the apparent superiority of group decision making is merely a function of the ability of one or more members to solve the problem in question. Put another way, interpersonal interactions have no synergistic effect. Instead, group performance is attributable solely to the abilities of the best decision maker in the group.[30]

This debate has been a long and contentious one in the literature, to which no satisfactory answer has yet emerged. The empirical evidence is mixed, with some studies supporting each side. One of the studies, which seems potentially relevant to the question of boards versus CEOs, however, suggests that group decision making does have synergistic effects. Larry Michaelsen and his team created a sample consisting of 222 team-learning groups gathered from organizational behavior courses. The subjects devoted the vast majority of class time to problem-solving tasks—some preformed by groups and others individually. Each student was randomly assigned to a single group and stayed there for the entire course. Group members spent at least 32 hours working together, and solved a variety of problems. The data collected were scores from objective tests taken by the

---

[29] Ernest J. Hall et al., *Group Problem Solving Effectiveness Under Conditions of Pooling vs. Interaction*, 59 J. Soc. Psych. 147 (1963).

[30] *See, e.g.*, Irving Lorge and Herbert Solomon, *Two Models of Group Behavior in the Solution of Eureka-type Problems*, 20 Psychometrika 139 (1955); Norman R. F. Maier and James A. Thurber, *Innovative Problem-solving by Outsiders: A Study of Individuals and Groups*, 22 Personnel Psych. 237, 248 (1969) (concluding that a group's product depends on having "one good problem-solver present").

students throughout the semester. The tests were taken first by individuals and then by groups. Both individual and group scores counted toward the grade. The mean group score was 89.9, which exceeded both the mean average individual score (74.2) and best individual score (82.6). Strikingly, all 222 groups outperformed their average-performing members and 215 of the 222 groups outperformed their best members. Both findings were statistically significant. These results tend to disprove both the pooling and best member hypotheses, while lending support to the claim that group decision making has synergistic effects.[31]

Note that several features of the Michaelsen team's experimental design replicate certain aspects of board decision making. As with boards, for example, the Michaelsen groups interacted episodically over an extended period. In addition, the task resembled the board's information-processing function. Group members were required to elicit information from one another, critically evaluate that information, and achieve consensus. Boards must engage in such processes with respect to both their strategic planning and monitoring functions. On the other hand, despite the researchers' efforts to devise tests that required a high degree of cognitive effort, the task at issue here differs from those of boards both in its simplicity and the existence of a single correct answer. Finally, the study also replicates organizational settings by linking both individual and group performance to a significant reward (higher grades), although the partial separability of the task diverges from the board setting.

My own view is that the best member hypothesis debate need not be resolved for us to draw some conclusions about the relative merits of boards and CEOs as the ultimate corporate decision maker. The ability of a group to identify the "best" individual decision maker is solely an artifact of the experimental design. In the corporate setting, there are no individual pre-tests that allow one to identify the best decision maker in a sample. Many organizational tasks involve team production in which task nonseparability and the infeasibility of effort-monitoring preclude identification of superior decision makers. Bias, information asymmetries, and various collective action problems can all skew selection of the superior individual decision maker. Members of subject groups,

---

[31] Larry K. Michaelsen et al., *A Realistic Test of Individual Versus Group Consensus Decision Making*, 74 J. App. Psych. 834 (1989).

for example, tend to believe they are superior to other group members.[32] Yet, because not all the children in Lake Wobegon really can be above average, the so-called overconfidence bias likely skews selection of superior decision makers. Other constraints on a group's ability to correctly identify its best decision maker include status differentials, social norms, and bounded rationality–based flaws in the evaluative process.

Put another way, an advantage of group decision making is that the group is sure to get the benefit of its best decision maker. A group that delegates decisions to the individual identified by the group as its best decision maker may not do so. Miner's study tested this hypothesis by requiring the subject groups to identify who among their members was the best decision maker. With four member groups, random selection would be correct 25 percent of the time. Although Miner's groups were slightly more accurate in selecting their best members than random chance, the difference was not statistically significant. If experimental groups cannot accurately identify the best decision maker in their midst, as Miner concludes, this finding casts doubt on the ability of shareholders to select an ideal single decision maker. Further doubt on the claim that one can ex ante identify a group's best decision maker is cast by Miner's additional finding that the average quality of group decisions exceeded the average quality of the decisions made by the individual selected by each group as its best decision maker.[33] On balance, it seems likely that shareholders are better off with a committee than an individual.

Individual v. Group Decision-Making Biases

Research in behavioral economics has identified a number of pervasive cognitive errors that bias decision making. According to the proponents of behavioral economics, these biases result in behavior that systematically departs from that predicted by the traditional rational choice model.[34]

---

[32] Neil Weinstein, *Unrealistic Optimism about Future Life Events*, 39 J. Personality & Social Psych. 806 (1980) (summarizing studies).

[33] Miner, *supra* note 13.

[34] Useful literature reviews include Christine Jolls et al., *A Behavioral Approach to Law and Economics*, 50 Stan. L. Rev. 1471 (1998); Korobkin and Ulen, *supra* note 27; Donald C. Langevoort, *Behavioral Theories of Judgment and Decision Making in Legal Scholarship: A Literature Review*, 51 Vand. L. Rev. 1499 (1998); Cass R. Sunstein, *Behavioral Law and Economics: A Progress Report*, 1 Am. L. & Econ. Rev. 115 (1999). The extent to which

It is the systematic nature of these biases that is critical. Standard economic analysis recognizes that individual decision makers may depart from rationality, but assumes that such departures come out in the wash—they cancel each other out so that the average or equilibrium behavior of large groups will be consistent with rational choice. By asserting that decision makers exhibit systematic biases, behavioral economics denies that claim. This literature draws extensively from experimental economics and cognitive psychology, which makes it a close cousin of the work on group versus individual decision making.

Several of the identified decision-making biases seem especially pertinent to managerial decision making. Two examples should suffice, however; namely, herding behavior and the overconfidence bias. In both cases, group decision making may counteract individual biases.

Herding. There is considerable evidence of herding behavior in corporate settings. As I have demonstrated elsewhere, the popularity of participatory management schemes among corporate managers owes much to herd behavior.[35] Judith Chevalier and Glenn Ellison found that young mutual fund managers tended to herd into popular market sectors and conventionally weighted portfolios.[36] Michael Klausner and Marcel Kahan contend that herding by lawyers helps to explain the persistence of sub-optimal provisions in bond indentures.[37]

Herd behavior occurs when a decision maker imitates the actions of others while ignoring his own information and judgment with regard to the merits of the underlying decision. Various explanations for herd behavior have been offered, such as the prospect that following the crowd

---

behavioral economics calls into question more traditional modes of economic analysis remains sharply contested. *See* Stephen M. Bainbridge, *Mandatory Disclosure: A Behavioral Analysis*, 68 U. Cin. L. Rev. 1023 (2000) (arguing that behavioral economics must be used with care). At the very least, however, it seems clear that attention must be paid to the possibility that a behavioral economics analysis might shed light on legal problems. *Id.*

[35] Stephen M. Bainbridge, *Privately Ordered Participatory Management: An Organizational Failures Analysis*, 23 Del. J. Corp. L. 979, 1002–4 (1998). Participatory management is a generic term for any system of industrial relations purporting to involve employees in workplace decision making; e.g., quality circles and self-directed work teams. *Id.* at 981.

[36] Judith Chevalier and Glenn Ellison, *Career Concerns of Mutual Fund Managers*, 114 Quart. J. Econ. 389 (1999).

[37] Marcel Kahan and Michael Klausner, *Path Dependence in Corporate Contracting: Increasing Returns, Herd Behavior, and Cognitive Biases*, 74 Wash. U.L.Q. 347 (1996) (to be clear, they posit herding as one of several reasons for that persistence).

may have a reputational payoff even if the chosen course of action fails. Because even a good actor can make decisions that lead to an adverse outcome, those who evaluate the actor look at both the outcome and the action before forming a judgment about the actor. If a bad outcome occurs but the action was consistent with approved conventional wisdom, the hit to the manager's reputation from the adverse outcome is reduced. As Keynes famously remarked, "it is better to fail conventionally than to succeed unconventionally."[38] If group decision making provides superior mechanisms for monitoring both the group itself and/or its subordinates, as the next section argues, the incentive to herd is reduced. An actor can depart from conventional wisdom with more confidence that an adverse outcome will be fairly evaluated.

Herding also can be a response to bounded rationality and information asymmetries. Under conditions of complexity and uncertainty, actors who perceive themselves as having limited information and can observe the actions of presumptively better-informed persons may attempt to free ride by following the latter's decisions. Importantly, this explanation for herding suggests that the introduction of new information may alter the equation. Hence, herding motivated by an information asymmetry produces short-lived fads in which consumer preferences prove quite brittle.[39] If group decision making is an efficient adaptation to bounded rationality, as the preceding section argued, the incentive to herd is again diminished.

Overconfidence. The old joke about the camel being a horse designed by a committee captures the valid empirical observation that individuals are often superior to groups when it comes to matters requiring creativity. Research on brainstorming as a decision-making process, for example, confirms that individuals working alone generate a greater number of ideas than do groups. Strikingly, this is especially true when the assigned task is "fanciful" rather than "realistic."[40]

Three factors might explain why groups are relatively worse at performing tasks requiring creativity or brilliance: First, some brilliant

---

[38] John Maynard Keynes, *The General Theory of Employment, Interest, and Money* 158 (1936).

[39] David Hirshleifer, *The Blind Leading the Blind: Social Influence, Fads, and Informational Cascades*, in *The New Economics of Human Behavior* 188, 191–93 (Mariano Tommasi and Kathryn Ierulli eds. 1995).

[40] Hill, *supra* note 20, at 527.

members of a group may proffer brilliant proposals that other members of the group simply fail to appreciate. Because groups decide questions only in ways that achieve a consensus, brilliant ideas which only one or two members of a group appreciate or understand are not likely to be the object of a group consensus. Second, some members of a group may oppose the brilliant proposals of others simply out of envy. Assuming the brilliant individuals would be singled out for praise or favorable recognition for coming up with the brilliant ideas, some individuals may oppose the ideas simply to prevent the more brilliant individuals from achieving reputational gains over them. Finally, some members of a group may adulterate brilliant proposals with sub-optimal amendments simply to exert their authority as members of the group. Many times, members of a decision-making body insist on making a proactive contribution to every matter that comes before the body for resolution. Such members may feel that if they do not personally alter or make a substantive contribution in some way to every solution that their bodies adopt, then other body members may start ignoring or disregarding their authority as members of the body. Such members constantly seek to reassert their power by rejecting a proposal as stated unless the body accepts one of their own ideas or amendments even when the proposal is essentially perfect and in need of no amendments.

Although individuals thus may well be better at devising a brilliant plan, individuals often become wedded to their plans and fail to see flaws that others might identify.[41] As with all decision makers, corporate managers likewise become heavily invested in their beliefs, which makes them unable to recognize that those beliefs may be biased.

This bias may be defused by group decision making. There is a widely shared view that groups are superior at evaluative tasks, which is largely confirmed by the winter survival exercise studies. Group decision making presumably checks individual overconfidence by providing critical assessment and alternative viewpoints, a hypothesis supported by Shaw's analysis of her experimental findings.

The assumption that group decision making constrains overconfident individuals is consistent with the standard account of the board's function. Recall that our taxonomy identified three basic board roles: monitoring, service, and resource gathering. At the core of the board's

---

[41] Peter M. Blau and W. Richard Scott, *Formal Organizations* 116–21 (1962).

service role is providing advice and counsel to the senior management team, especially the CEO. At the intersection of the board's service and monitoring roles is the provision of alternative points of view. Put another way, most of what boards do requires the exercise of critical evaluative judgment, but not creativity. Even the board's policymaking role entails judgment more than creativity, as the board is usually selecting from a range of options presented by subordinates.

As an admittedly anecdotal example, consider the saga of RJR Nabisco's efforts to develop a smokeless cigarette.[42] Unbeknownst to the board of directors, management spent millions of dollars on the project. When the board was finally informed, many directors reportedly were angered by management's failure to consult with them beforehand. Their anger was wholly justified, for the smokeless cigarette flopped. Managers who were responsible resigned to avoid being fired. The corporation would have been better served if the board had been advised of the project early in its development. Those responsible seem to have been wedded to the project, a tendency the board might have been able to counteract.

Countervailing Group Biases. The proposition that group decision making counteracts individual biases obviously overlaps with the claim that group decision making is an adaptive response to bounded rationality. Numerous studies suggest that groups benefit from both pooling information and from providing opportunities for one member to correct another's errors. If so, the benefits of group decision making should be present whether those errors arise from limitations on cognitive powers or biases in the exercise of those powers.

It must be acknowledged, however, that cohesive groups are subject to their own unique cognitive biases. A widely cited example is the so-called risky shift phenomenon. Although we might assume that group decision making has a moderating influence, social dilemma experiments demonstrate that groups actually make more extreme decisions than individuals. In early versions of these experiments, individual subjects were pre-tested by being presented with a story in which they were featured as the central character. The story placed them in a familiar social setting and asked them to choose between two options, one of which was described as being the riskier of the two, but also as having a potentially

---

[42] The following discussion is based on Bryan Burrough and John Helyar, *Barbarians at the Gate: The Fall of RJR Nabisco* 74–77 (1990).

higher return. Small groups were then presented with the same problem and asked to make a collective decision. Groups were significantly more likely to select the riskier option than were individuals. Given that individuals tend to be risk-averse, but that shareholder interests often require risk-preferring decisions, the risky shift phenomenon seems useful on first blush. Unfortunately, later experiments demonstrated that group shifts to greater caution could also be induced. The net effect is that there is a polarizing effect in group decision making, so that post discussion consensus is more extreme than the individual pre-test results, but not always in a predictable direction.[43]

The most significant group bias for our purposes, however, is the "groupthink" phenomenon.[44] Highly cohesive groups with strong civility and cooperation norms value consensus more than they do a realistic appraisal of alternatives. In such groups, groupthink is an adaptive response to the stresses generated by challenges to group solidarity. To avoid those stresses, groups may strive for unanimity even at the expense of quality decision making.

To the extent that groupthink promotes the development of social norms, it facilitates the board's monitoring function. It may also support other board functions, such as resource acquisition, to the extent that it promotes a sort of esprit de corps. The downside, though, is an erosion in the quality of decision making. The desire to maintain group cohesion trumps the exercise of critical judgment. Adverse consequences of groupthink thus include the prospect that the group will fail to examine alternatives, fail to be either self-critical or evaluative of others, and be selective in gathering information. Studies of meeting behavior, for example, conclude that people tend to prefer options that have obvious popularity.[45]

Boardroom culture encourages groupthink. Boards emphasize politeness and courtesy at the expense of oversight.[46] CEOs foster and channel groupthink through the exercise of their powers to control information flows, reward consensus, and discourage reelection of troublemakers.

---

[43] For discussion of the polarization effect, *see* Norbert L. Kerr, *Group Decision Making at a Multialternative Task: Extremity, Interfaction Distance, Pluralities, and Issue Importance*, 52 Org. Beh. and Human Decision Processes 64 (1992); Cass R. Sunstein, *Deliberative Trouble? Why Groups Go to Extremes*, 110 Yale L.J. 71 (2000).

[44] Irving Janis, *Victims of Groupthink* (1972) (discussing groupthink).

[45] Sara Kiesler & Lee Sproul, *Group Decision Making and Communication Technology*, 52 Org. Beh. & Human Decision Processes 96 (1992).

[46] Michael C. Jensen, *A Theory of the Firm: Governance, Residual Claims, and Organizational Forms* 49–50 (2000).

Not surprisingly, the groupthink phenomenon therefore has proven a major obstacle in translating the statutory model of director primacy into the real world of corporate governance. As we'll see in Chapter 4, however, various best practices have emerged design to deal with this problem.

Agency Costs

In a sense, the preceding discussion is a special case of the broader agency cost phenomenon. Individuals shirk, sometimes as a rational response to incentives and sometimes because of biased decision making. In either case, group decision making may help to constrain those tendencies.

Insofar as monitoring is concerned, group decision making has a bidirectional make-up. In the vertical dimension, is a group superior to an individual autocrat as a monitor of subordinates in the corporate hierarchy? In the horizontal dimension, do intra-group governance structures help to constrain shirking and self-dealing at the apex of the hierarchy?

Suppose the corporate hierarchy was capped by an individual autocrat rather than by a board of directors. Under such circumstances, a bilateral vertical monitoring problem arises. On the one hand, the autocrat must monitor his or her subordinates. On the other hand, someone must monitor the autocrat.

As we have seen, hierarchy is an adaptive governance response to the agency cost problem. Yet, as we also saw, that explanation raises the question: Who watches the watchers? Recall from Chapter 1 that economists Alchian and Demsetz solved this dilemma by requiring that the monitor be given the residual income left after all other workers have been paid.[47] Unfortunately, their model breaks down with respect to the public corporation. Although common stockholders are the corporation's residual claimants, they also are the corporate constituency perhaps least able to meaningfully monitor management behavior.[48]

---

[47] Armen A. Alchian and Harold Demsetz, *Production, Information Costs, and Economic Organization*, 62 Am. Econ. Rev. 777 (1972).

[48] Alchian and Demsetz tried to solve this problem by arguing that "the policing of managerial shirking [in the corporate context] relies on across-market competition from new groups of would-be managers as well as competition from members within the firm who seek to displace existing management." *Id.* at 788. In a world of passive shareholders and takeover defenses, however, this is a solution that does not solve.

Corporate law therefore provides a series of alternative accountability mechanisms designed to constrain agency costs without the need for an unending series of monitors. Chief among them is the board of directors. A hierarchy of individuals whose governance structures contemplate only vertical monitoring cannot resolve the problem of who watches the watchers. Instead, corporate law cuts the Gordian Knot by placing a group at the apex of the hierarchy.

Where an individual autocrat would have substantial freedom to shirk or self-deal, the internal dynamics of group governance constrain self-dealing and shirking both by individual team members and the group as a whole. At the most simplistic level, diffusion of responsibility in corporate decision making among a group constrains agency costs because it requires a conspiracy to make opportunism effective. Misconduct by a group commonly is harder to pull off than misconduct by a single individual. In addition, a multi-member board is inherently harder for misbehaving subordinates to suborn than would be a single autocrat. Instead of having to bribe or otherwise co-opt a single individual, the wrongdoers now must effect a conspiracy among a number of monitors. Because managers are less likely to capture a group than an individual, managers are less likely to self-deal with a corporation that is ultimately governed by a group rather than an individual.

More importantly, however, allocating decision making to a group rather than an individual brings key social norms into play. Within a production team, mutual monitoring and peer pressure provide a coercive backstop for a set of interpersonal relationships founded on trust and other non-contractual social norms. Of particular relevance here are effort and cooperation norms.

Behavior is regulated by both law and social norms. A standard example of the distinction between the two is that leaving a tip after one eats in a restaurant is a social norm, while paying for one's food is a legal requirement. Accordingly, we can roughly define a social norm as a social attitude specifying the behavior an actor ought to exhibit in a given situation. Although economists only recently began exploring the role norms play in regulating behavior, an astonishingly rich literature has developed in just a few years.

While the old adage opines, "familiarity breeds contempt," personal proximity to others in fact deeply affects behavior. As people become closer, their behavior tends to improve: "[S]omething in us makes it all but impossible to justify our acts as mere self-interest whenever those acts are seen by others as violating a moral principle;" rather, "[w]e want our actions to be seen by others—and by ourselves—as arising out of appropriate motives."[49] Small groups strengthen this instinct in several ways.

First, they provide a network of reputational and other social sanctions that shape incentives. Because membership in close-knit groups satisfies the human need for belongingness, the threat of expulsion gives the group a strong sanction by which to enforce compliance with group norms. Because a close-knit group presupposes a continuing relationship, the threat of punishment in future interactions deters the sort of cheating possible in one-time transactions:

> Informal peer group pressures can be mobilized to check malingering. . . . The most casual involves cajoling or ribbing. If this fails, rational appeals to persuade the deviant to conform are employed. The group then resorts to penalties by withdrawing the social benefits that affiliation affords. Finally, overt coercion and ostracism are resorted to.[50]

Mutual monitoring and social norms, enforced through peer pressure and reputational sanctions, thus provide important constraints on behavior, making it much harder for the top decision maker to self-deal or shirk when he or she is part of a group.

Second, because people care about how they are perceived by those close to them, communal life provides a cloud of witnesses whose good opinion we value. We hesitate to disappoint those people and thus strive to comport ourselves in accordance with communal norms. Effort norms will thus tend to discourage board members from simply going through the motions, but instead will encourage them to devote greater cognitive effort to their tasks.

Finally, there is a transaction cost explanation for the importance of closeness in trust relationships. The members of close-knit groups know a lot about one another, which reduces monitoring costs and thus further encourages compliance with group norms. These members therefore tend to internalize group norms.

---

[49] James Q. Wilson, *What is Moral and How Do We Know It?*, Commentary, June 1993, at 37, 39.
[50] Oliver E. Williamson, *Markets and Hierarchies: Analysis and Antitrust Implications* 48 (1975).

Taken together, these factors suggest that group decision making is a potentially powerful constraint on agency costs. It creates a set of high-powered incentives to comply with both effort and cooperation norms. The board of directors can be understood as an adaptive response to the problem of "who shall watch the watchers," providing a self-monitoring hierarch whose internal governance structures provide incentives for optimal monitoring of its subordinates.

Having said that, however, a few caveats are in order. First, monitoring actors' compliance with social norms becomes harder as the relevant community becomes larger and less closely knit. Social sanctions are also far more effective as applied within a close-knit group than among strangers.[51] Conversely, however, close-knit groups are also those most vulnerable to groupthink. Participation in group decision-making processes likely induces conformity with established or emergent group norms.

Second, collective action problems may impede the ability of decision-making groups to constrain agency costs. This concern seems especially pertinent to the board of directors. Because effective performance of the board's oversight duties requires collective action, we have a potential free riding problem. Even though faithful monitoring may be in an individual director's interest, he or she may assume that other directors will do the hard work of identifying sub-par performances, permitting the free rider to shirk. As in any free riding situation, this will tend to result in sub-optimal levels of monitoring. Put another way, as we have seen, group decision making can result in social loafing.

Even in cases of clearly sub-par management performance, moreover, other collective action problems may prevent the board from taking

---

[51] Cf. Donald McCloskey, *Bourgeois Virtue*, Am. Scholar, Spr. 1994, at 177, 183–84 (contending that the importance of trust to market exchange explains why members of the same ethnic group frequently can deal profitably with one another). Diamond exchanges, commodity trading associations, and the historical law merchant all exhibit norm compliance. Critically, however, each of these settings is characterized by a dense social network embedded in an intimate society that provides a framework for repeat transactions. Consequently, for example, Bernstein's classic study of the diamond market acknowledged that "geographical concentration, ethnic homogeneity, and repeat dealing may be necessary preconditions to the emergence of a contractual regime based on reputation bonds." Lisa Bernstein, *Opting Out of the Legal System: Extralegal Contractual Relations in the Diamond Industry*, 21 J. Leg. Stud. 115, 140 (1992). On the other hand, group research suggests that even ad hoc groups develop norms quite quickly. Hill, *supra* note 20, at 530. In any event, such conditions may not be necessary to the maintenance of such a regime once it has established itself. Instead, as the diamond industry departed from those conditions it shifted to a regime based on information technology and intermediaries. Bernstein, *supra*, at 143–44.

necessary remedial steps. Some director must step forward to begin building a majority in favor of replacing the incumbent managers, which again
raises a free rider problem. Furthermore, if an active director steps forward, he or she must not only overcome the forces of inertia and bias, but
also must likely do so in the face of active opposition from the threatened
managers who will try to cut off the flow of information to the board,
co-opt key board members, and otherwise undermine the disciplinary
process.

   None of these caveats suggest that corporations ought to be run by
an individual autocrat rather than a board of directors. On balance, effort
and cooperation norms within a small, close-knit group, such as the
board, provide high-level incentives. As we'll see in Chapter 4, however,
concerns about groupthink, social loafing, and collective action failures
all prove relevant to operationalizing group decision making in the
corporate setting.

CHAPTER 3

Director Primacy in the Courts

Because a model's ability to predict real world outcomes is the critical test of the model's validity, a key question is whether the director primacy model makes accurate predictions not only with respect to the statutory framework of corporate governance but also the case law in this area. As we saw in the opening chapters of this text, director primacy provides a coherent account of the statutory framework of corporate governance. In this chapter, we'll see that it likewise provides an account of the common law of corporate governance that has both descriptive and normative power. "Although 'Delaware has not explicitly embraced director primacy,' the relevant statutory provisions and the [cases] have largely intimated that directors retain authority and need not passively allow either exogenous events or shareholder action to determine corporate decision-making."[1] Director primacy thus provides a descriptive model that helps to predict the likely outcome of cases, as well as a normative model for criticizing decisions that go awry.

This text is not a treatise in corporate law, of course. To narrow our focus to a manageable level, we will examine two important doctrines that deeply implicate the authority of directors. First, to what extent do

---

[1] Harry G. Hutchison, *Director Primacy and Corporate Governance: Shareholder Voting Rights Captured by the Accountability/Authority Paradigm*, 36 Loy. U. Chi. L.J. 1111, 1194 (2005).

courts review the merits of operational decisions made by a disinterested board of directors? As we'll see, the director primacy model predicts that courts generally should refrain from reviewing such decisions and, pursuant to the business judgment rule, courts in fact generally do not review such decisions. Second, does the board of directors have a gatekeeping role with respect to unsolicited takeover bids? Under prevailing academic shareholder primacy-based models, the board has at best a limited role in this area. Curiously, however, Delaware courts have acknowledged a very broad role for the board, which has led to considerable academic criticism. In contrast to academic conventional wisdom, director primacy suggests that the Delaware cases strike an appropriate balance between two competing but equally legitimate goals of corporate law: on the one hand, because the power to review differs only in degree and not in kind from the power to decide, the discretionary authority of the board of directors must be insulated from shareholder and judicial oversight in order to promote efficient corporate decision making; on the other hand, because directors are obligated to maximize shareholder wealth, there must be mechanisms to ensure director accountability. Delaware's analytical framework provides courts with a mechanism for filtering out cases in which directors have abused their authority from those in which directors have not.

The Business Judgment Rule

The duty of care requires corporate directors to exercise "that amount of care which ordinarily careful and prudent men would use in similar circumstances."[2] Because the corporate duty of care thus resembles the tort law concept of reasonable care, one might assume the duty of care is violated when directors act negligently. Yet, the one thing about the business judgment rule on which everyone agrees is that it insulates directors from liability for negligence: "While it is often stated that corporate directors and officers will be liable for negligence in carrying out their corporate duties, all seem agreed that such a statement is misleading. . . . Whatever the terminology, the fact is that liability is rarely imposed upon corporate directors or officers simply for bad judgment and this reluctance to

---

[2] *See, e.g.*, Graham v. Allis-Chalmers Mfg. Co., 188 A.2d 125, 130 (Del. 1963).

ity for unsuccessful business decisions has been doctrinally labeled the business judgment rule."[3]

The business judgment rule thus is a curious doctrine. On the one hand, the duty of care tells directors to exercise reasonable care in making corporate decisions. On the other hand, the business judgment rule says that courts must defer to the board of directors' judgment absent highly unusual exceptions. Compare the liability of physicians, who are also held to a duty of care, but whose medical judgment gets no such deference. Why are directors of an incorporated business entitled to deference that physicians are denied? The question becomes all the more pressing when one recognizes that the business judgment rule is corporate law's central doctrine. It pervades every aspect of the state law of corporate governance, from negligence by directors to self-dealing transactions to termination of shareholder litigation and so on.[4]

The analysis herein proceeds from the premise that the business judgment rule, like all of corporate law, reflects an inherent tension between two competing values: the need to preserve the board of directors' decision-making discretion and the need to hold the board accountable for its decisions. Courts and commentators frequently focus almost solely on the latter value, emphasizing the need to deter and remedy misconduct by the firm's decision makers and agents. But while the separation of ownership and control in modern public corporations admittedly implicates important accountability concerns, accountability standing alone is an inadequate normative account of corporate law. A fully specified account of corporate law must incorporate the value of authority— i.e., the need to develop a set of rules and procedures that provides the most efficient decision-making system.[5] As it turns out, corporate decision-making efficiency can be ensured only by preserving the board's decision-making authority from being trumped by courts under the guise of judicial review.

Achieving an appropriate mix between these competing goals is a daunting—but necessary—task. As we have seen, there is an inescapable

---

Joy v. North, 692 F.2d 880, 885 (2d Cir.), cert. denied, 460 U.S. 1051 (1982).
[4] *See, e.g.,* Sinclair Oil Corp. v. Levien, 280 A.2d 717 (Del. 1971) (fiduciary duties of controlling shareholder); Shlensky v. Wrigley, 237 N.E.2d 776 (Ill. App. 1968) (operational decision); Auerbach v. Bennett, 393 N.E.2d 994 (N.Y. 1979) (dismissal of derivative litigation).
[5] *See generally* Michael P. Dooley, *Two Models of Corporate Governance*, 47 Bus. Law. 461 (1992).

tension between authority and accountability. The more you try to hold decision makers to account, the more you interfere with their decision-making processes. The more discretion you give decision makers, the less accountable they become. The task for corporate law makers is to find a happy medium that carefully balances these competing values.

Judicial Review of Operational Decisions

Suppose the board of directors made what has turned out, with the benefit of hindsight, to be a most unwise business decision. As a consequence thereof, the corporation's stock price has declined precipitously and, seemingly, persistently. Shareholders have brought suit, claiming that the board of directors acted negligently. The defendants move to dismiss for failure to state a claim, invoking the business judgment rule. How should the court rule?

At the outset, note that the fiduciary responsibilities of directors, and thus the appropriate degree of judicial review, depend "upon the specific context that gives occasion to the board's exercise of its business judgment."[6] Accordingly, a useful distinction can be drawn between operational issues, such as whether to install lighting in a baseball park, and structural choices, especially those creating a final period situation, such as takeovers.[7] This section focuses on the business judgment rule as it relates to operational decisions.

Speaking of the lighting in baseball parks, consider the wonderful old classic decision in *Shlensky v. Wrigley*.[8] Plaintiff William Shlensky was a minority shareholder in the corporation that owned the Chicago Cubs and operated Wrigley Field. Philip Wrigley was the majority stockholder (owning 80 percent of the stock) and president of the company. In the relevant period, 1961–1965, the Cubs consistently lost money. Shlensky alleged that the losses were attributable to their poor home attendance. In turn, Shlensky alleged that the low attendance was attributable to Wrigley's refusal to permit installation of lights and night baseball. Shlensky contended Wrigley refused to institute night baseball because the latter

---

[6]   McMullin v. Beran, 765 A.2d 910, 918 (Del. 2000).
[7]   *See* E. Norman Veasey, *The Defining Tension in Corporate Governance in America*, 52 Bus. Law. 393, 394 (1997) (drawing a similar distinction between "enterprise" and "ownership" decisions).
[8]   Shlensky v. Wrigley, 237 N.E.2d 776, 777–78 (Ill. App. 1968).

believed (1) that baseball was a daytime sport and (2) that night baseball might have a negative impact on the neighborhood surrounding Wrigley Field. The other defendant directors allegedly were so dominated by Wrigley that they acquiesced in his policy of day-only baseball, which allegedly violated their duty of care.

The defendants moved to dismiss for failure to state a claim, asserting "that the courts will not step in and interfere with honest business judgment of the directors unless there is a showing of fraud, illegality or conflict of interest." The court agreed. To be sure, the court took some pains to posit legitimate business reasons for the board's decision against lights. The court opined, for example, that "the effect on the surrounding neighborhood might well be considered by a director." Likewise, the court asserted that "the long run interest" of the firm "might demand" consideration of the effect night baseball would have on the neighborhood.

Does *Shlensky* thus suggest that courts will examine the substantive merits of a board decision? No. The court did not require defendants to show either that such shareholder wealth maximizing considerations motivated their decisions or that the decision in fact benefited the shareholders. To the contrary, the court acknowledged that its speculations in this regard were irrelevant dicta:

> By these thoughts we do not mean to say that we have decided that the decision of the directors was a correct one. That is beyond our jurisdiction and ability. We are merely saying that the decision is one properly before directors and the motives alleged in the amended complaint showed no fraud, illegality or conflict of interest in their making of that decision.[9]

In sum, if we may invoke an appropriate metaphor, the Illinois court did not even allow Shlensky to get up to bat.

To take a more modern example, in *Brehm v. Eisner*,[10] the Delaware Supreme Court reviewed a shareholder challenge to the compensation The Walt Disney Company had paid former president Michael Ovitz.

---

[9] The principle so announced is a very old one, indeed. *See, e.g.*, Dodge v. Ford Motor Co., 170 N.W. 668, 682 (Mich. 1919) (quoting authorities); Leslie v. Lorillard, 18 N.E. 363, 365 (N.Y. 1888) (opining that "courts will not interfere unless the [directors'] powers have been illegally or unconscientiously executed; or unless it be made to appear that the acts were fraudulent or collusive, and destructive of the rights of the stockholders. Mere errors of judgment are not sufficient. . . .").

[10] 746 A.2d 244 (Del. 2000).

Chief Justice Norman Veasey's opinion for the court explicitly rejected, as "foreign to the business judgment rule," plaintiffs' argument that the business rule could be rebutted by a showing that the directors failed to exercise "substantive due care," explaining that:

> Courts do not measure, weigh or quantify directors' judgments. We do not even decide if they are reasonable in this context. Due care in the decisionmaking context is *process* due care only. . . . Thus, directors' decisions will be respected by courts unless the directors are interested or lack independence relative to the decision, do not act in good faith, act in a manner that cannot be attributed to a rational business purpose or reach their decision by a grossly negligent process that includes the failure to consider all material facts reasonably available.

A presumption of judicial abstention from review of the merits of a board decision does not mean courts simply rubberstamp the board's decision. Both *Shlensky* and *Brehm* make clear that the business judgment rule has no application when fraud or self-dealing are present. Both cases also imply various other prerequisites must be satisfied before the rule may be invoked. References in some cases to preconditions like "non-feasance" suggest, for example, that the business judgment rule may only be invoked where the board has made a conscious business decision—a point that becomes especially significant with respect to the burgeoning class of board oversight cases.[11] The good faith and disinterested independence of the directors also are often identified as conditions on which the rule is predicated.[12] If these prerequisites are satisfied, however, the cases hold that the inquiry must end. There will be no judicial review of the substantive merits of the board's decision—whether those merits are measured in terms of fairness, reasonableness, wisdom, or care.[13]

---

[11] *See, e.g.,* Aronson v. Lewis, 473 A.2d 805, 813 (Del. 1984) (stating that the business judgment rule is inapplicable "where directors have either abdicated their functions, or absent a conscious decision, failed to act").

[12] *See, e.g.,* Auerbach v. Bennett, 393 N.E.2d 994, 999 (N.Y. 1979) (so long as directors were disinterested and acted in good faith, the business judgment rule required the court to defer to the board committee's recommendation to dismiss a shareholder derivative suit).

[13] To be sure, Delaware cases have not always hewed a line as sharp as that drawn in Brehm. *See generally* Stephen M. Bainbridge, *Corporation Law and Economics* 246–51 (2002) (discussing and criticizing Delaware's business judgment rule jurisprudence).

First Principles

Why are courts reluctant to assess the merits of board decisions? In *Kamin v. American Express Co.*,[14] in which plaintiff challenged the board's decision to declare an in-kind dividend of shares in a second corporation, the court opined that: "The directors' room rather than the courtroom is the appropriate forum for thrashing out purely business questions which will have an impact on profits, market prices, competitive situations, or tax advantages." But this is mere ipse dixit. Accordingly, let's turn to the basic principles on which this text has already built.

Because only shareholders are entitled to elect directors, boards of U.S. public corporations are substantially insulated from pressure by nonshareholder corporate constituencies, such as employees or creditors. At the same time, the diffuse nature of U.S. stockownership and regulatory impediments to investor activism substantially insulates directors from shareholder pressure. As such, the separation of ownership and control vests the board with virtually unconstrained freedom to exercise business judgment. In our theory of the firm, of course, this freedom is viewed as an essential attribute of efficient corporate governance.

The business judgment rule is an inevitable corollary of our explanation for the separation of ownership and control. Due to the limits on cognitive competence implied by bounded rationality, and the uncertainty and complexity inherent in long-term business relationships, such relationships inevitably confront the prospect of incomplete contracts, which in turn leaves greater room for opportunistic behavior, and thus inexorably leads to the need for coordination. According to our theory of the firm, firms arise when it is possible to resolve these difficulties by delegating to a central agency the power to direct how the various inputs will be utilized by the firm; in effect, allowing the central agency to constantly and, more important, unilaterally rewrite certain terms of the contract between the firm and its various constituents. Centralized decision making thus emerges as the defining characteristic of the public corporation. The board of directors and its subordinate top management team serve as the central decision making agency for corporations. In addition, to minimize opportunism, the governance structure must provide some mechanism for detecting and

---

[14] 383 N.Y.S.2d 807 (Sup. Ct. 1976), aff'd, 387 N.Y.S.2d 993 (App. Div. 1976).

punishing shirking by the firm's agents. The board of directors' monitoring function provides just such a mechanism.

The separation of ownership and control thus is a highly efficient solution to the decision-making problems faced by large corporations. Recall that authority-based decision-making structures arise where team members have different interests and amounts of information. Because collective decision making is impracticable in such settings, authority-based structures are characterized by the existence of a central agency to which all relevant information is transmitted and which is empowered to make decisions binding on the whole. The modern public corporation is a classic example of an authority-based decision-making structure. Neither shareholders nor any other constituency have the information or the incentives necessary to make sound decisions on either operational or policy questions. Overcoming the collective action problems that prevent meaningful shareholder involvement would be difficult and costly. Rather, shareholders will prefer to irrevocably delegate decision-making authority to some smaller group. Separating ownership and control by vesting decision-making authority in a centralized entity distinct from the shareholders is what makes the large public corporation feasible.

To be sure, this separation results in agency costs. A narrow focus on agency costs, however, can lead one astray. Corporate managers operate within a pervasive web of accountability mechanisms that substitute for monitoring by residual claimants. Important constraints are provided by a variety of market forces. The capital and product markets, the internal and external employment markets, and the market for corporate control all constrain shirking by firm agents. In addition, in the legal system there have evolved various adaptive responses to the ineffectiveness of shareholder monitoring, establishing alternative accountability structures to punish and deter wrongdoing by firm agents, such as the board of directors.

An even more important consideration, however, is that agency costs are the inevitable consequence of vesting discretion in someone other than the residual claimant. We could substantially reduce, if not eliminate, agency costs by eliminating discretion; that we do not do so suggests that discretion has substantial virtues. A complete theory of the firm thus requires one to balance the virtues of discretion against the need to require that discretion be used responsibly.[15] Neither discretion nor accountability

---

[15] Dooley, *supra* note 5, at 464–71.

can be ignored, because both promote values essential to the survival of business organizations. Unfortunately, they are ultimately antithetical: one cannot have more of one without also having less of the other. As Kenneth Arrow has observed, the power to hold to account is ultimately the power to decide:

> Clearly, a sufficiently strict and continuous organ of [accountability] can easily amount to a denial of authority. If every decision of A is to be reviewed by B, then all we have really is a shift in the locus of authority from A to B and hence no solution to the original problem.[16]

The board thus cannot be made more accountable without shifting some of its decision-making authority to shareholders or judges. Or, as former Delaware Chancellor Allen put it, "To recognize in courts a residual power to review the substance of business decisions for 'fairness' or 'reasonableness' or 'rationality' where those decisions are made by truly disinterested directors in good faith and with appropriate care is to make of courts super-directors."[17]

To be clear, this is not an argument for unfettered board authority. In some cases, accountability concerns become so pronounced as to trump the general need for deference to the board's authority. Establishing the proper mix of deference and accountability thus emerges as the central problem in applying the business judgment rule to particular situations.

Given the significant virtues of discretion, however, one must not lightly interfere with management or the board's decision-making authority in the name of accountability. There ought to be a rebuttable presumption in favor of preservation of managerial discretion. The separation of ownership and control mandated by U.S. corporate law has precisely that effect. Likewise, the business judgment rule exists because judicial review threatens the board's authority.[18]

This understanding of the rule's role is consistent with a passage from the Delaware Supreme Court's famed *Van Gorkom* decision that has received less attention than it deserves:

> Under Delaware law, the business judgment rule is the offspring of the fundamental principle, codified in [Delaware General Corporation

---

[16] Kenneth J. Arrow, *The Limits of Organization* 78 (1974).
[17] In re RJR Nabisco, Inc. Shareholders Litig. 1989 WL 7036 *13 n.13 (Del. Ch. 1989).
[18] Dooley, *supra* note 5, at 469–76.

Law] § 141(a), the business and affairs of a Delaware corporation are managed by or under its board of directors. . . . [T]he business judgment rule exists to protect and promote the full and free exercise of the managerial power granted to Delaware directors.[19]

In other words, the rule creates a presumption of deference to the board's authority as the corporation's central and final decision maker.

Defending Deference to Board Authority

Critics of the foregoing analysis likely would concede that judicial review shifts some power to decide to judges, but contend that that observation is normatively insufficient. To be sure, they might posit, centralized decision making is an essential feature of the corporation. Judicial review could serve as a redundant control on board decision making, however, without displacing the board as the primary decision maker.

An analogy to engineering concepts may be useful. If a mechanical system is likely to fail, and its failure likely to entail high costs, basic engineering theory calls for redundant controls to prevent failure. It would be naïve to assume that markets fully constrain director behavior. Why then is judicial review not an appropriate redundant control? If we assume that corporate law is generally efficient, the losses tolerated by judicial abstention must be outweighed by benefits elsewhere in the system. The following sections speculate as to the likely source of those benefits.

Encouraging Risk-Taking

In the American Law Institute's Principles of Corporate Governance, the drafters justify the business judgment rule as being necessary to protect "directors and officers from the risks inherent in hindsight reviews of their business decisions" and to avoid "the risk of stifling innovation and venturesome business activity."[20] This claim cannot be a complete

[19] Smith v. Van Gorkom, 488 A.2d 858, 872 (Del. 1985).
[20] American Law Institute, Principles of Corporate Governance: Analysis and Recommendations § 4.01 cmt. d at 141 (1994). Professor Dooley persuasively argues that the ALI Principles' version of the business judgment rule is flawed, inter alia, because it in fact encourages intrusive substantive review of business decisions. Dooley, *supra* note 5, at 471–86.

explanation of the business judgment rule. Duty of care litigation, after all, probably does far less to stifle innovation and business risk taking than does product liability and securities fraud litigation, but no equivalent of the business judgment rule exists in the latter contexts. Even so, however, encouraging optimal risk-taking is part of the story.

As the firm's residual claimants, shareholders do not get a return on their investment until all other claims on the corporation have been satisfied. All else being equal, shareholders therefore prefer high-return projects. Because risk and return are directly proportional, however, implementing that preference necessarily entails choosing risky projects.

Even though conventional finance theory assumes shareholders are risk-averse, rational shareholders still will have a high tolerance for risky corporate projects. First, the basic corporate law principle of limited liability substantially insulates shareholders from the downside risks of corporate activity. The limited liability principle, of course, holds that shareholders of a corporation may not be held personally liable for debts incurred or torts committed by the firm.[21] Because shareholders thus do not put their personal assets at jeopardy, other than the amount initially invested, they effectively externalize some portion of the business' total risk exposure to creditors.

Second, shareholders can largely eliminate firm-specific risk by holding a diversified portfolio. Accordingly, although investors are risk-averse and therefore demand a risk premium when investing, that premium will only reflect certain risks. Modern portfolio theory distinguishes systematic risks from unsystematic risks. Unsystematic risks are those specific to a particular firm, such as the risk that the CEO will have a heart attack or the firm's workers will go out on strike or that the plant will burn down. Systematic risks are those general to the market as a whole and thus affect all firms to one degree or another, such as changes in market interest rates or the prevailing economic climate. Investors can eliminate unsystematic risk by diversifying their portfolios, because things tend to come out in the wash. If one firm's plant burns down, another will hit oil, and so on. In contrast, no matter how well investors diversify their portfolios, they

---

[21] See, e.g., Mod. Bus. Corp. Act Ann. § 6.22 (1984 & supp) (stating that: "Unless otherwise provided in the articles of incorporation, a shareholder of a corporation is not personally liable for the acts or debts of the corporation except that he may become personally liable by reason of his own acts or conduct."). The limited liability rule, of course, is subject to the equitable exception most commonly known as "piercing the corporate veil."

cannot eliminate systematic risk, because it affects all stocks. Consequently, according to modern portfolio theory, while investors must be compensated for bearing systematic risk, they need not be compensated for bearing unsystematic risk. Returns on specific investments therefore differ not because the corporations involved have differing levels of firm-specific risk, but rather because firms differ insofar as their sensitivity to systematic risk is concerned. The Capital Asset Pricing Model (CAPM) uses the well-known beta coefficient to measure that relative sensitivity to systematic risk.[22]

Given limited liability and diversification, rational shareholders should be indifferent to changes in corporate policies that merely alter exposure to unsystematic risks. Instead, they should focus on (and prefer) policies that portend a higher rate of return by increasing the firm's beta. In contrast, rational corporate managers—and, to a lesser extent, directors—should be risk-averse with respect to such policies. Corporate managers typically have substantial firm-specific human capital.[23] Unfortunately for such managers, however, the risks inherent in firm-specific capital investments cannot be reduced by diversification; managers obviously cannot diversify their human capital among a number of different firms. As a result, managers will be averse to risks shareholders are perfectly happy to tolerate.

This difference between shareholder and managerial interests will be compounded if managers face the risk of legal liability, on top of economic loss, in the event a risky decision turns out badly. Business decisions rarely involve black-and-white issues; instead, they typically

---

[22] Richard A. Brealey & Stewart C. Myers, *Principles of Corporate Finance* 195 (7th ed. 2003). CAPM is somewhat controversial in the finance literature. *See id.* at 198–203 (discussing critiques of CAPM). It remains more-or-less the state of the art in the legal community, however, being especially widely used in valuation proceedings. *See, e.g.,* Le Beau v. M. G. Bancorporation, Inc., 1998 WL 44993 (Del. Ch. 1998), aff'd, 737 A.2d 513 (Del. 1999) (using CAPM to determine the discount rate); Gilbert v. MPM Enters., Inc., 709 A.2d 663 (Del. Ch. 1997), aff'd, 731 A.2d 790 (Del. 1999) (using CAPM to determine cost of equity capital); Ryan v. Tad's Enters., Inc., 709 A.2d 682 (Del. Ch. 1996), aff'd, 693 A.2d. 1082 (Del. 1997) (using CAPM to determine discount rate).

[23] Jeffrey N. Gordon, *What Enron Means for the Management and Control of the Modern Business Corporation: Some Initial Reflections*, 69 U. Chi. L. Rev. 1233, 1245 (2002) (explaining that "[m]anagers generally make large firm-specific human capital investments in their firms and thus are risk-averse"); Margaret M. Blair & Lynn A. Stout, *Director Accountability and the Mediating Role of the Corporate Board*, 79 Wash. U. L.Q. 403, 415 (2001) (explaining that "employees and managers often make large investments in firm-specific human capital").

involve prudential judgments among a number of plausible alternatives.[24] Given the vagaries of business, moreover, even carefully made choices among such alternatives may turn out badly.

At this point, the well-known hindsight bias comes into play. Decision makers tend to assign an erroneously high probability of occurrence to a probabilistic event simply because it ended up occurring.[25] If a jury knows that the plaintiff was injured, the jury will be biased in favor of imposing negligence liability even if, viewed ex ante, there was a very low probability that such an injury would occur and taking precautions against such an injury was not cost-effective. Even where duty of care cases are tried without a jury, as in Delaware, judges who know with the benefit of hindsight that a business decision turned out badly likewise could be biased toward finding a breach of the duty of care.[26]

Hence, there is a substantial risk that suing shareholders and reviewing judges will be unable to distinguish between competent and negligent management because bad outcomes often will be regarded, ex post, as having been foreseeable and, therefore, preventable ex ante. If liability results from bad outcomes, without regard to the ex ante quality of the decision and/or the decision-making process, however, managers will be discouraged from taking risks. If it is true that "lack of gumption is the single largest source of agency costs,"[27] rational shareholders will disfavor liability rules discouraging risk taking.

This analysis suggests that rational shareholders would be willing to pre-commit by contract to refrain from challenging the reasonableness of managerial business decisions. Obviously, however, the practicalities of running a large corporation with fluid stockownership preclude effecting such a policy by contract. The business judgment rule thus may be seen as providing a default off-the-rack rule that both shareholders

---

[24] James J. Hanks, Jr., *Evaluating Recent State Legislation on Director and Officer Liability Limitation and Indemnification*, 43 Bus. Law. 1207, 1232 (1988).

[25] Christine Jolls et al., *A Behavioral Approach to Law and Economics*, 50 Stan. L. Rev. 1471, 1523 (1998). For a useful analysis relating the hindsight bias to the business judgment rule, *see* Hal R. Arkes & Cindy A. Schipani, *Medical Malpractice v. the Business Judgment Rule: Differences in Hindsight Bias*, 73 Or. L. Rev. 587 (1994).

[26] Cf. Chris Guthrie et al., *Inside the Judicial Mind*, 86 Cornell L. Rev. 777, 799–805 (2001) (discussing empirical evidence that judicial decision making is tainted by the hindsight bias).

[27] Frank H. Easterbrook & Daniel R. Fischel, *The Economic Structure of Corporate Law* 99 (1991).

and managers would prefer, as Judge Ralph Winter opined in *Joy v. North*[28]:

> Although the rule has suffered under academic criticism, it is not without rational basis.
>
> First, shareholders to a very real degree voluntarily undertake the risk of bad business judgment. Investors need not buy stock, for investment markets offer an array of opportunities less vulnerable to mistakes in judgment by corporate officers. Nor need investors buy stock in particular corporations. In the exercise of what is genuinely a free choice, the quality of a firm's management is often decisive and information is available from professional advisors. Since shareholders can and do select among investments partly on the basis of management, the business judgment rule merely recognizes a certain voluntariness in undertaking the risk of bad business decisions.
>
> Second, courts recognize that after-the-fact litigation is a most imperfect device to evaluate corporate business decisions. . . .
>
> Third, because potential profit often corresponds to the potential risk, it is very much in the interest of shareholders that the law not create incentives for overly cautious corporate decisions. . . . Shareholders can reduce the volatility of risk by diversifying their holdings. In the case of the diversified shareholder, the seemingly more risky alternatives may well be the best choice since great losses in some stocks will over time be offset by even greater gains in others. . . . A rule which penalizes the choice of seemingly riskier alternatives thus may not be in the interest of shareholders generally.

Or, as Chancellor Allen similarly observed in *Gagliardi v. Trifoods Int'l, Inc.*[29]:

> Shareholders can diversify the risks of their corporate investments. Thus, it is in their economic interest for the corporation to accept in rank order all positive net present value investment projects available to the corporation, starting with the highest risk-adjusted rate of return first. Shareholders don't want (or shouldn't rationally want)

---

[28] Joy v. North, 692 F.2d 880, 885–86 (2d Cir. 1982), cert. denied, 460 U.S. 1051 (1983).
[29] 683 A.2d 1049, 1052 (Del. Ch. 1996).

directors to be risk-averse. Shareholders' investment interests, across the full range of their diversifiable equity investments, will be maximized if corporate directors and managers honestly assess risk and reward and accept for the corporation the highest risk-adjusted returns available that are above the firm's cost of capital.

Hence, when courts review the objective merits of a board decision, they effectively penalize "the choice of seemingly riskier alternatives."

Although Winter's analysis is compelling, it nevertheless is incomplete in several important respects. First, Winter's argument cannot be a complete explanation for the business judgment rule because it assumes that negligence by corporate directors must be a form of unsystematic risk. It must be so, because such negligence could not be diversified away otherwise. If so, however, why is not fraud or illegality on the part of such directors also a form of unsystematic risk? Just as a shareholder could protect herself against bad decisions, so could a shareholder protect herself against fraudulent decisions. Yet, the business judgment rule has never protected directors who commit fraud or self-dealing.

Second, the analysis thus far has fudged the distinction between directors and managers. To be sure, some commentators contend that directors have the same incentives for risk aversion as managers. As we'll see in Chapter 4, however, it has become very common for public corporations to require that newly appointed directors purchase substantial blocks of the corporation's shares and/or to compensate directors in the corporation's stock, which practice has been empirically linked to improved corporate performance, probably by its having aligned director and shareholder interests.[30] Hence, outside directors may not be quite as risk-averse as inside directors and other managers. Indeed, to the contrary, the incentives of outside director incentives may well be somewhat closer to shareholder preferences than to those of managers.

Finally, encouraging risk taking must be deemed an incomplete explanation because it fails to account for many of the rule's applications. Consider, for example, the business decision made in *Shlensky*. Was Wrigley an innovator making a venturesome business decision or an eccentric coot who was just behind the times? How can we know when

---

[30] *See generally* Sanjai Bhagat et al., *Director Ownership, Corporate Performance, and Management Turnover*, 54 Bus. Law. 885 (1999) (discussing trends in director stock-ownership); Charles M. Elson, *Director Compensation and the Management-Captured Board: The History of a Symptom and a Cure*, 50 SMU L. Rev. 127 (1996) (same).

the business judgment rule precluded Shlensky's even getting up to bat? In sum, encouraging risk-taking is part of the story, but only part. Something else is going on as well.

Judges Are Not Business Experts

In *Dodge v. Ford Motor Co.*,[31] the Michigan Supreme Court famously invoked the business judgment rule in refusing to enjoin Henry Ford's plans to expand production. As justification for its decision, the court modestly observed that: "*The judges are not business experts.*"[32] Although we shall see that this too is an incomplete explanation for the business judgment rule, at best, it has somewhat more plausibility than it is usually given in the literature.

A modern version of this rationale can be constructed by building on the burgeoning insights for legal analysis of cognitive psychology and behavioral economics. As applied to judicial decision making, the familiar cognitive limitations inherent in the concept of bounded rationality are reinforced both by the incentive structures familiar from agency cost economics and the well-known institutional constraints on adjudication (such as the necessity in many courts of general jurisdiction to provide speedy trials for criminal defendants).[33] In addition, of course, there is the problem of hindsight bias discussed above. Under such conditions, judges will shirk—i.e., look for ways of deciding cases with minimal effort.[34]

As we've seen, people conserve their limited cognitive resources by adopting institutional governance structures that promote more efficient decision making and by heuristic shortcuts. Is the business judgment rule an example of the latter tactic? When one considers the ease with which the *Shlensky* court disposed of plaintiff's claims, the idea seems not wholly implausible.

---

[31] 170 N.W. 668 (Mich.1919).

[32] *Id.* at 685 (emphasis supplied).

[33] *See generally* Stephen M. Bainbridge & Mitu Gulati, *How Do Judges Maximize? (The Same Way Everybody Else Does—Boundedly): Rules of Thumb in Securities Fraud Opinions*, 51 Emory L.J. 83 (2002) (discussing constraints and incentives that impact judicial decision making).

[34] The claim is not that judges do not work hard. Bainbridge & Gulati, *supra* note 33, at 106. The claim is only that judges have incentives to "delegate opinions to the clerks and focus their own attention on making sure that the opinions are 'good enough' so as to avoid negative attention." *Id.* at 109.

Business decisions are frequently complex and made under conditions of uncertainty. Accordingly, bounded rationality and information asymmetries counsel judicial abstention from reviewing board decisions. Judges likely have less general business expertise than directors. They also have less information about the specifics of the particular firm in question. Finally, most judges only rarely face business judgment issues. Most judges likely arrive on the bench with little expertise in corporate law and, equally likely, have little incentive to develop substantial institutional expertise in this area after they arrive. Because the legal and business issues are complex, and because judges are as subject as anyone to the cognitive limitations implied by bounded rationality, they have an incentive to duck these cases. In Eric Posner's useful phrase, they are "radically incompetent":

> [C]ourts have trouble understanding the simplest of business relationships. This is not surprising. Judges must be generalists, but they usually have narrow backgrounds in a particular field of the law. Moreover, they often owe their positions to political connections, not to merit. Their frequent failure to understand transactions is well-documented. One survey of cases involving consumer credit, for example, showed that the judges did not even understand the concept of present value. . . . Skepticism about the quality of judicial decisionmaking is reflected in many legal doctrines, including the business judgment rule in corporate law, which restrains courts from second-guessing managers and directors. . . .[35]

Although this line of analysis has some considerable traction, it too cannot be a complete explanation for the business judgment rule. In the first instance, business is not the only context in which judges are called upon to review complex issues arising under conditions of uncertainty. Reviewing Wrigley's refusal to install lights seems no more onerous than reviewing medical or product design decisions. Yet, as already noted, no "medical judgment" or "design judgment" rule precludes judicial review of malpractice or product liability cases. Something else must be going on.

In the second instance, Posner overlooks both the pervasive role Delaware plays in business judgment rule jurisprudence and the unique

---

[35] Eric A. Posner, *A Theory of Contract Law under Conditions of Radical Judicial Error*, 94 Nw. U. L. Rev. 749, 758 (2000) (footnote omitted).

incentive structure in which Delaware courts function.[36] The rationality of Delaware chancellors is bounded—just like that of everyone else. Like all judges, moreover, Delaware chancellors face significant resource constraints, especially with respect to the time available for decision making. In contrast to judges in other states, however, Delaware chancellors frequently have considerable prior corporate experience as practitioners.[37] Once on the bench, there is a substantial payoff for Delaware chancellors who continue to master corporate law. Delaware chancellors sit at "the center of the corporate law universe."[38] Corporate governance cases, heard episodically in other courts, make up a very high percentage of the Delaware chancellors' docket. The frequency with which the Delaware chancellors face such cases provides a strong incentive for them to master both doctrine and the business environment in which the doctrine works.[39] In particular, there is a strong reputational incentive for their doing so. Sitting without juries in a court of equity, Delaware chancellors put their reputations on the line whenever they make a decision. Because so many major corporations are incorporated in Delaware, chancery court cases are often high-profile and the court's decisions therefore are subject to close scrutiny by the media, academics, and practitioners. The reputation of a Delaware chancellor thus depends on his or her ability to decide corporate law disputes quickly and carefully.

For these reasons, the adage that "judges are not business experts" cannot be a complete explanation for the business judgment rule. Yet, many old adages have more than a grain of truth. So too does this one. Justice Robert Jackson famously observed of the Supreme Court: "We are not final because we are infallible, but we are infallible only because

---

[36] For a good analysis of the contribution the Delaware Court of Chancery makes to Delaware's dominance, see Jill E. Fisch, *The Peculiar Role of the Delaware Courts in the Competition for Corporate Charters*, 68 U. Cin. L. Rev. 1061 (2000); see generally Bainbridge & Gulati, *supra* note 33, at 149, on which the following discussion draws.

[37] See William T. Quillen & Michael Hanrahan, *A Short History of the Delaware Court of Chancery—1792–1992*, 18 Del. J. Corp. L. 819, 841–65 (1993) (describing in exhaustive detail the backgrounds of Delaware's twentieth century chancellors).

[38] D. Gordon Smith, *Chancellor Allen and the Fundamental Question*, 21 Seattle U.L. Rev. 577, 578 (1998).

[39] Cf. Rochelle C. Dreyfuss, *Forums of the Future: The Role of Specialized Courts in Resolving Business Disputes*, 61 Brook. L. Rev. 1, 5 (1995) (arguing that: "Cases cannot be adjudicated any more efficiently than Delaware is currently adjudicating them."); Fisch, *supra* note 36, at 1078 (opining that "Delaware chancery judges are known for their expertise in business matters, and the court has developed a reputation for its sophistication in corporate law.").

we are final."[40] Neither courts nor boards are infallible, but someone must be final. Otherwise we end up with a never-ending process of appellate review. The question then is simply who is better suited to be vested with the mantle of infallibility that comes by virtue of being final—directors or judges?

As we have seen, corporate directors operate within a pervasive web of accountability mechanisms, including competition in a number of markets. Granted, we've already acknowledged that only the most naïve would assume that these markets perfectly constrain director decision making, but it would be equally naïve to ignore the lack of comparable market constraints on judicial decision making. Market forces work an imperfect Darwinian selection on corporate decision makers, but no such forces constrain erring judges.[41] As such, rational shareholders will prefer the risk of director error to that of judicial error. Hence, shareholders will want judges to abstain from reviewing board decisions.

The shareholders' preference for abstention, however, extends only to board decisions motivated by a desire to maximize shareholder wealth. Where the directors' decision was motivated by considerations other than shareholder wealth, as where the directors engaged in self-dealing or sought to defraud the shareholders, however, the question is no longer one of honest error but of intentional misconduct. Despite the limitations of judicial review, rational shareholders would prefer judicial intervention with respect to board decisions so tainted.[42] The affirmative case for disregarding honest errors simply does not apply to intentional misconduct. To the contrary, given the potential for self-dealing in an organization characterized by a separation of ownership and control, the risk of legal liability may be a necessary deterrent against such misconduct.

Note the resulting link between the argument that that business judgment rule is necessary in light of the likelihood of judicial error and the alternate argument that the rule is necessary to encourage optimal risk taking. In theory, if judicial decision making could flawlessly sort out sound decisions with unfortunate outcomes from poor decisions,

---

[40] Brown v. Allen, 344 U.S. 443, 540 (1953) (Jackson, J., concurring).

[41] Easterbrook and Fischel, *supra* note 27, at 100.

[42] As Delaware Chief Justice Veasey observes, "investors do not want self-dealing directors or those bent on entrenchment in office. . . . Trust of directors is the key because of the self-governing nature of corporate law. Yet the law is strong enough to rein in directors who flirt with abuse of that trust." E. Norman Veasey, *An Economic Rationale for Judicial Decisionmaking in Corporate Law*, 53 Bus. Law. 681, 694 (1998).

and directors were confident that there was no risk of hindsight-based liability, the case for the business judgment rule would be substantially weaker. As long as there is some non-zero probability of erroneous second-guessing by judges, however, the threat of liability will skew director decision making away from optimal risk-taking. Because loss aversion and regret avoidance commonly affect decision makers, even a small risk of liability can be expected to have a large deterrent effect on directors who are already risk-averse by virtue of their non-diversifiable investment in firm-specific human capital.

Impact on the Board's Internal Dynamics

As the discussion in the preceding section acknowledges, variants of the encouraging risk-taking and judicial expertise rationales for the business judgment rule are well accepted in the literature, if not in the precise form offered here. In recent scholarship, I have suggested a third rationale for the rule, which is based on the potential implications of judicial review for the internal governance of boards.[43]

Recall that the corporate governance is a superb exemplar of Kenneth Arrow's authority form of decision making. Information flows up a branching hierarchy to a central office and binding decisions flow back down. At the apex of that decision-making pyramid is not a single hierarch, however, but a multi-member committee—the board—that usually functions by consensus.

We've seen that the board of directors is a good example of the so-called relational team, which is defined by two key characteristics: (1) team members make large investments in firm-specific human capital and (2) their productivity is costly to measure because of task nonseparability. Members of such a team often develop idiosyncratic working relationships with one another; they develop not only firm-specific human capital but also team-specific human capital.

Although teams can be a highly effective decision-making mechanism, they are difficult to monitor. Because relational teams arise when the production process results in nonseparable outputs, the productivity of individual team members, by definition, cannot be measured on an

---

[43] Stephen M. Bainbridge, *Why a Board? Group Decision Making in Corporate Governance*, 55 Vand. L. Rev. 1 (2002).

output basis. Yet, at the same time, individual productivity may be quite costly to measure from an input perspective. How does one measure how well a board member cooperates in responding to changed circumstances or emergencies, for example? Because neither input nor output can be measured effectively, judicial review of board decision making cannot be an effective monitoring mechanism.

The key problem for present purposes, and the one that differentiates this line of argument from that of the preceding section, however, is that judicial review could interfere with—or even destroy—the internal team governance structures that regulate board behavior. Relational teams are not only hard to monitor, they also are hard to discipline. As they develop team-specific human capital, members of a production team develop idiosyncratic ways of working with one another that generate a form of synergy. Under such circumstances, dismissal becomes a highly undesir-able sanction, because no team member can be replaced without disrupt-ing the entire team. Because relational teams often become insular,[44] moreover, even external sanctions falling short of dismissal may have ripple effects throughout the team.[45] Insular workplace teams often fail to deal effectively with outsiders. In particular, relational teams often respond to external monitoring efforts by "circling the wagons" around the intended target of sanctions.[46]

In light of these considerations, relational teams are better monitored by a combination of mutual motivation, peer pressure, and internal monitoring than by external reviewers. Accordingly, shareholders will therefore prefer a rule under which judges abstain from reviewing board decisions.

Note that this line of analysis justifies several aspects of the business judgment rule unexplained by alternative theories. Under it, for example, the inapplicability of the business judgment rule to fraud or self-dealing is readily explicable. Duty of care litigation is typically concerned with collective actions by the board of directors as a whole. In taking such

---

[44] See Charles Heckscher, *The Failure of Participatory Management*, Across the Board, Nov. 1995, at 16 (citing empirical studies).

[45] Cf. Raghuram G. Rajan and Luigi Zingales, *The Tyranny of the Inefficient: An Enquiry into the Adverse Consequences of Power Struggles*, Nat'l Bureau Econ. Research Working Paper 5396 (Dec. 1995) (demonstrating the inefficiency of power struggles by sub-units of an organization).

[46] Cf. Zapata Corp. v. Maldonado, 430 A.2d 779, 787 (Del. 1981) (opining that directors tasked with deciding whether the corporation should sue one or more of their fellow directors might be affected by "a 'there but for the grace of God go I' empathy").

actions, we have seen, the board is constrained to exercise reasonable care by a combination of external market forces and internal team governance structures. When an individual director decides to pursue a course of self-dealing, however, he or she usually acts alone and, moreover, betrays his or her fellow directors' trust.[47] It makes sense for courts to be less concerned with damage to internal team governance when the defendant director's misconduct has already harmed that governance structure through betrayal. Instead, by providing a set of external sanctions against self-dealing, the law encourages directors to refrain from such betrayals.[48]

Corporate Decisions Affect Nonshareholder Constituencies, But So What?

In rejecting the business judgment rule's traditional explanation, we observed that judges are unlikely to be medical or engineering experts; yet no "medical judgment rule" or "designer judgment rule" insulates doctors from malpractice claims or manufacturing firms from product liability claims. We further implied that judicial review of business decisions would not differ from judicial review of medical or product design decisions. In terms of the technical complexity of the decisions at bar, that assertion is doubtless true. Yet, business decisions do differ in an important way from those other sorts of claims.

Imagine an automobile manufacturer whose cars have a defective gas tank. Fixing the design problem would cost the manufacturer $50 per car. Injuries caused by the defective product average $75 per car. Suppose that under a negligence-based tort liability regime, the manufacturer would be held liable for an average of only $25 per car. Because such a negligence-based regime does not compel the manufacturer to fully internalize the social costs of its conduct, it would be economically irrational for the manufacturer to fix the defect. A socially sub-optimal outcome thus results. An important justification for the strict liability-based products liability regime thus is that it is more likely to lead manufacturers to

---

[47] Cf. Robert J. Haft, *The Effect of Insider Trading Rules on the Internal Efficiency of the Large Corporation*, 80 Mich. L. Rev. 1051, 1062–63 (1982) (describing the deleterious effects on board effectiveness of director self-dealing).

[48] *See* William W. Bratton, *Game Theory and the Restoration of Honor to Corporate Law's Duty of Loyalty*, in *Progressive Corporate Law* 139, 146 (Lawrence E. Mitchell ed. 1995) (arguing for a "coercive [legal] backstop" to prevent self-dealing).

internalize the costs of their activities than is a negligence-based regime.[49]

As a society, we probably want manufacturers and physicians to fully internalize the costs of their activities. Tort liability arguably is a reasonably efficient way of accomplishing that desirable outcome. While we also likely want directors to internalize the social costs of their decisions, however, corporate law in general and fiduciary obligation in particular are not appropriate vehicles for achieving that result.

The point is not that director decision making has no externalities. It does. Board decisions can adversely affect not only true outsiders to the corporation but also nonshareholder constituencies. As we saw in Chapter 1, however, the interests of such parties are more appropriately dealt with by contract and general welfare legislation.

The Limits of Abstention

The argument is not for judicial abnegation but only for judicial abstention. The distinction is a significant one. Abstention contemplates judicial reticence, but leaves open the possibility of intervention in appropriate circumstances. Yet again, Kenneth Arrow is instructive:

> [Accountability mechanisms] must be capable of correcting errors but should not be such as to destroy the genuine values of authority. . . .
>
> To maintain the value of authority, it would appear that [accountability] must be intermittent. This could be periodic; it could take the form of what is termed "management by exception," in which authority and its decisions are reviewed only when performance is sufficiently degraded from expectations. . . .[50]

The problem then is to identify the circumstances in which intervention is necessary. Put another way, the task is to define the conditions under which accountability concerns ought to trump preservation of the board's authority.

If the business judgment rule is treated as a substantive standard of review, judicial intervention all too easily could become the norm rather than the exception. How one frames the question matters a lot. In polling,

---

[49] Cf. Robert Cooter & Thomas Ulen, *Law and Economics* 319 (2d ed. 1997).

[50] Arrow, *supra* note 16, at 78.

for example, both the order in which questions are asked and the way in which they are phrased can affect the outcome. The same is true of legal standards. These effects follow, in part, from the phenomena known in behavioral economics as framing and anchoring. Framing refers to the process by which people formulate options as involving potential gains or losses. People tend to be risk-averse with respect to potential gains, but risk-preferring with respect to potential losses. Consequently, people will prefer a certain $100 gain to a 50 percent chance of gaining $200, but prefer a 50 percent chance of losing $200 to a certain loss of $100, even though the expected outcomes are the same in both cases. Anchoring refers to the effect initial reference points have on subsequent decision making. Actors presented with options framed with an initial reference demonstrably allow that reference point to affect their decision-making processes.[51] One study asked professional accountants to estimate the prevalence of management fraud. One group of subjects was asked whether they believed management fraud occurred in more than 10 of every 1,000 companies audited, while a second group was asked whether they believed management fraud occurred in more than 200 of every 1,000 companies. Both groups were then asked to estimate the actual number of fraud cases per 1,000 companies. Accountants in the latter group gave a significantly higher response to the second question than accountants in the former, showing that the subjects failed to adequately adjust their estimate of the incidence of fraud from the initial reference point to which they were exposed.[52] There is evidence that judges are subject to both types of cognitive error.[53]

Although tests of the anchoring phenomenon have concentrated on the effect of numbers as reference points, it seems plausible that verbal cues—like the phrasing of a legal standard—will have a similar effect. Consequently, both the phrasing of the legal standard and the ordering of the questions it asks are likely to effect outcomes.

All of which suggests that, no matter how gingerly courts apply a substantive standard, measuring the "quantity" of negligence is a task

---

[51] Marcel Kahan & Michael Klausner, *Path Dependence in Corporate Contracting: Increasing Returns, Herd Behavior, and Cognitive Biases*, 74 Wash. U.L.Q. 347, 362 (1996) (citing studies).

[52] Russell B. Korobkin & Thomas S. Ulen, *Law and Behavioral Science: Removing the Rationality Assumption from Law and Economics*, 88 Cal. L. Rev. 1051, 1100–2 (2000).

[53] Chris Guthrie et al., *Inside the Judicial Mind*, 86 Cornell L. Rev. 777 (2001).

best left untried.[54] Courts will find it difficult to resist the temptation to tweak the standard so as to sanction honest decisions that, with the benefit of hindsight, proved unfortunate and/or appear inept. All of the adverse effects of judicial review outlined in the preceding sections are implicated, however, whether or not the board exercised reasonable care. The business judgment rule thus builds a prophylactic barrier by which courts pre-commit to resisting the temptation to review the merits of the board's decision. Put another way, the business judgment rule creates a very strong presumption that deference to and preservation of the board's decision-making primacy trumps accountability concerns in the context of ordinary business decisions, which is precisely what the director primacy model recommends.

The Rule of Undivided Loyalty

In a classic 1944 decision, *Bayer v. Beran*,[55] a New York judge explained the business judgment rule in terms that almost seem to anticipate the director primacy model:

> To encourage freedom of action on the part of directors, or to put it another way, to discourage interference with the exercise of their free and independent judgment, there has grown up what is known as the "business judgment rule." "Questions of policy of management, expediency of contracts or action, adequacy of consideration, lawful appropriation of corporate funds to advance corporate interests, are left solely to their honest and unselfish decision, for their powers therein are without limitation and free from restraint, and the exercise of them for the common and general interests of the corporation may not be questioned, although the results show that what they did was unwise or inexpedient."

The court went on, however, to explain that the business judgment rule "yields to the rule of undivided loyalty." The business judgment rule "presupposes that the directors have no conflict of interest."[56] Hence,

---

54 Henry G. Manne, *Our Two Corporation Systems: Law and Economics*, 53 Va. L. Rev. 259, 271 (1967).
55 49 N.Y.S.2d 2 (1944).
56 Lewis v. S. L. & E., Inc., 629 F.2d 764, 769 (2d Cir. 1980).

self-dealing is one of the classic ways in which the business judgment rule's presumptions are rebutted.

"A director is interested if he will be materially affected, either to his benefit or detriment, by a decision of the board, in a manner not shared by the corporation and the shareholders."[57] Consequently, for example, a director who sells or leases property to or from the corporation is interested in that transaction. Similarly, a director who contracts to provide services to the corporation is interested in that transaction.

Directors also can be interested in a transaction by virtue of indirect connections. In *Bayer*, for example, the corporation hired the wife of its president. Their spousal relationship gave the president an indirect interest in the transaction. Similarly, in *Globe Woolen Co. v. Utica Gas & Electric Co.*,[58] a director of the defendant corporation was also the president and chief stockholder of the plaintiff. By virtue of those business relationships, he was deemed interested in the transaction between the plainitff and defendant even though he was not a party to their contract.

In addition to lacking a personal interest in the transaction in question, a director must be independent. "A director is independent if he can base his decision 'on the corporate merits of the subject before the board rather than extraneous considerations or influences.'"[59] In particular, a director who is beholden to, or under the influence of, an interested party lacks the requisite independence.[60]

The Presumption in Favor of Authority

If the business judgment rule has no application to conflicted interest transactions in either theory or doctrine, how then should judges review

---

[57] Seminaris v. Landa, 662 A.2d 1350, 1354 (Del. 1995). *See also* In re RJR Nabisco, Inc. Shareholders Litig., 1989 WL 7036 at *14 (Del. Ch. 1989) (a disqualifying interest "is a financial interest in the transaction adverse to that of the corporation or its shareholders").

[58] 121 N.E. 378 (N.Y. 1918). Consequently, directors are deemed to be interested when they "stand in a dual relation which prevents an unprejudiced exercise of judgment." Stoner v. Walsh, 772 F. Supp. 790, 802 (S.D.N.Y. 1991) (quoting United Copper Sec. Co. v. Amalgamated Copper Co., 244 U.S. 261, 264 (1917)).

[59] Seminaris v. Landa, 662 A.2d 1350, 1354 (Del. 1995) (quoting Aronson v. Lewis, 473 A.2d 805, 816 (Del. 1984)).

[60] *See* In re MAXXAM, Inc., 659 A.2d 760, 773 (Del. Ch. 1995) ("To be considered independent a director must not be 'dominated or otherwise controlled by an individual or entity interested in the transaction.'").

board of director decisions tainted by such interests? Do concerns about accountability automatically trump the principle of deference to board authority?

Critics of the director primacy model sometimes suggest that it over-states the importance of authority. One of the truly striking things about U.S. corporation law, however, is the extent to which the balance between authority and accountability in fact leans towards the former. As we've just seen, the business judgment rule is designed "to protect and promote the full and free exercise of the managerial power granted to Delaware directors."[61]

In the closely related context of the procedural rules governing share-holder derivative litigation, the New York Court of Appeals stated in *Marx v. Akers:* "By their very nature, shareholder derivative actions infringe upon the managerial discretion of corporate boards. . . . Consequently, we have historically been reluctant to permit shareholder derivative suits, noting that the power of courts to direct the management of a corporation's affairs should be 'exercised with restraint.'"[62] The *Marx* court further noted the need to strike "a balance between preserving the discretion of directors to manage a corporation without undue interference, through the demand requirement, and permitting shareholders to bring claims on behalf of the corporation when it is evident that directors will wrongfully refuse to bring such claims," which is precisely the balance between authority and accountability the director primacy model predicts.

We observe similar rules seemingly designed to protect the board's authority in statutory provisions, such as those governing transactions in which the directors are personally interested, including management buyouts, which involve a significant conflict of interest and therefore tend to get close judicial scrutiny, but which receive judicial deference in appropriate cases.[63]

As a final example, consider the role of the board in negotiated acquisitions. Because approval by the target's board of directors is a nec-essary prerequisite to most acquisition methods, the modern corporate statutory scheme allows the target board to function as a gatekeeper who

---

[61] Smith v. Van Gorkom, 488 A.2d 858, 872 (Del. 1985).
[62] Mark v. Akers, 666 N.E.2d 1034, 1037 (N.Y. 1996) (quoting Gordon v. Elliman, 119 N.E.2d 331, 335 (N.Y. 1954)); *see also* Pogostin v. Rice, 480 A.2d 619, 624 (Del. 1984) ("[T]he derivative action impinges on the managerial freedom of directors. . . .").
[63] *See* Stephen M. Bainbridge, *Independent Directors and the ALI Corporate Governance Project*, 61 Geo. Wash. L. Rev. 1034, 1074–81 (1993).

decides which bids will be presented to the shareholders. To purchase the board's cooperation, the bidder may offer side payments, such as an equity stake in the surviving entity, employment or non-competition contracts, substantial severance payments, continuation of existing fringe benefits, or other compensation arrangements. Although it is undoubtedly rare for side payments to be so large as to materially affect the price the bidder would otherwise be able to pay target shareholders, side payments may affect the board's decision making by causing its members to agree to an acquisition price lower than that which could be obtained from hard bargaining or open bidding.

Even where management is not consciously seeking side payments from the bidder, a conflict of interest can still arise:

> There may be at work [in negotiated acquisitions] a force more subtle than a desire to maintain a title or office in order to assure continued salary or prerequisites. Many people commit a huge portion of their lives to a single large-scale business organization. They derive their identity in part from that organization and feel that they contribute to the identity of the firm. The mission of the firm is not seen by those involved with it as wholly economic, nor the continued existence of its distinctive identity as a matter of indifference.[64]

In game theory terms, the problem is that a negotiated corporate acquisition is a classic final period problem. In repeat transactions, the risk of self-dealing by one party is constrained by the threat that the other party will punish the cheating party in future transactions. In a final period transaction, this constraint—i.e., the threat of future punishment—disappears because the final period transaction is the last in the series.

As such, some of the various extrajudicial constraints on board discretion present in the operational context break down in corporate acquisitions. The target board is no longer subject to shareholder discipline because the target's shareholders will be bought out by the acquirer. The target board is no longer subject to market discipline because the target, by definition, will no longer operate in the market as

---

[64] Paramount Commc'ns, Inc. v. Time, Inc., [1989 Transfer Binder] Fed. Sec. L. Rep. (CCH) ¶ 94,514, at 93,268–69 (Del. Ch. July 14, 1989), reprinted in 15 Del. J. Corp. L. 700, 715 (1990), aff'd, 571 A.2d 1140 (Del. 1990).

an independent agency. As a result, the board is less vulnerable to both shareholder and market penalties for self-dealing.

Despite this well-known conflict of interest, Delaware corporate law definitively allocates decision-making authority to the board and, moreover, provides both substantive and procedural mechanisms ensuring a substantial degree of judicial deference to the board. The target's board possesses broad authority to determine whether to merge the firm and to select a merger partner. The initial decision to enter into a negotiated merger transaction is thus reserved to the board's collective business judgment, with shareholders having no statutory power to initiate merger negotiations.[65] The board also has sole power to negotiate the terms on which the merger will take place and to arrive at a definitive merger agreement embodying its decisions as to these matters. Finally, while courts may inspect such decisions slightly more closely than they do standard operational decisions, the business judgment rule continues effectively to ensure that the considerable latitude conferred upon the board by statute may be exercised without significant risk of judicial intervention.[66]

Does this analysis mean that the board should have unfettered authority? No. In some cases, accountability concerns become so pronounced as to trump the general need for deference to the board's authority. Recall Arrow's comment that "[t]o maintain the value of authority, it would appear that [accountability] must be intermittent. This could be periodic; it could take the form of "management by exception," in which authority and its decisions are reviewed only when performance is sufficiently degraded from expectations. . . ."[67] Given the significant virtues of discretion, however, one must not lightly interfere with the board's decision-making authority in the name of accountability. Instead, there ought to be a presumption in favor of judicial deference to decisions made by a disinterested and independent board of directors even when the transaction involves a conflict of interest on the part of some of the corporation's officers or directors.

---

[65] Smith v. Van Gorkom, 488 A.2d 858, 873 (Del. 1985).

[66] *See* Veasey, *supra* note 7, at 394 (drawing a distinction between "enterprise" and "ownership" decisions with respect to judicial review of board actions).

[67] Arrow, *supra* note 16, at 78.

The Paradigm Conflict of Interest: The Unsolicited Takeover Bid

The conflict of interest present in negotiated acquisitions is vastly exacerbated when the target company's board of directors receives an unsolicited takeover bid. As Judge Richard Posner observed:

> When managers are busy erecting obstacles to the taking over of the corporation by an investor who is likely to fire them if the takeover attempt succeeds, they have a clear conflict of interest, and it is not cured by vesting the power of decision in a board of directors in which insiders are a minority. . . . No one likes to be fired, whether he is just a director or also an officer.[68]

Likewise, the Delaware Supreme Court observed in *Bennett v. Propp* that "[w]e must bear in mind the inherent danger in the purchase of shares with corporate funds to remove a threat to corporate policy when a threat to control is involved. The directors are of necessity confronted with a conflict of interest, and an objective decision is difficult."[69]

Because the conflict of interest is so serious in this context, the board's response to an unsolicited takeover bid provides another ideal test bed for applying the principles of director primacy to judicial review. As we have seen, measures intended to promote accountability inevitably implicate the values of authority. Are the accountability concerns presented in this context so severe as to trump authority considerations?

The Academics' Balance(s)

In the early 1980s, there came a veritable flood of academic writing on target board resistance to unsolicited takeover bids. Despite the voluminous debate, however, a relatively narrow set of policy proposals emerged; as Michael Dooley aptly put it, the literature "produced policy prescriptions running the gamut from A to B."[70] Ronald Gilson proposed an auction approach to takeover defenses, under which the incumbent board would be allowed to use only those tactics intended to secure a better offer for the shareholders, such as releasing information relevant

---

[68] Dynamics Corp. of Am. v. CTS Corp., 794 F.2d 250, 256 (7th Cir. 1986), rev'd on other grounds, 481 U.S. 69 (1987).
[69] 187 A.2d 405, 409 (Del. 1962).
[70] Michael P. Dooley, *Fundamentals of Corporation Law* 549 (1995).

to the offer's adequacy or delaying an offer while an alternative bidder is sought.[71]

Frank Easterbrook and Daniel Fischel proposed an even more restrictive regime that's been called the passivity or no-resistance rule.[72] Easterbrook and Fischel would allow incumbent directors and managers of a target company no role in unsolicited offers; they argued for complete passivity on the part of target incumbents in the face of a hostile tender offer. In their view, the tender offer presents not just a situational conflict of interest but also acts as the principal systemic constraint on unfaithful or inefficient corporate managers. In other words, they argued, the mere threat of corporate takeovers acts as an important check on agency costs that overcomes the collective action problems that plague shareholder oversight. The company is most vulnerable to hostile bids when its stock price is low due to management incompetence and there is room for improving the company's value by displacing the incumbent management team. Put another way, a company will only appear attractive, and therefore will only be acquired, if the stock is undervalued compared to its potential. Knowing this, corporate managers will pursue superior performance and high stock prices to preserve their own jobs. Hence, Easterbrook and Fischel claim, "[i]nvestors benefit even if their corporation never becomes the subject of a tender offer."[73]

Given this analysis, Easterbrook and Fischel's hostility toward management resistance to takeovers is hardly surprising. They argued that defensive tactics make monitoring by outsiders less profitable and thus

---

[71] *See, e.g.,* Ronald J. Gilson, *Seeking Competitive Bids Versus Pure Passivity in Tender Offer Defense,* 35 Stan. L. Rev. 51 (1982) [hereinafter Gilson, *Seeking Competitive Bids*]; Ronald J. Gilson, *The Case Against Shark Repellent Amendments: Structural Limitations on the Enabling Concept,* 34 Stan. L. Rev. 775 (1982). While Gilson's concern for the board's conflict of interest is apparent, his approach did not effectively resolve that problem. It is very difficult to distinguish ex ante between defensive tactics that will promote a corporate auction and those that will preserve target board independence. Dooley, *supra* note 70, at 555 (criticizing Gilson's approach). In addition, because Gilson's proposal only addressed incumbent tactics undertaken after an unsolicited offer is expected, it did nothing to prevent incumbent directors and managers from erecting defenses long before any offer is on the horizon.

[72] *See, e.g.,* Frank H. Easterbrook & Daniel R. Fischel, *Auctions and Sunk Costs in Tender Offers,* 35 Stan. L. Rev. 1 (1982); Frank H. Easterbrook & Daniel R. Fischel, *The Proper Role of a Target's Management in Responding to a Tender Offer,* 94 Harv. L. Rev. 1161 (1981) [hereinafter Easterbrook & Fischel, *The Proper Role*].

[73] Easterbrook & Fischel, *supra* note 27, at 173.

also less common.[74] Put another way, takeover defenses attenuate outsiders' incentives to play a monitoring role by eroding the expected return on identifying suitable takeover targets. Instead of being able to capture the returns of their monitoring activities, bidders are forced to share their gains with shareholders of the target company and with other bidders.

Delaware's Balance

The Delaware Supreme Court never adopted either the auction or the passivity model.[75] At the same time, however, the court recognized that the traditional doctrinal options were inadequate to the task at hand. Characterizing the action of a corporation's board of directors as a question of care or of loyalty has vital, potentially outcome-determinative, consequences. If the court treated takeover defenses as a loyalty question, with its accompanying intrinsic fairness standard, takeover defenses would rarely pass muster. The defendant directors would be required, subject to close and exacting judicial scrutiny, to establish that the transaction was objectively fair to the corporation.[76] Because this burden is an exceedingly difficult one to bear and would likely result in routine judicial invalidation of takeover defenses, a duty of loyalty analysis makes sense only if we think all takeovers are socially undesirable and that all takeover defenses are therefore bad social policy.

On the other hand, if the court treated takeover defenses as a care question, virtually all takeover defenses would survive judicial review. Before the target's directors could be called to account for their actions, plaintiff would have to rebut the business judgment rule's presumptions by showing that the decision was tainted by fraud, illegality, self-dealing, or some other exception to the rule. Absent the proverbial smoking gun,

---

[74] *Id.* In contrast to Gilson's preference for auctions, Easterbrook and Fischel contended that defensive tactics that induce auctions are especially problematic. *Id.* at 173–75. The first bidder expends time and effort monitoring potential targets. Second bidders essentially get a free ride on the first bidder's efforts. If the first bidder is unable to earn an adequate return on those efforts, however, the incentive to bid is reduced. *Id.*

[75] Unocal Corp. v. Mesa Petroleum Co., 493 A.2d 946, 955 n.10 (Del. 1985) (acknowledging academic suggestions that "a board's response to a takeover threat should be a passive one" and dismissing them as "clearly . . . not the law of Delaware").

[76] *See* Robert M. Bass Group, Inc. v. Evans, 552 A.2d 1227, 1239 (Del. Ch. 1988) (observing where "fiduciaries charged with protecting the interest of the public shareholders have a conflicting self interest, those fiduciaries must establish the transaction's 'entire fairness' to the satisfaction of the reviewing court").

plaintiff is unlikely to prevail under this standard. A duty of care analysis thus makes sense only if we think management resistance to takeovers is always appropriate.

In *Unocal Corp. v. Mesa Petroleum Co.*,[77] the Delaware Supreme Court attempted to steer a middle course by promulgating what has been called an "intermediate" or "enhanced business judgment" standard of judicial review but is perhaps best described as a "conditional business judgment rule."[78] In doing so, the court strongly reaffirmed the target board's general decision-making primacy, which includes an obligation to determine whether an unsolicited offer is in the shareholders' best interests:

> *The board has a large reservoir of authority upon which to draw.* Its duties and responsibilities proceed from the inherent powers conferred by . . . § 141(a), respecting management of the corporation's "business and affairs." Additionally, the powers here being exercised derive from . . . § 160(a), conferring broad authority upon a corporation to deal in its own stock. From this it is now well established that in the acquisition of its shares a Delaware corporation may deal selectively with its stockholders, provided the directors have not acted out of a sole or primary purpose to entrench themselves in office.
>
> Finally, the board's power to act derives from its fundamental duty and obligation to protect the corporate enterprise, which includes stockholders, from harm reasonably perceived, irrespective of its source. . . . Thus, we are satisfied that *in the broad context of corporate governance, including issues of fundamental corporate change, a board of directors is not a passive instrumentality.*[79]

Note the strong emphasis on the authority of the board of directors as a core principle of corporate governance; indeed, it is treated as such an important principle as to mandate substantial judicial deference to boards.

At the same time, however, the court recognized the especially pronounced tension between authority and accountability present in this transactional context. "Because of the omnipresent specter that a board may be acting primarily in its own interests, rather than those of

---

[77] 493 A.2d 946 (Del. 1985).

[78] Dooley, *supra* note 5, at 515.

[79] *Unocal*, 493 A.2d at 953–54 (emphasis added; citations and footnotes omitted).

the corporation and its shareholders, there is an enhanced duty which calls for judicial examination at the threshold before the protections of the business judgment rule may be conferred."[80]

The initial burden of proof is on the directors, who must first show they had reasonable grounds for believing that the unsolicited posed a danger to corporate policy or effectiveness. The directors satisfy this burden by showing they acted in good faith and conducted a reasonable investigation. The good faith element requires a showing that the directors acted in response to a perceived threat to the corporation and not for the purpose of entrenching themselves in office. The reasonable investigation element requires a demonstration that the board was adequately informed, with the relevant standard being one of gross negligence. Assuming the directors carry their first step, they next must prove the defense was reasonable in relation to the threat posed by the hostile bid. Both the decision to adopt a takeover defense and any subsequent decision to implement it are independently subject to challenge and judicial review.

Not surprisingly, the board's "initial" burden of proof quickly became the whole ball game. If the directors carried their two-step burden, the business judgment rule applied, but if the directors failed to carry their initial burden, the duty of loyalty's intrinsic fairness test applied.[81] It is for this reason the *Unocal* test is more properly seen as a conditional version of the business judgment rule, rather than an intermediate standard of review lying between the duties of care and of loyalty. The *Unocal* standard solved the problem of outcome determination not so much by creating a different standard of review, but rather by creating a mechanism for determining on an individual basis which of the traditional doctrinal standards was appropriate for the particular case at bar.

As the *Unocal* standard evolved, it culminated in *Paramount Communications Inc. v. QVC Network Inc.*,[82] in which Chief Justice Veasey interpreted *Unocal* and its many progeny as articulating that a reasonableness inquiry was to be applied on a case-by-case basis: "The key features of an enhanced scrutiny test are: (a) a judicial determination regarding the adequacy of the decisionmaking process employed by the directors, including the information on which the directors based their

---

[80] *Id.* at 954.
[81] *See* Shamrock Holdings, Inc. v. Polaroid Corp., 559 A.2d 257, 271 (Del. Ch. 1989).
[82] 637 A.2d 34 (Del. 1994).

decision; and (b) a judicial examination of the reasonableness of the directors' action in light of the circumstances then existing." The burden of proof is on the directors with respect to both issues. They need not prove that they made the right decision, but merely that their decision fell within the range of reasonableness. The implicit assumption is that a reasonable decision is unlikely to be motivated by conflicted interest or, at least, that improper motives are irrelevant so long as the resulting decision falls within a range of reasonable outcomes. The operating norm seems to be "no harm, no foul," which seems sensible enough.

Given the Delaware courts' "normal sensitivity to conflicts of interest[s],"[83] the evidence that target board resistance to unsolicited tender offers is, at best, a risky proposition for shareholders and, at worst, economically disastrous,[84] and the undeniable fact that the passivity rule does a more thorough job of removing management's conflicted interests from the tender offer process than does *Unocal*, it may seem surprising that the Delaware courts adopted a standard that permits target resistance. The Delaware courts' consistent rejection of the passivity rule suggests the courts have perceived some dimension to the puzzle that has escaped the attention of academics.

Analysis should begin, then, with the proposition that all doctrinal responses to corporate conflict of interest transactions have two features in common. First, so long as the board of directors is disinterested and independent, it retains full decision-making authority with respect to the transaction. Second, the board's independence and decision-making process is subject to judicial scrutiny. Here, again, we see the competing influences of authority and accountability.

In a sense, Delaware's takeover cases do no more than simply bring this traditional corporate governance system to bear on target resistance to tender offers.[85] Admittedly, the form of review is unique, but so too is

---

[83] See Dooley, *supra* note 5, at 515 ("Given ... the courts' normal sensitivity to conflicts of interest, many have been perplexed and some dismayed by the courts' refusal to ban or at least severely limit target board resistance.").

[84] See Dooley, *supra* note 70, at 555–57 (summarizing data on wealth effects of takeovers and of target board resistance).

[85] The point is made obvious by the Delaware Supreme Court's decision in *Williams v. Geier*, 671 A.2d 1368, 1371–74 (Del. 1996), in which an anti-takeover dual class stock plan received approval by the disinterested shareholders. In light of the shareholder action, the court held that the *Unocal* standard was "inapplicable here because there was no unilateral board action." *Id.* at 1377. As with all other conflicted interest transactions, shareholder approval provides substantial protection from judicial review for the board's decision. *See id.* at 1371.

the context. Just as has been the case with all other corporate conflicts of interest, Delaware decisions in the unsolicited tender offer context strive to find an appropriate balance between authority and accountability. We see evidence of the Delaware courts' concern for accountability in, for example, *Unocal*'s explicit recognition of the conflict of interest that target directors and officers face in an unsolicited takeover bid. As a doctrinal matter, the Delaware Supreme Court concretely demonstrated its sensitivity to management's conflicted interests by placing the preliminary burden of proof on the board. This action demonstrated considerable judicial sensitivity to the board's conflicted interests because, outside of areas traditionally covered by the duty of loyalty, putting the initial burden of proof on the board of directors is a very unusual—indeed, essentially unprecedented—step.

At the same time, however, we see much evidence that Delaware courts are also concerned with the value of authority. *Unocal*'s express rejection of the passivity model, for example, made clear that the board retains an important gatekeeping function even with respect to a transaction so obviously redolent with the potential for conflicts of interest. Likewise, we see deference to the board's role in *QVC*'s holding that a court should not second-guess a board decision that falls within the range of reasonableness, "even though [the board] might have decided otherwise or subsequent events may have cast doubt on the board's determination." Even plainer evidence of the Delaware courts' concern for authority came when Chancellor Allen wrote that unless *Unocal* was carefully applied, "courts—in exercising some element of substantive judgment—will too readily seek to assert the primacy of their own view on a question upon which reasonable, completely disinterested minds might differ."[86] Is it not striking how precisely Allen echoes our recurring mantra that one cannot make an actor more accountable without simultaneously transferring some aliquot of his decision-making authority to the entity empowered to hold him accountable?

---

[86] City Capital Assocs. Ltd. P'ship v. Interco Inc., 551 A.2d 787, 796 (Del. Ch. 1988). Chief Justice Veasey's *QVC* opinion likewise emphasized that a court should not second-guess a board decision falling within the range of reasonableness "even though it might have decided otherwise or subsequent events may have cast doubt on the board's determination." Paramount Commc'ns, Inc. v. QVC Network Inc., 637 A.2d 34, 45 (Del. 1994).

Why Not Passivity?

In contrast to the Delaware balance, virtually all of the policy prescriptions to emerge from the academic accounts of the tender offer's corporate governance function would create an entirely new and radically different system of corporate governance, in which the board is stripped of some or all of its normal decision-making authority. The academic proposals not only reflect an overriding concern with accountability; they also reject the very notion that authority values have any legitimate role to play in developing takeover doctrine. Deciding whether the judiciary or the academy has the better argument is the task to which this section is devoted.

The key to our inquiry is whether the unsolicited tender offer differs in kind, and not just in degree, from any other conflicted interest transaction. If so, perhaps a special governance scheme applicable only to unsolicited tender offers can be justified. If not, however, we would expect the law to treat unsolicited tender offers just as it treats other conflicted interest transactions. In other words, the law should develop mechanisms for policing the incumbent directors' conflicts of interests, but it should not deny the incumbents a role in the process.

A commonly advanced justification for treating the tender offer differently from other conflicted interested transactions, such as negotiated acquisitions, rests on the tender offer's provision of a takeover vehicle that does not require the cooperation of the target board of directors. As discussed above, the target board's gatekeeper role in negotiated acquisitions creates a conflict of interest, which is constrained in part by the ability the tender offer gives a bidder to bypass the target's board by purchasing a controlling share block directly from the stockholders. According to some, authority values are only appropriate in the negotiated acquisition context if the board is denied the ability to resist tender offers.[87]

This argument has a certain superficial appeal, but ultimately is unpersuasive. Tender offers are not the only vehicle by which outsiders

---

[87] *See, e.g.,* Easterbrook & Fischel, *The Proper Role, supra* note 72, at 1200 ("The performance of the board in its role as agent is policed by market forces. . . . [T]he tender offer, therefore, is an essential safety valve to ensure that managers evaluate merger proposals in the best interests of the shareholders."); Gilson, *supra* note 71, at 850 ("Restricting management's role in a tender offer does not deny the value of management's expertise in evaluating and negotiating complex corporate transactions, but rather validates the unfettered discretion given management with respect to mergers and sales of assets.").

can appeal directly to the shareholders. Proxy contests similarly permit a would-be acquirer to end-run management. Yet, nobody expects a board to be passive in the face of a proxy contest.[88] To the contrary, the incumbent board's role is very active indeed, because the incumbent board members remain in office and therefore also remain legally obligated to conduct the business, unless and until they are displaced. Complete passivity in the face of a proxy contest would be inconsistent with the directors' obligation to determine and advance the best interests of the corporation and its shareholders.

The same is true of a tender offer. While the analogy between tender offers and proxy contests is unconvincing for most purposes, "the courts may have correctly sensed a fit at the most basic level."[89] As with a proxy contest, directors of a target of an unsolicited tender offer will remain in office unless and until the offer succeeds. Therefore, unless and until they are removed by a successful bidder, the board of directors has a "fundamental duty" to protect shareholders from harm,[90] which can include resisting an unsolicited tender offer they truly believe is not in the shareholders' best interests. As *Unocal* recognized, complete board passivity in the face of such an offer would be inconsistent with the directors' fiduciary duties. To the contrary, their fiduciary duty obliges them to seek out alternatives. At the bare minimum, it thus would be appropriate for the board to use takeover defenses to delay an inadequate bid from going forward while the board seeks out an alternative higher-valued offer. Until the board has time to arrange a more attractive alternative, there is a risk that the shareholders will "choose the inadequate tender option only because the superior option has not yet been presented."[91]

A related but more substantial argument against authority values in the unsolicited tender offer context contrasts the board's considerable control in negotiated acquisitions with the board's lack of control over secondary market transactions in the firm's shares. Corporate law generally provides for free alienability of shares on the secondary trading markets. Mergers and related transfers of control are treated quite differently, however, with the target board being given considerable legal responsibility

---

[88] *See* Dooley, *supra* note 5, at 516 ("No one would expect an incumbent management team to vacate their offices at the first hint of an election challenge.").

[89] Dooley, *supra* note 70, at 563.

[90] MacAndrews & Forbes Holdings, Inc. v. Revlon, Inc., 501 A.2d 1239, 1251 (Del. Ch. 1985), aff'd, 506 A.2d 173 (Del. 1986).

[91] Shamrock Holdings, Inc. v. Polaroid Corp., 559 A.2d 278, 289 (Del. Ch. 1989).

and latitude in negotiating a merger agreement. The question thus is whether unsolicited tender offers are more like secondary market trading or more like mergers.

The so-called structural argument, also known as the shareholder choice argument, asserts that the tender offer is much more closely analogous to secondary market transactions. According to its proponents, an individual shareholder's decision to tender his shares to the bidder no more concerns the institutional responsibilities or prerogatives of the board than does the shareholder's decision to sell his shares on the open market or, for that matter, to sell his house.[92] Both stock and a home are treated as species of private property that are freely alienable by their owners.

The trouble is that none of the normative bases for the structural argument proves persuasive. The idea that shareholders have the right to make the final decision about an unsolicited tender offer does not necessarily follow, for example, from the mere fact that shareholders have voting rights. While notions of shareholder democracy permit powerful rhetoric, corporations are not New England town meetings. Put another way, we need not value corporate democracy simply because we value political democracy. Indeed, as Chapter 5 will argue, we need not value shareholder democracy very much at all. What is most striking about shareholder voting rights is the extensive set of limitations on those rights. Chapter 5 argues that these limitations reflect the presumption in favor of authority. They are designed to minimize the extent to which shareholders can interfere in the board of directors' exercise of its discretionary powers.

Nor is shareholder choice a necessary corollary of the shareholders' ownership of the corporation. As Chapter 1 argued, because shareholders are simply one of many constituencies bound together by a web of explicit and implicit contracts, ownership simply is not a meaningful concept as applied to the corporate entity. Hence, a shareholder's ability to dispose of his stock is defined and limited by the terms of the corporate contract, which in turn are provided by the firm's organic documents and the state of incorporation's corporate statute and common law. "[S]hareholders

---

[92] *See, e.g.,* Dynamics Corp. of Am. v. CTS Corp., 794 F.2d 250, 254 (7th Cir.1986), rev'd on other grounds, 481 U.S. 69 (1987); Hanson Trust PLC v. ML SCM Acq'n Inc., 781 F.2d 264, 282 (2d Cir. 1986); Norlin Corp. v. Rooney, Pace Inc., 744 F.2d 255, 258 (2d Cir. 1984).

do not possess a contractual right to receive takeover bids. The share-holders' ability to gain premiums through takeover activity is subject to the good faith business judgment of the board of directors in structuring defensive tactics."[93]

This insight suggests another way of looking at the problem; namely, to ask whether the passivity rule or something like the Delaware regime would emerge from the hypothetical bargain as the majoritarian default. The empirical evidence suggests that the latter would do so. It is well-established, for example, that the combination of a poison pill and a stag-gered board of directors is a particularly effective takeover defense.[94] Yet, about 70 percent of public corporations now have staggered boards.[95] The incidence of staggered boards has increased dramatically among firms going public, while activist shareholders have made little headway in efforts to "de-stagger" the board. These findings are highly suggestive:

> Although agency costs are high, many managerial teams are scru-pulously dedicated to investors' interests. . . . By increasing the value of the firm, they would do themselves a favor (most managers' compensation is linked to the stock market, and they own stock too). Nonexistence of securities said to be beneficial to investors is telling.[96]

The existence of securities having certain features seems equally telling. Indeed, if what investors do matters more than what they say, one must

---

[93] Moran v. Household Int'l, Inc., 490 A.2d 1059, 1070 (Del. Ch.), aff'd, 500 A.2d 1346 (Del. 1985). Accord Shamrock Holdings, Inc. v. Polaroid Corp., 559 A.2d 257, 272 (Del. Ch. 1989) (observing "stockholders have no contractual right to receive tender offers or other takeover proposals").

[94] Lucian Arye Bebchuk et al., *The Powerful Antitakeover Force of Staggered Boards: Theory, Evidence, and Policy,* 54 Stan. L. Rev. 887, 931 (2002) (combining a staggered board and a poison pill almost doubled the chances of a target corporation remaining independent); Robert B. Thompson, *Shareholders as Grown-Ups: Voting, Selling, and Limits on the Board's Power To "Just Say No,"* 67 U. Cin. L. Rev. 999, 1017-18 (1999) (using legal treatment of poison pill and classified board provisions as a measure of jurisdictional commitment to shareholder primacy); Neil C. Rifkind, Note, *Should Uninformed Shareholders Be a Threat Justifying Defensive Action by Target Directors in Delaware?: "Just Say No" After* Moore v. Wallace, 78 B.U. L. Rev. 105, 111 (1998) (observ-ing that "[w]hen poison pills and classified boards are used in tandem, the bidder either must mount two consecutive proxy contests to elect a majority of directors, or convince a court that the target directors' opposition to the offer constitutes a breach of the direc-tors' fiduciary duties").

[95] Robin Sidel, *Staggered Terms for Board Members Are Said to Erode Shareholder Value, Not Enhance It,* Wall Street Journal, Apr. 1, 2002, at C2.

[96] Easterbrook & Fischel, *supra* note 27, at 205.

conclude that IPO investors are voting for director primacy with their wallets.[97]

Finally, and most importantly, the structural argument also ignores the risk that restricting the board's authority in the tender offer context will undermine the board's authority in other contexts. As a previous section demonstrated, even the most casual examination of corporate legal rules offers plenty of evidence that courts value preservation of the board's decision-making authority. The structural argument, however, ignores the authority values reflected in these rules. To the contrary, if accepted, the structural argument would necessarily undermine the board's unquestioned authority in a variety of areas. Consider, for example, the board's authority to negotiate mergers. If the bidder can easily bypass the board by making a tender offer, hard bargaining by the target board becomes counterproductive. It will simply lead the bidder into making a low-ball tender offer to the shareholders. This offer, in turn, would probably be accepted due to the collective action problems that preclude meaningful shareholder resistance. Restricting the board's authority to resist tender offers thus indirectly restricts its authority with respect to negotiated acquisitions.

Indeed, taken to its logical extreme, the structural argument requires direct restrictions on management's authority in the negotiated acquisition context. Suppose management believes that its company is a logical target for a hostile takeover bid. One way to make itself less attractive is by expending resources in acquiring other companies. Alternatively, the board could effect a preemptive strike by agreeing to be acquired by a friendly bidder. In order to assure that such acquisitions will not deter unsolicited tender offers, the structural argument would require exacting judicial review of the board's motives in any negotiated acquisition.

To take but one more example, a potential target can make itself less vulnerable to a takeover by eliminating marginal operations or increasing the dividend paid to shareholders, either of which would enhance the value of the outstanding shares. Thus, a corporate restructuring can be seen as a preemptive response to the threat of takeovers. Although such transactions may aid incumbents in securing their positions, it is hard to imagine valid objections to incumbents doing so through transactions

---

[97] Lynn A. Stout, *Bad and Not-So-Bad Arguments for Shareholder Primacy*, 73 S. Cal. L. Rev. 1189, 1206 (2002) (summarizing evidence "shareholders display a revealed preference for rules that promote director primacy at early stages of a firm's development").

that benefit shareholders.[98] Why should it matter if the restructuring occurs after a specific takeover proposal materializes? On the contrary, the structural argument not only says that it does matter, but taken to its logical extreme, it would require close judicial scrutiny of all corporate restructurings.[99]

Lastly, restrictions on the board's authority to function as a gate-keeper with respect to unsolicited tender offers might have a multiplicative effect on the board's authority generally. Because "the efficiency of organization is affected by the degree to which individuals assent to orders, denying the authority of an organization communication is a threat to the interests of all individuals who derive a net advantage from their connection with the organization."[100] Hence, by calling into question the legitimacy of the central decision-making body's authority in this critical decision-making arena, a passivity rule might reduce the incentive for subordinates to assent to that body's decisions in other contexts as well, thereby undermining the efficient functioning of the entire firm.

The final and perhaps most important argument for treating negotiated and hostile acquisitions differently with respect to the scope of the target board's authority comes down to the conflicted interests inherent in corporate takeovers. Put succinctly, accountability concerns are so severe in this context, they must trump authority values. Here we thus come to an argument that directly challenges the principles of director primacy.

Unsolicited tender offers admittedly implicate accountability concerns in at least two ways, which might be referred to, respectively, as transactional and systemic. The former relates to the effect of a hostile takeover on the target in question, while the latter relates to the effect resistance to hostile takeovers can have on public corporations as a whole.

---

[98] *See* Dooley, *supra* note 5, at 517 (making this point); cf. Shamrock Holdings, Inc. v. Polaroid Corp., 559 A.2d 257, 276 (Del. Ch. 1989) (upholding an employee stock ownership plan despite its anti-takeover effects, because the plan was "likely to add value to the company and all of its stockholders").

[99] A related cost of shareholder choice is that it may encourage directors and managers to refrain from investments that have a positive net present value but also make the firm more attractive to potential hostile acquirers. *See* Richard E. Kihlstrom & Michael L. Wachter, *Why Defer to Managers? A Strong-Form Efficiency Model*, available at http://ssrn.com/abstract= 803564.

[100] Chester I. Barnard, *The Functions of the Executive* 169 (30th anniversary ed. 1968).

Neither justifies wholly barring authority values from playing a part in developing the governing legal rules.

Let's first consider the question of transactional accountability. No one disputes Judge Posner's claim that an unsolicited takeover offer poses a serious conflict between the interests of target managers and target shareholders. If the deal goes forward, shareholders stand to gain a substantial premium for their shares, while incumbent directors and managers face a substantial risk of losing their jobs. Any defensive actions by the incumbents are thus tainted by the specter of self-interest.

A key failing of the academic literature on takeovers, however, is the almost universal conflation of the roles of corporate officers and directors. The legal literature speaks of management resistance and management defensive tactics,[101] rarely recognizing any separate institutional role for the board. To the limited extent that it does differentiate between directors and managers, the literature tends to assume naïvely that even independent directors are in thrall to senior managers and will ignore shareholder interests if necessary to preserve their patrons' jobs.[102]

In contrast, the Delaware courts take the board of directors' distinct role quite seriously, especially with respect to its independent members. As a doctrinal matter, the board's burden of proof is more easily carried if the key decisions are made by independent directors.[103] As a practical matter, the court's assessment of the outside directors' role often is outcome-determinative.[104]

Why have the Delaware courts insisted on drawing such sharp distinctions between the board's role and that of management? While the conflict of interest unsolicited tender offers pose for the target company's managers is inescapable, the independent director's conflict of interest is merely a potential problem. Indeed, for the independent directors, the conflicts posed by unsolicited tender offers are no different than those

---

[101] *See, e.g.,* Easterbrook & Fischel, *The Proper Role, supra* note 72, at 1199 n.108; Gilson, *supra* note 71, at 881.

[102] *See, e.g.,* Dynamics Corp. of Am. v. CTS Corp., 794 F.2d 250, 256 (7th Cir.1986), rev'd on other grounds, 481 U.S. 69 (1987); Norlin Corp. v. Rooney, Pace Inc., 744 F.2d 255, 266 n.12 (2d Cir. 1984); Panter v. Marshall Field & Co., 646 F.2d 271, 300 (7th Cir.) (Cudahy, J., concurring in part and dissenting in part), cert. denied, 454 U.S. 1092 (1981).

[103] Moran v. Household Int'l, Inc., 500 A.2d 1346, 1356 (Del. 1985); Unocal Corp. v. Mesa Petroleum Co., 493 A.2d 946, 955 (Del. 1985).

[104] William T. Allen, *Independent Directors in MBO Transactions: Are They Fact or Fantasy?,* 45 Bus. Law. 2055, 2060 (1990).

posed by freeze-out mergers, management buyouts, interested director transactions, or a host of similar situations. Corporate law neither prohibits these transactions nor requires complete board passivity in connection with them simply because they potentially involve conflicts of interest. Instead, it regulates them in ways designed to constrain self-interested behavior. Unless one makes a living on the buying side of corporate takeovers, it is not clear why hostile takeovers should be treated differently.

Consider, for example, the somewhat analogous case of management-sponsored leveraged buyouts. Like unsolicited tender offers, these transactions inherently involve a strong risk of management self-dealing. While management is acting as the sellers' agents and, in that capacity, is obliged to get the best price it can for the shareholders, it is also acting as a purchaser and, in that capacity, has a strong self-interest to pay the lowest possible price. Like unsolicited tender offers, management buyouts also create conflicts of interest for the independent directors. Just as an independent director may resist an unsolicited tender offer to avoid being fired by the hostile bidder, he may go along with a management buyout in order to avoid being fired by the incumbent managers. Alternatively, if an independent director is inclined to resist a hostile takeover because of his friendship with the insiders, should he not go along with a management-sponsored buyout for the same reason?

Strikingly, the empirical evidence indicates shareholder premiums are essentially identical in management-sponsored leveraged buyouts and arm's length leveraged buyouts.[105] This evidence suggests that the potentially conflicted interests of independent directors are not affecting their ability to successfully constrain management misconduct. Accordingly, while judicial review of management buyouts tends to be rather intensive, courts have allowed such transactions and have addressed the problem of conflicted interests by encouraging an active role for the firm's independent directors in approving a management buyout proposal. Why should the same not be true of the board's response to unsolicited tender offers?

In summary, the conflict of interest present when the board responds to an unsolicited tender offer differs only in degree, not kind, from any

---

[105] Jeffrey Davis & Kenneth Lehn, *Information Asymmetries, Rule 13e-3, and Premiums in Going-Private Transactions*, 70 Wash. U. L.Q. 587, 595–96 (1992).

other corporate conflict.[106] Although skepticism about board motives is appropriate, the board members' conflict of interest does not necessarily equate to blameworthiness. Rather, it is simply a state of affairs inherently created by the necessity of conferring authority on the board of directors to act on behalf of the shareholders. To be sure, proponents of the passivity rule will respond that such a state of affairs could be avoided if the law refused to confer such authority on the board in this context. Yet, if the legal system deprives the board of authority here, it will be hard-pressed to decline to do so with respect to other conflict transactions. As has been the case with other situations of potential conflict, we would expect the courts to develop standards of review for takeover defenses that are designed to detect, punish, and deter self-interested behavior. Because the risk may be greater in this context, stricter-than-normal policing mechanisms may be required, but this does not mean that we must set aside authority values by divesting the board of decision-making authority.

Because the target board of directors' transactional conflict of interest thus is neither so severe nor so unusual as to justify a passivity requirement, opponents of the target board's gatekeeping function must find some other basis for denying in this context the board's normal decision-making authority. For most critics of takeover defenses, such a basis is found in the systemic agency cost effects of target resistance.

The tension between authority and accountability arises because we need some mechanism for enforcing those rights for which shareholders have contracted; most notably, of course, we need a mechanism for ensuring director and management compliance with the shareholder wealth maximization norm. Unfortunately, like many intra-corporate contracts, the shareholder wealth maximization norm does not lend itself to judicial enforcement absent self-dealing. To the contrary, for the reasons discussed above, in most cases the business judgment rule precludes courts from reviewing alleged departures from that norm. Instead, the norm generally must be enforced indirectly through a complex and varied set of extrajudicial accountability mechanisms.

Disciplinary actions against employees and mid-level managers normally take the form of dismissals, demotions, or salary adjustments imposed by senior management. Where it is top management that must be disciplined, however, alternative mechanisms become necessary.

---

[106]   Dooley, *supra* note 5, at 517.

According to the standard academic account, hostile takeover bidders provide such a mechanism. Making the standard efficient capital market assumption that poor corporate performance will be reflected in the corporation's stock price, opponents of target resistance claim that a declining market price sends a signal to prospective bidders that there are gains to be had by acquiring the corporation and displacing the incumbent managers.[107] The signal, of course, will not always be correct. Sometimes the firm's market price may be declining despite the best efforts of competent management, for example, where some exogenous shock like technological change or new government regulation has permanently altered the corporation's fundamentals. If close examination by a prospective bidder reveals that the declining market price is, in fact, attributable to shirking by the top management team, however, a disciplinary takeover could produce real gains to divide between the target's shareholders and the successful acquirer. This prospect creates positive incentives for potential bidders to investigate when the market signals that a firm is in distress. Conversely, because keeping the stock price up is the best defense managers have against being displaced by this outside searcher, the market for corporate control—more specifically, the unsolicited tender offer—is an important mechanism for preventing shirking by top management.

By making possible target resistance to unsolicited takeover bids, takeover defenses thus supposedly undermine the very foundations of corporate governance.[108] The first prospective bidder to identify a prospective target incurs significant search costs, which become part of the bidder's overall profit calculation. Further, by announcing its offer, the first bidder also identifies the prospective target to all other potential bidders. Subsequent bidders thus need not incur the high search costs carried by the first bidder, perhaps allowing them to pay a higher price than is possible for the first bidder. If target resistance delays closing of the offer, additional bidders have an even greater opportunity to enter the fray. At the very least, target resistance may force the initial bidder to raise its offer, thereby reducing other bidders' incentives to search out takeover targets. Reductions in bidders' search incentives result in fewer opportunities for shareholders to profit from takeover premia. More important, a

---

[107] See Henry Manne, *Mergers and the Market for Corporate Control*, 73 J. Pol. Econ. 110, 112 (1965).

[108] Alan E. Garfield, *Paramount: The Mixed Merits of Mush*, 17 Del. J. Corp. L. 33, 50 (1992).

reduction in search incentives also reduces the effectiveness of inter-firm monitoring by outsiders. In turn, that reduces the market for corporate control's disciplinary effect. A rule prohibiting target resistance, therefore, is likely to decrease agency costs and increase stock prices, benefiting shareholders of all firms, even those whose companies are never targeted for a takeover bid.

The difficulty with this line of argument is that a passivity rule, in effect, creates a kind of private eminent domain: bidders can effectively "condemn" target shares by offering even a slight premium over the current market price.[109] Awarding the lion's share of the gains to be had from a change of control to the bidder, though, only makes sense if all gains from takeovers are created by bidders through the elimination of inept or corrupt target managers, and none is attributable to the hard work of efficient target managers. Unfortunately for proponents of the passivity rule, the evidence is that "takeovers produce gains for a variety of reasons that are likely to differ from case to case."[110]

In order for a no-resistance rule to make sense, the unsolicited tender offer also must be the critical mechanism by which incumbents are disciplined. Unsolicited tender offers, however, are so rare and sporadic that a top manager who shirks his responsibilities by playing golf when he should be working is undoubtedly more likely to be struck by lightning while on the course than to be fired after a hostile takeover. As a result, the disciplinary effect of takeovers likely has been overstated by proponents of the passivity rule. Instead, as my analysis of Delaware's takeover jurisprudence will suggest, the critical disciplinary mechanism is the board of directors, especially when these directors are independent. In turn, the tenure and reputation of outside board members are determined by the performance of the top inside managers, which gives independent directors further incentives to be vigilant in overseeing management's conduct.

If independent directors were the sole bulwark against managerial shirking, concerns about structural and actual bias might be troubling, but they do not stand alone. Important accountability mechanisms are supplied by the product market in which the firm operates and

---

[109]   Lucian Arye Bebchuk, *The Sole Owner Standard for Takeover Policy*, 17 J. Legal Stud. 197, 200 (1988). As Bebchuk notes, the taking implications of the no-resistance rule are inconsistent with the passivity model's chief proponents' strong preference in other contexts for property rights and freedom of contract. *Id.* at 200–3.

[110]   Dooley, *supra* note 70, at 553.

the internal and external job markets in which the firm's managers compete.[111] Top corporate managers do not get ahead by being associated with sub-par performance in the product markets: "[H]ow do managers get ahead, both in rising through a particular firm's hierarchy or in obtaining a better position with another firm? The answer is surely not by being associated with failed projects, sub-par performance and personal venality."[112] Indeed, as between shareholders and managers, it is the latter who have the greatest incentives to ensure the firm's success. Shareholders can and should hold diversified portfolios, so that the failure of an individual firm will not greatly decrease their total wealth. Managers, on the other hand, cannot diversify their firm-specific human capital (or their general human capital, for that matter). If the firm fails on their watch, it is the top management team that suffers the principal losses.

For this reason, the capital markets also have a disciplinary function. Incompetent or even unlucky management eventually shows up in the firm's performance. These signs are identified by potential debt or equity investors, who (if they are willing to invest at all) will demand a higher rate of return to compensate them for the risks of continued suboptimal performance. In turn, this demand makes the firm more likely to founder and take the incumbent managers down with it.

The point here is not that the tender offer has no disciplinary effect but merely that the tender offer is only one of many mechanisms by which management's behavior is constrained. Evidence that those constraints are effective despite the Delaware courts' failure to adopt a passivity rule abounds. Indeed, the director primacy–based system of U.S. corporate governance has served investors and society well:

> Despite the alleged flaws in its governance system, the U.S. economy has performed very well, both on an absolute basis and particularly relative to other countries. U.S. productivity gains in the past decade have been exceptional, and the U.S. stock market has consistently outperformed other world indices over the last two decades, including the period since the scandals broke. In other words, the broad

---

[111]   Barry D. Baysinger & Henry N. Butler, *Antitakeover Amendments, Managerial Entrenchment, and the Contractual Theory of the Corporation*, 71 Va. L. Rev. 1257, 1272 (1985).

[112]   Dooley, *supra* note 5, at 525.

evidence is not consistent with a failed U.S. system. If anything, it suggests a system that is well above average.[113]

Given the importance of Delaware to the U.S. corporate governance system, it is equally difficult to imagine that the system would be functioning so well if the critics of its takeover jurisprudence were correct.

Summation

The emphasis on conflicted interests reflects the Delaware courts' solution to the irreconcilable tension between authority and accountability. Concern for accountability drives the courts' expectation that the board will function as a separate institution independent from and superior to the firm's managers. The courts will inquire closely into the role actually played by the board (especially the outside directors), the extent to which they were supplied with all relevant information and independent advisors, and the extent to which they were insulated from management influence. Only if the directors had the ultimate decision-making authority, rather than incumbent management, will the board's conduct pass muster. But if it does, respect for authority values will require the court to defer to the board's substantive decisions. The board has legitimate authority in the takeover context, just as it has in proxy contests and a host of other decisions that nominally appear to belong to the shareholders. Nor can the board's authority be restricted in this context without impinging on the board's authority elsewhere. Authority thus cannot be avoided anymore than can accountability; the task is to come up with a reasonable balance. Properly interpreted, that is precisely what the Delaware cases have done.

---

[113] Bengt R. Holmstrom & Steven N. Kaplan, *The State of U.S. Corporate Governance: What's Right and What's Wrong?* 1 European Corporate Governance Institute-Finance Working Paper No. 23/2003, available at http://ssrn.com/abstract_id=441100.

CHAPTER 4

The Shift from Managerialism to Director Primacy

Let's review. The corporation is properly understood to be a legal fiction representing a web of contracts among multiple classes of stakeholders. As such, the law's principal function with respect to corporate governance is facilitating private ordering by providing a set of off-the-rack default rules. While the parties appropriately remain free to modify those rules as they see fit, the default rules should be designed to minimize transaction costs. In most cases, doing so means selecting the majoritarian default as the legal rule; i.e., the rule most people would select if they could costlessly bargain with one another.

There is good reason to think that the default rules of corporate law are generally efficient. Even if one thinks long-term survival is inadmissible evidence of a rule's merits, the evidence that state competition for charters results in a race to the top suggests that corporate law rules generally tend to evolve toward the majoritarian default.

In every state, the default rule calls for the corporation to be run neither by shareholders nor executives, but by a board of directors elected by the shareholders and responsible for maximizing shareholder wealth. Assuming that this separation of ownership and control is the majoritarian default, it was necessary to develop a theory as to why this was the governance structure most corporate stakeholders would select if they could have costlessly bargained over the issue when the corporation was being formed.

Analysis begins with the observation that the size and complexity of the public corporation ensures that stakeholders face significant collective action problems in making decisions, suffer from intractable information asymmetries, and have differing interests. Under such conditions, consensus-based decision-making structures are likely to fail. Instead, it is cheaper and more convenient to assign the decision-making function to a central decision maker wielding the power to rewrite intra-corporate contracts by fiat.

The analysis to this point, of course, suggests only that the decision-making structure should be one based on authority rather than participatory democracy. Yet, it turns out that corporate law also was wise to assign ultimate decision-making authority to a group—i.e., the board of directors—rather than a single individual. Groups turn out to have significant advantages vis-à-vis individuals at exercising critical evaluative judgment, which is precisely the principal skill set needed at the top of the corporate hierarchy. In addition, the default rule's reliance on group decision making solves the problem of "who watches the watchers" by placing a self-monitoring body at the apex of the corporate hierarchy. We thus have a rather compelling story explaining why the default rules of corporate governance envision a system of director primacy.

As we have seen, however, a model is only as good as the predictions it makes possible. Not surprisingly, here is where the critics of director primacy have focused their ire. Jeremy Telman, for example, opines that:

> While director primacy has the normative edge over managerialism, managerialism seems to have a far stronger empirical basis than the director-primacy model, and thus the director-primacy model is more vulnerable to criticism on the descriptive level than it is on the normative level. Directors do not run corporations; for the most part, they simply approve decisions made by executives. Although those executives are, in theory, chosen by and accountable to the board, in reality, boards are generally dominated by corporate executives who do not have the time, the interest, the expertise, or the incentive to act as significant checks on managerial decision-making authority.[1]

---

[1]   D. A. Jeremy Telman, *The Business Judgment Rule, Disclosure, and Executive Compensation*, 81 Tul. L. Rev. 829, 859 (2007).

Likewise, George Dent contends that "the evidence is overwhelming that most boards are passive, dominated by CEOs who exert their power in their own interests."[2]

In response to the critics, we need to delineate precisely what it is that we expect of the board of directors as an institution of corporate governance. Unfortunately, one of the major problems faced by anyone trying to develop a theory of the board of directors' role is that that role has changed radically over time. It is only in recent decades that boards were expected to act "as significant checks on managerial decision-making authority." More important for our purposes, during those decades there have been a number of changes in the law and best practice that have empowered boards and delegitimated managerialism. If real world practice does not yet entirely comport with the statutory ideal, the two are growing ever closer to one another.

The Evolving Role of the Board of Directors

The board of directors is a remarkably old institution. New York's 1811 statute authorizing general incorporation of manufacturing corporations granted broad management powers over the corporation to a board of trustees, a term that was borrowed from a 1784 statute authorizing general incorporation of religious congregations.[3] As this example suggests, we can trace the history of the board back to organizational forms that long predated the modern business corporation. Specifically, as the Supreme Court noted in 1809, we can look back to to early English forms: "As our ideas of a corporation, its privileges and its disabilities, are derived entirely from the English books, we resort to them for aid in ascertaining its character."[4]

Unfortunately, any "attempt to trace the history of the board of directors and officers back to their origins plunges one into a maze of problems."[5] The modern board of directors evolved from organizational forms in which the governing body performed functions very different from those

---

[2] George W. Dent, Jr., *Academics in Wonderland: The Team Production and Director Primacy Models of Corporate Governance* at 14 (June 2007), available at http://papers. ssrn.com/sol3/papers.cfm?abstract_id=995186.
[3] Ronald E. Seavoy, *The Origins of the American Business Corporation 1784–1855: Broadening the Concept of Public Service During Industrialization* 65 (1982).
[4] Bank of the United States v. Deveaux, 9 U.S. (5 Cranch) 61, 88 (1809).
[5] Cyril O'Donnell, *Origins of the Corporate Executive*, 26 Bull. Bus. Hist. Soc'y 55 (1952).

of today's corporate board.[6] Accordingly, history doesn't tell us very much about the merits of director primacy. Put another way, evolutionary theorists tell us that a bird's feathers changed functions from display and thermoregulation to flight as the avian class of animals evolved. Likewise, the board of directors has evolved over time as the corporate form has evolved in response to changing economic conditions.

Subject only to very minor exceptions, all modern state corporate codes require that the corporation establish a board of directors, which is charged in varying language with directing the affairs and business of the corporation. All state corporate codes also allow the formation of board committees, and the delegation of most decisions to board committees or corporate employees. Beyond this, corporate law has not attempted to define either the composition or function of the board or its committees.

Did boards ever manage public corporations, as early corporation statutes commanded? Perhaps, but not any time recently. In his magisterial history, *The Visible Hand*, Alfred Chandler related that boards of early nineteenth century banks actually made loan decisions. By the 1880s, however, boards of publicly held railroads were comprised mainly of representatives of large investors who served only part-time. Where boards of such companies exercised real power, it was mainly with respect to major financial decisions. Operational decisions were made by professional managers. Chandler observed a similar evolution in manufacturing corporations, although in this class of firms there was an even clearer transition from family capitalism, in which the firm was owned and managed by a dominant family, to managerial capitalism, in which the firm was managed by professionals unrelated to the original founders.[7]

Managerial capitalism reached its high-water mark in the 1950s. The boards of this era were largely "an extension of management."[8] Eight out of ten directors in this period were either employees (insiders) or outsiders closely affiliated with the corporation, such as the firm's lawyers

[6] Frank Gevurtz has done yeoman service in tracing the evolution of the board of directors from such early forms as medieval town councils. Franklin A. Gevurtz, *The Historical and Political Origins of the Corporate Board of Directors*, 33 Hofstra L. Rev. 89 (2004).
[7] Alfred D. Chandler, *The Visible Hand: The Managerial Revolution in American Business* (1977).
[8] Jeffrey N. Gordon, *The Rise of Independent Directors in the United States, 1950–2005: Of Shareholder Value and Stock Market Prices*, 59 Stan. L. Rev. 1465, 1514 (2007).

and bankers. The boards of this era saw their function mainly as advisory rather than as being comprised of either management or monitoring. Their low compensation and modest stock ownership (if any) combined with strong "don't rock the boat" social norms ensured that most boards were passive.[9]

The comfortable world of mid-twentieth century boards began to unravel in the 1970s. Events such as the financial collapse of Penn Central and the questionable payment scandals exposed during Watergate made clear that all too many boards were essentially supine.[10] In the wake of these revelations, corporate governance came under attack from two directions.

On one side, Ralph Nader and other radical social reformers claimed that public confidence in American corporations was declining precipitously in the face of antisocial corporate behavior. Pollution, workplace hazards, discrimination, unsafe products, corporate crime, and a host of other antisocial corporate social behaviors (and their effects) were attributable to lack of management accountability. In turn, lack of management accountability was attributable to state corporate law, which had been "reduced to reflecting the preferences of the managers of the largest corporations."[11] Accordingly, Nader called for a federal corporation law, displacing state law, which would make management more accountable to society.

At the same time, corporate governance was also under attack from the intellectual descendants of Adolf Berle, who argued for greater management accountability to shareholder interests. During the 1970s, many of these "traditionalists" concluded that corporate law was moving away from, not toward, greater accountability. Former Securities and Exchange Commission (SEC) Chairman William Cary argued, for example, that competition among states for incorporations produced a "race to the bottom" in which shareholder interests were sacrificed.[12] In response, Cary urged adoption of a federal statute designed to promote greater management accountability to shareholders, although not going so far as to require federal incorporation.

---

[9] *See generally* Charles M. Elson, *Director Compensation and the Management-Captured Board—The History of a Symptom and a Cure*, 50 SMU L. Rev. 127 (1996).

[10] Gordon, *supra* note 8, at 1514–17.

[11] Ralph Nader et al., *Taming the Giant Corporation* 60 (1976).

[12] William L. Cary, *Federalism and Corporate Law: Reflections Upon Delaware*, 83 Yale L.J. 663 (1974).

Cary and other traditionalist critics of corporate governance believed that the radical reformers' critique, coupled with the wave of scandals in the 1970s, had eroded public confidence in the modern business corporation and, as a result, had brought into question the very legitimacy of the economic system in which the corporation was the dominant actor.[13] Much of what followed flowed from this central belief that greater management accountability was essential if the corporation was to survive as an economic entity.

The Emergence of the Monitoring Board

In the midst of the 1970s ferment in corporate governance, Melvin Eisenberg developed a so-called monitoring model of the board, according to which corporate governance norms should explicitly call for a separation of the task of managing large publicly held corporations and that of monitoring those who do the managing.[14] Eisenberg argued that corporate statutes required the board to manage the corporation, but (he also argued) in the real world the board was essentially passive, with most of its functions being performed by senior executives. Arguing further that the board's principal remaining function was the selection and monitoring of the firm's chief executive, Eisenberg claimed that most boards failed to adequately perform even that residual task.

The monitoring model was embraced in the early drafts of the American Law Institute's Principles of Corporate Governance.[15] Tentative Draft No. 1 of the Principles, for example, required that independent directors comprise a majority of the board of directors of a large publicly held corporation.[16] This was intended to ensure objective board evaluation of management's performance. The same concern led the drafters to urge that, as a matter of good corporate practice, the independent directors

---

[13] *See, e.g.*, Melvin Aron Eisenberg, *The Modernization of Corporate Law: An Essay for Bill Cary*, 37 U. Miami L. Rev. 187, 209–10 (1983); Roswell B. Perkins, *The Genesis and Goals of the ALI Corporate Governance Project*, 8 Cardozo L. Rev. 661, 667 (1987).

[14] Melvin Aron Eisenberg, *The Structure of the Corporation* 139–41 (1976).

[15] Stephen M. Bainbridge, *Independent Directors and the ALI Corporate Governance Project*, 61 Geo. Wash. L. Rev. 1034 (1993).

[16] American Law Institute, Principles of Corporate Governance: Analysis and Recommendations § 3.03(a) (Tent. Draft No. 1 1982) [hereinafter "Project"]. The Project's eleven Tentative Drafts will be cited herein as follows: "TD No. X at [section or page]."

should not have outside employment or other commitments that would interfere with their performance of their duties. Likewise, the provisions' allowing of the independent directors to call upon corporate employees for assistance, to retain separate council or other experts on special issues, and to inspect corporate records and interview corporate personnel, were designed to enable the independent directors to bypass the company's senior executives when gathering information.

As espoused by Eisenberg and others, the monitoring model required directors to take on a very active role in the corporation. Yet, their role did not primarily involve decision making or even policy making, because the firm was to be managed by its senior executives. Instead, the board's principal function was to monitor the performance of the company's senior executives.[17]

The monitoring model was an important advance in corporate governance theory, with both explanatory and justificatory power, yet it nevertheless was incomplete. Although monitoring the performance of senior executives admittedly is the board's major function, that task necessarily entails activities best described as managerial. "The activities of the participating board involve it in strategic and important policy decisions affecting the future development of the company." Although "it remains clear that the management directs operations," "the board's participation in strategic planning can enhance the quality of strategic decisions and empower the board better to understand and evaluate management performance."[18]

Boards Today

The modern board of directors thus is properly understood as a production team whose product consists of a unique combination of advice giving, ongoing supervision, and crisis management. To the extent the board makes discrete decisions, those decisions typically entail some form of monitoring. The board reviews and approves major business decisions, sets executive compensation, hires and fires senior management, and the like. Rarely does the board engage in day-to-day managerial

---

[17] *Id.* at § 3.02.
[18] Kenneth R. Andrews, "Rigid Rules Will Not Make Good Boards," *Harvard Business Review*, Nov.–Dec. 1982, at 35, 44.

decision making. Instead, that role is reserved to the CEO and the other members of the top management team.

As we saw in Chapter 2, the efficiency of this allocation of corporate power is confirmed by the literature on group decision making. Creative planning is a task best left to individuals; hence, it is not surprising that the board does little in that area. In contrast, groups excel at tasks requiring the exercise of critical evaluative judgment, team learning, institutional memory, and the like. This is precisely the skill set desirable in an effective monitor. As a supervisory agent, the board develops an institutional memory that allows it to measure performance over time, while its critical evaluative judgment allows it to assess that performance.

To be sure, the performance of many boards with respect to these tasks is sub-optimal. Indeed, the complaint that "directors . . . do not direct" has a long and distinguished pedigree.[19] Most recently, of course, much of the blame for Enron and the other corporate scandals of the early years of the new millennium was laid at the feet of corporate directors. For example, the New York Stock Exchange's leadership opined that, during the early years of this century, we observed a "'meltdown' of significant companies due to failures of diligence, ethics and controls" on the part of directors and senior managers.[20] At Enron, perhaps the most notorious example, the report of an internal investigation concluded that Enron's "Board of Directors failed . . . in its oversight duties" with "serious consequences for Enron, its employees, and its shareholders."[21]

Nevertheless, boards today face pressures that their predecessors likely never even imagined. As a result, some commentators argue, at "a growing number of companies, the corporate board, once a sleeping giant, is waking up and flexing its intellectual muscle."[22]

We can divide the relevant pressures into five basic, albeit somewhat overlapping, areas. First, influential groups set out guides to best practices

---

[19] See, e.g., William O. Douglas, Directors Who Do Not Direct, 47 Harv. L. Rev. 1305 (1934).

[20] New York Stock Exchange, Corporate Governance Rule Proposals Reflecting Recommendations from the NYSE Corporate Accountability and Listing Standards Committee, as Approved by the NYSE Board of Directors, at http:// www.nyse.com/ pdfs/corp_gov_pro_b.pdf (Aug. 1, 2002).

[21] William C. Powers, Jr. et al., Report of Investigation by the Special Investigative Committee of the Board of Directors of Enron Corp., available at http://news.findlaw. com/hdocs/docs/enron/sicreport/sicreport020102.pdf (Feb. 1, 2002).

[22] Ram Charan, Boards at Work: How Corporate Boards Create Competitive Advantage 3 (1998).

that redefined the norms of expected board behavior. Second, director compensation practices evolved to better match director incentives with shareholder interests. Third, a variety of market forces made directors more concerned for their reputations as good corporate stewards. Fourth, courts ratcheted up the perceived legal expectations of directors. Finally, stock exchange and securities law rules mandated increased director independence and activism.

Best Practices

The corporate governance ferment of the 1970s produced three highly influential studies of the board of directors. In 1978, the American Bar Association (ABA) Section of Corporation, Banking and Business Law's Committee on Corporate Laws produced a *Corporate Director's Guidebook*, which detailed emerging best practices. In the same year, the prestigious Business Roundtable issued a *Statement on the Role and Composition of the Board of Directors of the Large Publicly Owned Corporation*. The following year, the ABA Committee on Corporate Laws issued a report entitled *The Overview Committees of the Board of Directors*.

The Committee on Corporate Laws' *Guidebook* proved especially influential, eventually becoming the most frequently cited handbook of its sort.[23] The ABA contemplated a role for the board that was in contrast to what is contained in the narrow monitoring model and according to which monitoring is one of several key functions, including:

- Reviewing and monitoring performance of the corporation's business and its operating, financial and other corporate plans, strategies and objectives, and changing plans and strategies as appropriate;
- Adopting policies of ethical conduct and monitoring compliance with those policies and with applicable laws and regulations;
- Understanding the risk profile of the corporation and reviewing and overseeing risk management programs;

---

[23] American Bar Association Section of Corporation, Banking and Business Law's Committee on Corporate Laws, *Corporate Director's Guidebook* vii (4th ed. 2004).

- Understanding the corporation's financial statements and monitoring the adequacy of its financial and other internal controls as well as its disclosure controls and procedures;
- Choosing, setting goals for, regularly evaluating and establishing the compensation of the chief executive officer and the most senior executives, and making changes in senior management when appropriate;
- Developing, approving and implementing succession plans for the chief executive officer and the most senior executives;
- Reviewing the process for providing adequate and timely financial and operational information to the corporation's decision makers (including directors) and shareholders;
- Evaluating the procedures, operation and overall effectiveness of the board and its committees; and
- Establishing the composition of the board and its committees, including choosing director nominees who will bring appropriate expertise and perspectives to the board, recognizing the important role of independent directors.

The *Guidebook* goes on to offer detailed best practices with respect to each of these areas.

Although it has been particularly influential, the *Guidebook* is but part of a "best practices industry" that has grown dramatically over the last 25-odd years. Today, for example, the Conference Board publishes an annual *Corporate Governance Handbook*, providing up-to-date treatment of best practices and legal standards. In the 2005 edition, the Conference Board counseled that:

> Boards of directors can no longer act as passive advisors for the CEOs who have handpicked them, often in an effort to keep control of the company. Members of corporate boards must take an increasingly active role in fulfilling their fiduciary responsibilities of oversight. They are no longer "window dressing," and they should act effectively to add value to the company.[24]

The *Handbook* annually provides the latest guidance for carrying out these functions in a host of areas, including: selecting director nominees,

---

[24] The Conference Board, *Corporate Governance Handbook 2005* 8 (2005).

director election procedures, ensuring diversification of professional expertise and background, when and how to delegate authority to board committees, how to conduct board meetings, adopting company-specific governance guidelines, planning for CEO succession, setting CEO and other executive compensation, using outside consultants, ensuring that the company has appropriate disclosure procedures and internal controls, conducting general oversight, designing corporate strategy, and managing risk.

The growth of the governance business also has made it possible for boards to draw on corporate governance consultants for firm-specific advice. The National Association of Corporate Directors (NACD), for example, offers company-specific advisory services to boards that are designed to provide "a cost-efficient, customized, and confidential way for your board to review good governance practices, learn more about roles and responsibilities, develop processes, and engage specific committees more effectively."[25] The NACD program is just one of a number of such services accredited by the Institutional Shareholder Services' (ISS) Accredited Director Education Program.

To be sure, violating best practices will not give rise to legal liability. As the Delaware Supreme Court explained in *Brehm v. Eisner*:

> All good corporate governance practices include compliance with statutory law and case law establishing fiduciary duties. But the law of corporate fiduciary duties and remedies for violation of those duties are distinct from the aspirational goals of ideal corporate governance practices. Aspirational ideals of good corporate governance practices for boards of directors that go beyond the minimal legal requirements of the corporation law are highly desirable, often tend to benefit stockholders, sometimes reduce litigation and can usually help directors avoid liability. But they are not required by the corporation law and do not define standards of liability.[26]

---

[25] http://www.nacdonline.org/services/
[26] Brehm v. Eisner, 746 A.2d 244, 256 (Del. 2000). *See also* Report and Recommendations of the Blue Ribbon Committee on Improving the Effectiveness of Corporate Audit Committees 27 (1999) [hereinafter cited as Blue Ribbon Report] (stating that: "It is not the Committee's intention or belief that such additional disclosure requirements [as it recommended] would impose greater liability on the audit committee or full board under state law. Rather the current standards for liability under the business judgment rule—in essence, gross negligence—would continue to apply.").

As statements of best practices became more common and detailed, however, they become part of the behavioral norms directors expect of themselves and their colleagues. Directors thus can be expected to internalize accepted best practices. Hence, the mere existence of such practices should help promote better corporate governance. As Norman Veasey observes, most directors try "to do what is right, what is professional, what is honorable, and what is profitable" most of the time.[27]

In recent years, moreover, core best practices have not been left to reputational sanctions or directors' self-esteem for enforcement. Instead, they have taken on real teeth via ISS's Corporate Governance Quotient. Since 2002, the CGQ has measured "the strengths, deficiencies and overall quality of a company's corporate governance practices and board of directors" at "more than 8,000 companies across 31 countries."[28] Although ISS was founded to provide services to institutional investors, it extensively markets the CGQ to companies:

> Subject companies may, in ISS's words, "use CGQ dynamically to evaluate their governance structures, benchmark their governance performance and conduct peer analysis." The "dynamic" use refers to a subject company's ability to, for a fee, use ISSue Blueprint, a corporate governance analytic tool that allows companies to compare governance standards to peers and against "best practices." Through the web interface, a client company may input various governance changes to test how the change would impact the company's CGQ. Essentially, the client clicks a box indicating that its directors receive annual education and training on their responsibilities, for example, and the CGQ score increases. Combine the roles of chairman and CEO and the CGQ decreases.

> ISS also offers a separate tool for compensation plans—ISSue Compass—which similarly uses a web interface to allow a company the opportunity to test a provision with ISS before submitting it to shareholders for approval in the proxy statement. A client company

---

[27] E. Norman Veasey, *Law and Fact in Judicial Review of Corporate Transactions*, 10 U. Miami Bus. L. Rev. 1, 4 (2002).
[28] http://www.issproxy.com/esg/cgq.html.

can thus know whether or not ISS will support the compensation plan when ISS is asked for its recommendation.[29]

In addition, many consulting firms advertise that they can help managers raise their firm's CGQ score. Because "many of the world's largest and most respected financial institutions have incorporated ISS's CGQ data and ratings into various aspects of their operations" and are using CGQ "as a tool in equity and credit research, to perform risk analysis, manage portfolios, conduct due diligence and support buy/sell decisions,"[30] firms with low CGQ scores can suffer real world costs. Not surprisingly, public corporation directors and officers increasingly tweak their firm's corporate governance rules so as to maximize their CGQ score.

Compensation Practices

One hundred years ago, it was actually illegal to compensate directors for their services as board members. Because most boards at that time consisted mainly of founding entrepreneurs, insiders, or representatives of major shareholders, their members had alternative incentives for good performance. As independent outside directors became more common, however, legislatures and courts recognized that compensation was a necessary incentive. By the mid-1970s, almost all public corporations paid their directors. The amount of director compensation grew rapidly in the following years.[31]

In the mid-1990s, prominent corporate governance expert Charles Elson, who himself served on several boards of directors, began arguing that the prevailing norm of cash compensation failed adequately to incentivize directors. Indeed, he contended that the growing levels of cash compensation actually created perverse incentives:

> Today's director compensation with its emphasis on substantial cash payments and employee-type benefits, including insurance and retirement programs, acts to align the interests of the outside directors with current management rather than with the shareholders,

---

[29] Paul Rose, *The Corporate Governance Industry*, 32 J. Corp. L. 887, 902–3 (2007).

[30] *Corporate Governance Data Plays Critical Role in Fundamental Analysis*, PR Newswire, Sept. 17, 2003.

[31] *See* Elson, *supra* note 9, at 135–48 (tracing history of director compensation practices).

making necessary management oversight an almost impossible task. Why? Because the outside directors are compensated in a way that makes them, in effect, salaried employees of the corporation—or, in reality, the management—rather than the representatives and fiduciaries of the corporation's owners, the stockholders. . . . The message . . . to the director would seem to be not to rock the boat. . . .

. . . . [D]irectors whose remuneration is unrelated to corporate performance have little personal incentive to challenge their management benefactors. Eager not to "bite the hand that feeds them," particularly when such an action may lead to discharge from a lucrative position, it is little wonder that boards have become so passive and subject to management domination.[32]

Elson's solution was to change the form of director compensation:

To ensure that directors will examine executive initiatives in the best interest of the business, the outside directors must become substantial shareholders. To facilitate this, directors' fees should be paid primarily in company stock that is restricted as to resale during their term in office. No other form of compensation, which serves to compromise their independence from management, should be permitted. The goal is to create within each director a personally based motivation to actively monitor management in the best interest of corporate productivity and to counteract the oversight-inhibiting environment that management appointment and cash-based/benefit-laden fees create.[33]

In 1996, a NACD blue ribbon panel adopted many of Elson's ideas, recommending the use of stock-based compensation and further opining that directors should personally invest an amount in company stock sufficiently large so as to decouple the director's financial interests from those of management.[34]

Although few firms have gone so far as to eliminate all cash compensation and benefits, Elson is widely credited with having encouraged a substantial number of firms to provide at least part of director compensation

[32] *Id.* at 162–64.
[33] *Id.* at 165.
[34] National Association of Corporate Directors, Report of the NACD Blue Ribbon Commission on Director Professionalism (1996).

in stock and/or to require directors to hold some specified amount of stock as a qualification for board service. According to a 2007 report by the Conference Board, 90 percent of surveyed companies make some form of stock-based compensation to directors, with 38 percent paying all of part of the basic retainer in stock.[35]

In theory, this change in board compensation practices should align director incentives with the interests of shareholders. Lucian Bebchuk and Jesse Fried, however, claim that the incentives thereby created are minimal:

> Consider, for example, a director who owns 0.005 percent of the company's shares. And suppose that the director is contemplating whether to approve a compensation arrangement requested by the CEO that would reduce shareholder value by $10 million. Given the director's fraction of total shares, the reduction in the value of the director's holdings that would result from approval of the CEO's request would be only $500. Such a cost, or even one several times larger, is highly unlikely to overcome the various factors exerting pressure on the director to support the CEO's request.[36]

Bebchuk and Fried's critique is unpersuasive for several reasons. First, although Bebchuk and Fried elsewhere invoke behavioral research on social and psychological factors in support of various arguments, here they fail to take into account the behavioral research that suggests that most individuals are loss-averse. Because directors are loss-averse, small losses to a director's stock portfolio will have greater psychological weight than small incentives provided by the CEO, all else being equal. Second, Bebchuk and Fried's hypothetical amount of stock ownership, while perhaps not an uncommon level, fails to take into account the possibility that for many directors the shares they own in the company on whose board they serve will constitute a substantial part of that director's net worth. A director who owns $100,000 worth of stock in a corporation with a market float of $1 billion will have considerable incentives to resist even changes that will make a small reduction in the value of those shares if his total portfolio amounts to only $200,000.

---

[35] The Conference Board, *Directors' Compensation and Board Practices in 2006* 6–8 (2007).
[36] Lucian Bebchuk & Jesse Fried, *Pay Without Performance: The Unfulfilled Promise of Executive Compensation* 34 (2004).

Bebchuk and Fried also claim that a director will not oppose shareholder value–destroying projects because the loss from those projects will be less than their annual compensation.[37] But this fails to take into account the effect such projects would have on the director's total portfolio, which in many cases may be a substantial multiple of their annual compensation. The incentives of such directors will be to encourage value-creating projects.

Jeffrey Gordon identifies a more serious concern; namely, that stock-based compensation may create the same sort of perverse incentives for directors that it famously did for the managers of Enron.[38] Importantly, however, much stock-based director compensation takes the form of restricted stock grants rather than stock options. Some economists argue that recipients of restricted stock are less likely to engage in earnings management and other forms of financial fraud than are recipients of stock options.[39] Whether that's true or not, note that stock options only reward their recipients in the event that the stock price goes up. In contrast, holders of restricted stock have the potential not only for upside gains but also downside losses. Because preventing downside losses from materializing is just as much a part of the monitoring job as promoting potential upside gains, restricted stock seems likely to strike the correct incentive balance.

Does compensation matter? A literature review published in 2000 identified five studies providing empirical support for the proposition that increased director stockownership leads to better decision making by directors.[40] Subsequently, a 2005 study found that banks paying a high percentage of compensation in stock exhibited higher performance and growth than competitors emphasizing cash compensation.[41] As such, it seems plausible to conclude that the trend toward paying directors in stock has tended to better align director incentives with shareholder interests. Put another way, paying directors in stock encourages directors to behave in the real world, as the director primacy model predicts.

---

[37] *Id.* at 205.
[38] Gordon, *supra* note 8, at 1488.
[39] *See e.g.,* Natasha Burns & Simi Kedia, *The Impact of Performance-Based Compensation on Misreporting,* 79 J. Fin. Econ. 35 (2006).
[40] R. Franklin Balotti et al., *Equity Ownership and the Duty of Care: Convergence, Revolution, or Evolution?,* 55 Bus. Law. 661, 672–77 (2000) (summarizing studies).
[41] David A. Becher et al., *Incentive Compensation for Bank Directors: The Impact of Deregulation,* 78 J. Bus. 1753 (2005).

Reputational Concerns

Shareholder activist Nell Minow claims that public corporation directors are "the most reputationally sensitive people in the world."[42] Certainly, a reputation as a poor corporate steward adversely affects the director's self-esteem, his or her relationships with peers, and his or her employability with other corporations. Directors thus have strong incentives to care about their reputations. Indeed, directors whose performance is below par have never faced a greater risk of public obloquy than they do today.

David Skeel has identified a number of ways in which so-called shaming sanctions come into play in corporate governance, several of which apply in full measure to the board of directors.[43] First, the "perp walk" beloved of prosecutors not only shames the individual defendants in a given case, but also chills others considering similar misconduct. Second, a criminal conviction subjects defendants to criticism from the bench. Finally, Skeel notes, activist shareholders publicly identify firms and/or individual managers and directors believed to be underperforming. CalPERS' annual focus list of firms alleged to have poor corporate governance is the most famous—and probably most successful—example of this phenomenon. According to Skeel, attention from CalPERS frequently "spurs the companies [on the list] to make immediate changes such as separating the CEO and board chair positions or adding independent directors."

To Skeel's list, we might add the 24/7 media environment. Today, there is "a bigger audience for business news than ever before, and a greater capacity to deliver it."[44] Cable TV networks, newspapers, websites, and blogs provide nonstop coverage. Although this coverage often amounts to cheerleading that creates celebrity CEOs, the post-Enron "drumbeat of revelations of excessive executive pay and perks and forgiven loans, with directors winking at each other or simply looking the other way, has provided sensational grist for the business press."[45] Reputations that took years to construct can now be unmade in moments.

---

[42] David A. Skeel, Jr., *Shaming in Corporate Law*, 149 U. Pa. L. Rev. 1811, 1812 n.3 (2001).
[43] David A. Skeel, Jr., *Corporate Shaming Revisited: An Essay for Bill Klein*, 2 Berkeley Bus. L.J. 105 (2005).
[44] Gregory J. Millman, *No Longer Just Gray: Business Journalism Takes Off*, Fin. Exec., Oct 1, 2006, at 18.
[45] Tom Horton, *Integrity*, Directors & Boards, Jan. 1, 2003, at 10.

Finally, as the leading center of corporation law in the United States, the Delaware courts play an important role in establishing behavioral norms by naming names. As Edward Rock explains:

> Delaware courts generate in the first instance the legal standards of conduct (which influence the development of the social norms of directors, officers, and lawyers) largely through what can best be thought of as "corporate law sermons." These richly detailed and judgmental factual recitations, combined with explicitly judgmental conclusions, sometimes impose legal sanctions but surprisingly often do not. Taken as a whole, the Delaware opinions can be understood as providing a set of parables—instructive tales—of good managers and bad managers, of good lawyers and bad lawyers, that, in combination, fill out the normative job description of these critical players. . . . [T]hese standards of conduct are communicated to managers by corporate counsel, and . . . play an important role in the evolution of (nonlegal) norms of conduct.[46]

Of course, judicial decisions not only help set norms, but also deter misconduct via the threat of legal liability.

The potential seriousness of reputational sanctions is confirmed by a study by Suraj Srinivasan of the University of Chicago School of Business. Srinivasan studied a sample of 409 companies that had restated earnings during the period 1997–2001 to determine whether there was any impact on outside directors. Srinivasan found that director turnover was higher for firms that restated earnings downward and that the likelihood of director turnover increased proportionately with the severity of the restatement. Srinivasan also found that directors of firms that restated their earnings downward tended to lose their board positions at other firms. Srinivasan concluded that the evidence showed that outside directors, especially those who served on the audit committee, experienced significant labor market reputational costs for financial reporting failures.[47]

---

[46] Edward B. Rock, *Saints and Sinners: How Does Delaware Corporate Law Work?*, 44 UCLA L. Rev. 1009, 1016–17 (1997).

[47] Suraj Srinivasan, *Consequences of Financial Reporting Failure for Outside Directors: Evidence from Accounting Restatements and Audit Committee Members*, 43 J. Accounting Research 291 (2005).

Further evidence of reputational effects is provided by a study of uncontested board elections. The authors found that directors attending fewer than 75 percent of board meetings and those receiving negative ISS recommendations receive 14 percent and 19 percent fewer votes, respectively, than their counterparts. Although the authors could not identify direct effects on the reputations of the directors who received reduced votes, at the very least it seems likely that their self-esteem suffers. In any case, reduced votes had several positive effects, including higher CEO turnover, reduced compensation. And removal of poison pills and classified boards.[48]

Judicial Insistence on Informed Decision Making

Until the mid-1980s, so long as they refrained from self-dealing, shareholder litigation held few fears for corporate directors. As Yale law professor Joseph Bishop observed in a widely cited 1968 law review article, "The search for cases in which directors of industrial corporations have been held liable in derivative suits for negligence uncomplicated by self-dealing is a search for a very small number of needles in a very large haystack."[49] In the 1980s, however, the Delaware Supreme and Chancery Courts began to emphasize the need for directors to avail themselves, "prior to making a business decision, of all material information reasonably available to them."[50] As we saw in the previous chapter, where the directors have so availed themselves, judicial review of their decisions and actions is precluded by the duty of care's chief corollary—the business judgment rule. At least in theory, however, where the directors failed to do so, they now faced the prospect of personal monetary liability.

Although the Delaware cases dealing with the nascent duty to be informed were aptly described as "a long-overdue judicial affirmation of

---

[48] Jie Cai et al., *Electing Directors* (May 2007), available at http://papers.ssrn.com/sol3/papers.cfm?abstract_id=910548.

[49] Joseph W. Bishop Jr., *Sitting Ducks and Decoy Ducks: New Trends in the Indemnification of Corporate Directors and Officers*, 77 Yale L.J. 1078, 1099 (1968).

[50] Aronson v. Lewis, 473 A.2d 805, 811 (Del. 1984); *see also* Smith v. Van Gorkom, 488 A.2d 858, 872 (Del. 1985). In addition to an informed decision, there are a number of other preconditions that must be satisfied in order for the business judgment to insulate a board's decisions or actions from judicial review. *See generally* Stephen M. Bainbridge, *Corporation Law and Economics* 270–83 (2002) (discussing preconditions).

the need for better informed directors,"[51] they tended to arise in the context of specific transactions. Hence, for example, directors were expected to gather all reasonably available material information about the company's value when selling the company in a merger or other acquisition. But what about the board's more general oversight role, in which monitoring of management takes place outside the context of a particular transaction?

In the seminal 1996 *Caremark* decision, Delaware Chancellor Allen made clear that the board's duty to be informed extended to its general oversight duties. Specifically, Allen opined that the directors' duty of care includes an affirmative obligation to ensure "that appropriate information will come to [their] attention in a timely manner as a matter of ordinary operations."[52] In *Caremark*, the corporation had no program of internal controls to ensure that the corporation complied with key federal statutes governing its operations. When the corporation ran afoul of one of those statutes and was obliged to pay a substantial fine, a derivative suit was brought against the directors. In reviewing the merits of that claim for purposes of evaluating the settlement, Allen rejected the defendants' argument that "a corporate board has no responsibility to assure that appropriate information and reporting systems are established by management. . . ."[53] Instead, he imposed an affirmative obligation for management and the board to implement systems of internal control. Although Allen's analysis was mere dicta given the procedural posture of the case, the Delaware Supreme Court subsequently affirmed that *Caremark* articulates the necessary conditions for assessing director oversight liability."[54]

In *Guttman v. Huang*, Delaware Vice Chancellor Leo Strine noted that *Caremark* had proven enormously influential and "is rightly seen as a prod towards the greater exercise of care by directors in monitoring their corporations' compliance with legal standards."[55] In that case, Strine applied *Caremark* to allegations that the board of directors had failed adequately to exercise oversight over the company's internal accounting controls, holding that liability might be imposed where there was evidence

---

[51] Krishnan Chittur, *The Corporate Director's Standard of Care: Past, Present, and Future,* 10 Del. J. Corp. L. 505, 543 (1985).

[52] *In re Caremark Int'l Inc. Deriv. Litig.,* 698 A.2d 959, 970 (Del. Ch. 1996).

[53] *Id.* at 969–70.

[54] Stone v. Ritter, 911 A.2d 362, 365 (Del. 2006).

[55] Guttman v. Huang, 823 A.2d 492, 506 (Del. Ch. 2003).

that "the company lacked an audit committee, that the company had an audit committee that met only sporadically and devoted patently inadequate time to its work, or that the audit committee had clear notice of serious accounting irregularities and simply chose to ignore them or, even worse, to encourage their continuation."[56]

Granted, as a practical matter, the liability risk faced by independent directors probably remains low.[57] "Nevertheless the directors' perception of risk seems to have increased over the period, perhaps because of lawyers' exaggerations, perhaps because of scare-mongering by liability insurers, or perhaps because of the saliency of outlier cases like Enron and WorldCom, in which outside directors paid out-of-pocket to settle claims."[58] Accordingly, the fear of litigation encourages boards to establish a "tone at the top" that encourages honesty, integrity, and compliance with legal requirements. In particular, board members are cautioned not to rely passively on management and outside advisors. While board members are not private investigators charged with conducting corporate espionage to detect wrongdoing, they are obliged to make a candid inquiry before accepting the reports they receive from management and outside advisors. As the Delaware Supreme Court observed in *Smith v. Van Gorkom*, the board must "proceed with a critical eye in assessing information" provided by others.[59]

Judicial Pressure for Director Independence

As we've seen, state corporate law mandates no particular board composition. Along with mandating that boards become better informed, however, the evolving common law of corporate governance creates significant incentives for corporations to include a substantial number of independent directors on the board. It has long been the case, for example, that approval of related party and other conflicted interest transactions by vote of a majority of the disinterested and independent directors effectively immunizes such transactions from judicial review— by invoking the defendant-friendly business judgment rule as the standard

---

[56] *Id.* at 507.
[57] *See* Bernard Black et al., *Outside Director Liability*, 58 Stan. L. Rev. 1055 (2006).
[58] Gordon, *supra* note 8, at 1484.
[59] Smith v. Van Gorkom, 488 A.2d 858, 872 (Del. 1985).

of review.[60] In connection with going private transactions initiated by a controlling shareholder, the Delaware Supreme Court called upon boards to create "an independent negotiating committee of its outside directors to deal with [the buyer] at arm's length."[61] Indeed, the Court went on to equate "fairness in this context" to the conduct that might be expected from "a theoretical, wholly independent, board of directors acting upon the matter before them." Similarly, with respect to antitakeover defenses, the court has held that the validity of such defenses is "materially enhanced... where, as here, a majority of the board favoring the proposal consisted of outside independent directors."[62] Taken together with similar decisions in other areas of corporate law, these judicially-created safe harbors provide substantial incentives for both boards and managers to favor director independence.

Sarbanes-Oxley and the Board of Directors

The opening years of the first decade of the twenty-first century were not kind to Wall Street. The stock market ended the year lower for three years running during 2000–2002, which was the first time this had happened since the 1930s. The problem was not just a weak economy, however. During this period, every week seemed to bring new reports of misdeeds at leading U.S. corporations and financial institutions. The now infamous scandal at Enron turned out not to be an isolated case, as news of corporate shenanigans at companies such as WorldCom, Global Crossing, Tyco, Adelphia, and others soon followed.

By mid-2002, Congress decided it was time to clean house. In July 2002, it passed the "Public Company Accounting Reform and Investor Protection Act" of 2002—popularly known as the Sarbanes-Oxley Act or SOX. When President George W. Bush signed the act later that month, he praised it for making "the most far-reaching reforms

---

[60] Puma v. Marriott, 283 A.2d 693 (Del. Ch. 1971). *See also* Marciano v. Nakash, 535 A.2d 400, 405 n.3 (Del. 1987) (opining that "approval by fully-informed disinterested directors under section 144(a)(1)... permits invocation of the business judgment rule and limits judicial review to issues of gift or waste with the burden of proof upon the party attacking the transaction").

[61] Weinberger v. UOP, Inc., 457 A.2d 701, 709 n.7 (Del. 1983).

[62] Moran v. Household Intern., Inc., 500 A.2d 1346, 1356 (Del. 1985).

of American business practices since the time of Franklin Delano Roosevelt."[63]

Although the SOX reforms covered virtually the entire corporate governance waterfront, it's fair to say that empowering boards of directors and insisting that they become more effective were key major goals. As the *Wall Street Journal* said of concomitant corporate governance proposals by the New York Stock Exchange, they "anointed boards of directors, especially 'independent directors' as the capitalist cavalry."[64]

To be sure, SOX itself did relatively little to reform boards of directors. Besides some minor tweaking of rules such as those governing disclosure of stock transactions by directors and so on, the only substantive changes worked by SOX dealt with the audit committee of the board of directors. Instead, Congress and the SEC left the heavy lifting on board reform to the stock exchanges. All three major exchanges—the New York Stock Exchange (NYSE), NASDAQ, and the American Stock Exchange (AMEX)—amended their corporate governance listing requirements to:

- Require that a majority of the members of the board of directors of most listed companies must be independent of management
- Define independence using very strict bright-line rules
- Expand the duties and powers of the independent directors
- Expand the duties and powers of the audit committee of the board of directors

The Majority Independent Board and Its Committees

The NYSE's pre-SOX listing standards treated a director as independent unless, inter alia: (1) the director was employed by the corporation or its affiliates in the past three years; (2) the director had an immediate family member who, during the past three years, was employed by the corporation or its affiliates as an executive officer; (3) the director had a direct business relationship with the company; or (4) the director was a partner, controlling shareholder, or executive officer of an organization that had a business relationship with the corporation, unless the corporation's

---

[63] George W. Bush, *Remarks on Signing the Sarbanes-Oxley Act of 2002* (July 30, 2002), in 38 Weekly Comp. Pres. Doc. 1283, 1284 (Aug. 5, 2002).

[64] Editorial, *The Capitalist Cavalry*, Wall Street Journal, June 7, 2002, at A10 (describing the NYSE committee as "barons of Wall Street").

board determined in its business judgment that the relationship did not interfere with the director's exercise of independent judgment. The NYSE required that all listed companies have at least three such independent directors. In addition, listed companies had to have an audit committee comprised solely of independent directors. The committee had to have at least three members, all of whom were to be "financially literate." At least one committee member had to have expertise in accounting or financial management.

In its post-SOX listing standards, the NYSE now mandates that all listed companies "must have a majority of independent directors."[65] In addition, as we'll see below, the NYSE has mandated the use of several board committees comprised of independent directors. Finally, the NYSE requires that: "To empower non-management directors to serve as a more effective check on management, the non-management directors of each listed company must meet at regularly scheduled executive sessions without management."[66] Although the rule does not indicate how many times per year the outside directors must meet to satisfy this requirement, emerging best practice suggests that there should be such a meeting held in conjunction with every regularly scheduled meeting of the entire board of directors. In fact, most companies—whether NYSE-listed or not—now regularly conduct such sessions. As early as 1996, a Korn/Ferry survey found that the boards of 62 percent of respondents met in executive session at least once a year. By 2003, that figure had risen to "an astounding 87 percent."[67] Two years later, the figure was 94 percent.[68]

The NYSE requires that the identity of the outside director who chairs the mandatory executive sessions must be disclosed in the listed company's Form 10-K. In addition, the Form 10-K or the company's annual proxy statement must include a statement of how interested parties can make concerns known to the outside directors. As a matter of best practice, this requirement should be incorporated into the company's whistleblower policy.

---

[65] NYSE Listed Company Manual § 303A.01. Note that both the NYSE and NASDAQ exempt controlled companies—i.e., those in which a shareholder or group of shareholders acting together control 50 percent or more of the voting power of the company's stock—from the obligation to have a majority independent board.

[66] NYSE Listed Company Manual §303A.03.

[67] *Korn/Ferry Int'l, 30th Annual Board of Directors Study* 5 (2003); *Korn/Ferry Int'l, 24th Annual Board of Directors Study* 21 (1996).

[68] *Korn/Ferry Int'l, 32nd Annual Board of Directors Study* (2005).

Relatedly, in July 2006, the SEC amended its disclosure rules to require disclosure of: (1) whether each director and each person nominated to be nominee is independent of management; (2) any transactions, arrangements, or other relationships considered by the board of directors in determining if an individual satisfied the applicable independence standards; and (3) the names of any members of the audit, nominating, or compensation committees who are not independent.

The NASDAQ and AMEX standards are substantially similar. One wrinkle is that NASDAQ expressly states an expectation that executive sessions of the outside directors will be held at least twice a year.

In addition to imposing new substantive requirements, the post-SOX stock exchange listing standards significantly tightened the definition of director independence. State corporation law traditionally used a rather vague standard to decide whether a given director was independent of management. As one Delaware judicial opinion put it, the question is whether "through personal or other relationships the directors are beholden to" management. In contrast, the new NYSE and NASDAQ listing requirements adopt strict bright-line rules for deciding whether a director is adequately independent to count toward the requisite majority. In addition to the extensive prophylactic rules, the standard generally requires that the board of directors determine that a nominee has no material direct or indirect relationship with the listed company. The NASDAQ and Amex rules are substantially similar.

The third major set of post-SOX changes are statutory and stock exchange requirements for board committees. State corporation law allows a board of directors to establish committees to which some board powers may be delegated, although a number do so only on an opt-in basis pursuant to which committee formation must be authorized by the articles of incorporation or the bylaws. Section 141(c)(2) of the Delaware General Corporation Law, for example, provides that the board may set up one or more committees consisting of one or more members. The jurisdiction and powers of the committee must be specified in either the bylaws or the board resolution creating the committee. The board may delegate all of its powers and authority to such committees, except that board committees are barred from acting on matters requiring shareholder approval or changes to the bylaws. Beyond this, however, state corporation law codes do not mandate formation of any specific committees or set out rules on committee composition.

In contrast, SOX required all the stock exchanges to adopt a listing standard that in turn required all listed companies to have an audit committee. The NYSE went even further by also mandating the establishment of a Nominating and Corporate Governance Committee and a Compensation Committee.

NYSE Listed Company Manual § 303A.04 requires that listed companies set up "a nominating/corporate governance committee composed entirely of independent directors." The Committee must have a written charter specifying how it will go about identifying candidates for board membership and selecting those candidates to be nominated. The Committee should have sole power to select headhunters and negotiate their fees.

NASDAQ gives companies an alternative. Under Marketplace Rule 4350(c), new directors must be nominated either by a majority of the independent directors or a nominating committee comprised solely of independent directors. Both the NYSE and NASDAQ exempt companies in which a shareholder or group of shareholders acting together control 50 percent or more of the voting power of the company's stock from the nominating committee requirement.

In addition to nominating director candidates, many companies assign responsibility for selecting new CEOs to the nominating committee. In cooperation with the compensation committee, the nominating committee may take the lead in negotiating the terms of a newly appointed CEO's employment agreement. Finally, the nominating committee may be tasked with setting director compensation, although many firms assign that job to the compensation committee.

Note that the NYSE listing requirement includes "corporate governance" as part of the nominating committee's job. This aspect of the committee's duties remains poorly defined. In general, however, the intent seems to be that the nominating committee should serve as the board of directors' principal point of contact with shareholders. As a practical matter, one common task given this committee is the assignment of directors to other board committees (typically subject to approval by the entire board).

The nominating power is vitally important. Board of director elections usually look a lot like old Soviet elections—there is only one slate of candidates and the authorities know how each voter voted. Absent the very unusual case of a proxy contest, in which a dissenting shareholder puts forward an alternative slate of director candidates, the slate nominated by the outgoing board of directors will be reelected by default.

Corporate reformers long complained that boards simply rubber stamped the CEO's choices of new director candidates. Having a separate committee of independent directors who are in charge of the nomination process should weaken the CEO's grip on power. James Westphal and Edward Zajac demonstrated that as board power increases relative to the CEO—measured by such factors as the percentage of insiders and whether the CEO also served as chairman—newly appointed directors become more demographically similar to the board.[69]

The second major new committee is the compensation committee, which is tasked with reviewing and approving (or recommending to the full board) the compensation of senior executives and generally oversees the corporation's compensation policies. Proponents of a separate compensation committee that deals with such matters, rather than the board as a whole, argue that inside directors, even if recused from considering their own compensation, cannot objectively evaluate the compensation of other senior executives in light of the close relationship between one executive's compensation and that of another.

Under NYSE Listed Company Manual § 303A.05, the board of directors of all listed companies must have a compensation committee. The committee must be comprised solely of independent directors. Only listed companies in which a shareholder or group of shareholders acting together own 50 percent or more of the stock are exempt from this requirement.

The NYSE also tweaked the definition of director independence to prevent the oft-complained-about problem of compensation committee interlocks. Specifically, the NYSE definition of "independent director" excludes a "director or an immediate family member [who] is, or has been within the last three years, employed as an executive officer of another company where any of the listed company's present executive officers at the same time serves or served on that company's compensation committee." Suppose, for example, that Jane is a director of Ajax Corporation. Jane is also the CFO of Zeus Corporation. Donna is Ajax's CLO (a.k.a. general counsel), a member of Zeus' board of directors, and a member of Zeus' compensation committee. Under the NYSE rule, because Donna is on Zeus' compensation committee, Jane cannot be deemed an independent director of Ajax. Donna can be deemed an

---

[69] James D. Westphal & Edward J. Zajac, *Who Shall Govern? CEO/Board Power, Demographic Similarity, and New Director Selection*, 40 Admin. Sci. Q. 60 (1995).

independent director of Zeus, however, because the interlock rule runs in only one direction.

The NYSE also requires that the compensation committee adopt a written charter setting out the committee's purpose, responsibilities, and powers. At a minimum, the compensation committee must have power to:

- Set performance goals for the CEO, evaluate the CEO's performance in light of those goals, and set the CEO's pay. If the board wishes, the compensation committee may simply recommend a pay figure for the CEO—the appropriateness of which would then be decided by all the independent directors. Notice that, in either case, only independent directors are involved in setting the CEO's salary.
- Make recommendations to the board of directors with respect to the pay of other executive officers and any incentive or stock-based compensation plans that are subject to board approval.
- Produce a compensation committee report on executive officer compensation, to be included in the listed company's annual proxy statement or annual report on Form 10-K.

It's become quite common for companies to get advice from consultants in setting executive pay. The NYSE expects that the charter will vest the power to hire, fire, and compensate such consultants in the compensation committee rather than the CEO.

As with its provisions on the nominating committee, the NASDAQ rule on compensation gives firms the option of establishing a separate compensation committee or having senior executive compensation set by a majority of the independent directors on the board. In either case, the rule forbids the CEO from being present during voting or deliberations. NASDAQ allows the company to appoint a single non-independent board member to the compensation committee (for a period of up to two years), so long as the company discloses why it believes doing so is in the company's interest. Again, both the NYSE and NASDAQ exempt from the compensation committee rules a company that has a shareholder or group of shareholders acting together that own more than 50 percent of the voting power of the company's equity securities.

Effective July 2006, the SEC began requiring a "Compensation Committee Report" in which the company states whether the compensation committee has discussed the Compensation Discussion and Analysis (CD&A) disclosures with management and whether the committee recommended that the CD&A be included in the company's annual Form 10-K and its proxy statement.

An influential report by former SEC Chairman Richard Breeden to the WorldCom board of directors, in which he made numerous recommendations for improving WorldCom's corporate governance, provides an overview of emerging best practices for compensation committees:

- Pertaining to committee membership: Breeden recommended that the committee "consist of not less than three members, each of whom should be an independent director who possesses experience with compensation and human resources issues."
- Pertaining to meeting requirements: The committee should meet not less than four times per year to evaluate the performance of the CEO and other top management. At least once a year, the committee should get a training session on how to evaluate executive performance and otherwise comply with its various duties.
- Pertaining to compensation consultants: Any outside consultants should be hired and fired by the committee, which also should have sole power to set the consultant's pay.
- Pertaining to turnover: To prevent the committee members from getting too cozy with management, there should be regular turnover of the committee membership. In particular, the chair of the committee should rotate at least once every three years.
- Pertaining to compensation committee compensation: The pay of committee members should be high enough to encourage them to devote substantial effort to their duties. For WorldCom, Breeden recommended that Committee members receive at least $35,000 per year and the chairman receive at least $50,000 per year.
- Pertaining to oversight: "At least twice each year the Compensation Committee should meet with the Director of Human Resources and the General Counsel to review (i) compliance with the Company's prohibitions against any related party transactions between directors or employees and their families and the Company or any of its affiliates; (ii) compliance with SEC proxy disclosure standards; and (iii) all employee complaints, disputes or issues regarding human resources or compensation issues."[70]

---

[70] www.thedirectorscollege.com/images/downloads/Breeden%20Report%20Restoring%20Trust.pdf.

Do all these new rules matter? A study by Cornell University economists found that corporate compliance with the SOX compensation rules was causally linked to a significant decrease in CEO compensation, suggesting that the rules in fact are resulting in board members who are becoming more effective.[71]

Finally, we come to the centerpiece of the post-SOX changes in the board of directors; namely, the audit committee. The data contained in a corporation's financial statements are the market's best tool for evaluating how well a firm's managers perform. But because management prepares the financial statements, how can the market trust those statements to represent fairly and accurately the company's true financial picture? Would managers really tell the truth if it meant losing their jobs?

To ensure that the financial statements are accurate and complete, the SEC requires corporations to have those statements audited by an independent firm of certified public accountants. In order to keep management and the outside auditor from getting too cozy with one another, it's long been good practice for the corporation's board of directors to have an audit committee. Ideally, the audit committee provides a forum for independent directors to discuss the firm's financial results outside of management's presence and ensures that the audited financial statements fairly and accurately represent the company's financial picture.

Enron, WorldCom, and the various other scandals of 2000–2002, especially those involving former Big 6 accounting firm Arthur Andersen, demonstrated that there were serious problems with all of the key players: management, the outside auditor, and the board of directors and its audit committee. The wave of restated financials in 2001–2002 confirmed that there were basic, widespread problems with the financial disclosures provided by many companies. Congress, the SEC, and the stock exchanges struck back in various ways.

When Sarbanes-Oxley was under consideration by Congress, a consensus quickly formed in favor of imposing a tougher version of the NYSE requirements on all public corporations. SOX § 301 therefore ordered the SEC to adopt rules requiring that the stock exchanges and

---

[71] Vidhi Chhaochharia & Yaniv Grinstein, *CEO Compensation and Board Structure* (Nov. 2006), available at http://icf.som.yale.edu/pdf/seminar06-07/GRINSTEIN.PDF.

NASDAQ adopt listing requirements mandating the creation by listed companies of audit committees that met the following specifications:

- Pertaining to committee responsibilities: The audit committee is responsible for appointing, compensating, and supervising the company's outside auditor. The outside auditor "shall report directly to the audit committee." The committee also must resolve "disagreements between management and the auditor regarding financial reporting."
- Pertaining to independence: All members of the audit committee must be independent, which § 301 defines as barring the committee member from being an "affiliated person" of the company and from accepting any "consulting, advisory, or other compensatory fee" from the company except for directors' fees.
- Pertaining to whistleblowers: The audit committee must establish procedures for handling complaints about the way the company conducts its accounting, internal audit controls, and outside audits. The procedure must include a mechanism for "the confidential, anonymous submission by employees . . . of concerns regarding questionable accounting or auditing matters."
- Pertaining to the hiring of advisors: In addition to empowering the audit committee to hire and pay the outside auditor, the company also must empower the committee to hire "independent counsel and other advisors, as it determines necessary to carry out its duties," with the outside advisor's fees paid by the company.

These reforms were effected mainly through changes in the stock exchange listing standards. For example, new NYSE Listed Company Manual § 303A.06 says that each listed company must have an audit committee. Unlike the nominating and compensation committee requirements, even companies with a controlling shareholder must comply with the audit committee rules.

In § 303A.07, the NYSE sets out additional committee requirements. The committee must have at least three members. (Note that a growing number of firms are appointing as many as five individuals to the audit committee so as to help to allocate the heavy workload imposed on this committee's members.) All committee members must be independent, both as defined in SOX § 301 and the NYSE Listed Company Manual. All committee members must be "financially literate" and at least one

member "must have accounting or related financial management expertise." It's left up to the company's board of directors to decide what that
means and whether the members qualify. The audit committee must
have a written charter specifying its duties, role, and powers. The committee is charged with oversight of "(1) the integrity of the listed company's financial statements, (2) the listed company's compliance with
legal and regulatory requirements, (3) the independent auditor's qualifications and independence, and (4) the performance of the listed company's internal audit function and independent auditors." The committee
must prepare an annual report on the audit process to be included in the
company's annual proxy statement. The audit committee must establish
procedures for receiving and dealing with complaints "regarding
accounting, internal accounting controls, or auditing matters" and set
up a process for confidential, anonymous submission by employees "of
concerns regarding questionable accounting or auditing matters."
(Because of this requirement, many companies assign responsibility for
oversight of their compliance programs generally to the audit committee.
Firms that chose not to do so, typically so as to avoid overloading the
audit committee's members with work, commonly assign this task to the
Nominating and Corporate Governance committee.) The audit committee must have the power to engage independent counsel and other
advisors and to pay such advisors. The committee must have the power
to set the compensation of the outside auditor. At least once a year, the
committee must receive a report from the outside auditor on the adequacy of the company's internal controls. The committee is to review the
company's annual and quarterly disclosure reports, specifically including the MD&A section, as well as the financial statements. The committee
is to review earnings announcements and other guidance provided ana-
lysts. The committee must meet periodically in executive session with
both the company's internal and outside auditors. The committee must
review any disagreements between management and the auditors. The
NASDAQ rules are less detailed but substantially similar to the NYSE
provisions.

According to the Conference Board, in 2006 98 percent of the surveyed companies had an audit committee. The median number of audit
committee meetings per year was seven. Ninety-four percent had a
compensation committee. Sixty-three percent had a nominating committee. Forty-six percent had a separate corporate governance committee. The median number of annual meetings for each of the last three

(compensation committees, nominating committees, and corporate governance committees) was four.[72]

Is an Independent Board Essential for Director Primacy?

Even before SOX and the concomitant stock exchange listing standard changes mandated that most public companies have a majority independent board, the ratio of independent-to-inside directors had been shifting toward the former for decades as a result of the pressures we identified above. In his important article, *The Rise of Independent Directors in the United States*, Jeffrey Gordon provides the following data that show the steady decline in the mean percentage of insiders who serve on public company boards:[73]

Year	Mean percentage of inside directors	Decade-to-decade % change
1950	49%	n/a
1955	47%	
1960	43%	−12%
1965	42%	
1970	41%	−5%
1975	39%	
1980	33%	−20%
1985	30%	
1990	26%	−21%
1995	21%	
2000	16%	−38%

Jeffrey N. Gordon, The Rise of Independent Directors in the United States, 1950-2005: Of Shareholder Value and Stock Market Prices, 59 Stanford Law Review 1465, 1473 n.9 (2007). Used by Permission.

---

[72] Conference Board, *supra* note 35, at 23, 29.
[73] Gordon, *supra* note 8. According to a 1990 Conference Board survey, the number of manufacturing companies having a majority of nonemployee directors increased from 63% in 1966, to 71% in 1972, to 86% in 1989. The trend for nonmanufacturing companies was less dramatic, but probably only because they started from a higher base, moving from 85% in 1966, to 86% in 1972, to 91% in 1989. The Conference Board, *Membership and Organization of Corporate Boards* (1990).

Gordon further illustrated the shift graphically in the following figure:

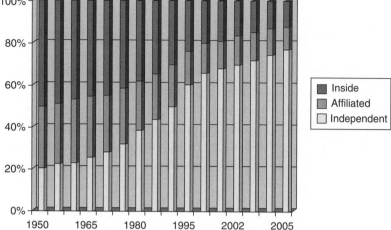

Figure 3 Board Composition from 1950 to 2004 (smoothed)
Source: Jeffrey N. Gordon, The Rise of Independent Directors in the United States, 1950–2005: Of Shareholder Value and Stock Market Prices, 59 Stanford Law Review 1465 (2007).

As Figure 3 suggests, the trend toward board independence continued post-2000. Indeed, today it is common at many companies for the CEO to be the only insider on the board of directors.[74] Thirty percent of surveyed companies had an outsider serving as Chairman of the Board, moreover, while 48 percent had a lead independent director with specified leadership duties.[75]

Is the modern supermajority independent board more likely to behave as the corporation's Platonic master than the insider-dominated boards of yesteryear? At first blush, one might assume that the answer to that question ought to be an affirmative one. Yet, on close examination, the problem turns out to be quite difficult to answer. Two functions of independence are especially relevant to the analysis: providing interlocks and constraining agency costs.

---

[74] A Conference Board survey found that in 2006 the median number of directors at the surveyed public manufacturing companies was nine, eight of whom were outsiders. Conference Board, *supra* note 35, at 35.
[75] *Id.* at 33.

Interlocks and Decision Making. Independent directors might not be necessary—indeed, might be a detriment—in a world of perfectly loyal managers. An executive committee comprised of full-time senior employees would seem to have the advantages of group decision making combined with the obvious informational advantages insiders possess over a board comprised of outsiders who devote but a small portion of their time and effort to the firm. The former's decisions are much more likely to be informed ones than are those made by the latter.[76]

More subtly, and perhaps more importantly, long-term employees make significant investments in firm-specific human capital. Any employee who advances to senior management levels necessarily invests considerable time and effort in learning how to do his job more effectively. Much of this knowledge will be specific to the firm for which he works. The longer he works for the firm, moreover, the more firm-specific his human capital becomes. Such an employee is likely to make better decisions for the firm than an outsider, even assuming equal levels of information relating to the decision at hand. The insider can put the decision in a broader context, seeing the relationships and connections it has to the firm as whole.

This analysis implicates our argument that the board of directors is best understood as a collegial body using consensus-based decision making. Recall that Arrow demonstrated that consensus works only where team members have equal information and comparable interests. Insiders are more likely to have comparable access to information and similar interests than are disparate outsiders. Among other things, insiders have many informal contacts with one another, which promotes team formation and provides additional access to information. Hence, in Arrow's model, consensus decision making should work best in insider-dominated boards.

On the other hand, putting outside directors on the board creates value by providing interlocks with a variety of potential strategic partners. This is relevant not only to the board's resource gathering function, but also to its monitoring and service functions. Complex business decisions can call for knowledge in many areas, some relatively arcane.

---

[76] At the minimum, the presence of outsiders on the board increases decision-making costs simply because the process takes longer. Outsiders by definition need more information and are likely to take longer to persuade than are insiders. Michael P. Dooley and E. Norman Veasey, *The Role of the Board in Derivative Litigation: Delaware Law and the Current ALI Proposals Compared*, 45 Bus. Law. 503, 533 (1989).

Providing access to such knowledge can be seen as part of the board's resource gathering function. Board members may either possess such knowledge themselves or have access to credible external sources thereof. Specialization of this sort is a rational response to bounded rationality. The expert in a field makes the most of his limited capacity to absorb and master information by limiting the amount of information that must be processed and (concomitantly) the breadth of the field in which he specializes. As applied to the corporate context, more diverse boards likely contain more specialists, and therefore should get greater benefits from specialization.

Independence and Agency Costs. The conventional justification for director independence is grounded in agency cost economics. Recall, however, that the very centralization of management making possible the large corporation also introduces the potential for agency costs. Corporate law therefore provides a series of accountability mechanisms designed to constrain agency costs. Chief among them is the board of directors, especially the independent directors. To be sure, outsiders have neither the time nor the information necessary to be involved in the minutiae of day-to-day firm management. What outsiders can do, however, is to monitor senior managers and replace those whose performance is sub-par. Hence the emphasis on the board's monitoring role in the taxonomy of board functions.

If independent directors effectively constrain agency costs, however, there should be an identifiable correlation between the presence of outsiders on the board and firm performance. Yet, the empirical data on this issue are decidedly mixed. Some early studies found such correlations. Stuart Rosenstein and Jeffrey Wyatt, for example, found that shareholder wealth increased when independent directors were appointed.[77] Michael Weisbach studied board decisions to remove a CEO and found that boards comprised mainly of independent directors were more likely to base the removal decision on poor performance, as well as more likely to remove an under-performing CEO, than were insider-dominated boards.[78] He also found that CEO removals by outsider-dominated boards added to firm value, whereas CEO removals by insider-dominated boards

[77] Stuart Rosenstein & Jeffrey G. Wyatt, *Outside Directors, Board Independence, and Shareholder Wealth*, 26 J. Fin. Econ. 175 (1990).
[78] Michael S. Weisbach, *Outside Directors and CEO Turnover*, 20 J. Fin Econ. 431 (1988).

did not. Barry Baysinger and Henry Butler found that corporate financial performance tends to increase (up to a point) as the percentage of independent directors increases.[79] James Cotter found that boards dominated by outsiders generate higher shareholder gains from tender offers.[80]

Other studies, however, are to the contrary. A well-known report by Paul MacAvoy, for example, found that board composition had no effect on profitability.[81] April Klein likewise found little evidence of a general association between firm performance and board composition, but found a positive correlation between the presence of insiders on board finance and investment committees and firm performance.[82] A meta-analysis of numerous studies in this area concluded that there was no convincing evidence that firms with a majority of independent directors outperform other firms.[83] It further concluded that there is some evidence that a "moderate number" of insiders correlates with higher performance. Another meta-analysis reported at about the same time (1998) likewise found no evidence that board composition affects financial performance.[84] Finally, a 2007 literature review concluded that "the econometric research on whether independent directors enhance financial performance for the shareholders is, at best, inconclusive."[85] The authors of that survey also conducted their own study of 254 public companies in 50 industry sectors and found no evidence that "it makes any difference at all to shareholders' financial return whether a board has a higher or lower percentage of independent directors."[86]

---

[79] Barry D. Baysinger & Henry N. Butler, *Revolution Versus Evolution in Corporation Law: The ALI's Project and the Independent Director*, 52 Geo. Wash. L. Rev. 557, 572 (1984).

[80] James F. Cotter et al., *Do Independent Directors Enhance Target Shareholder Wealth During Tender Offers?*, 43 J. Fin. Econ. 195 (1997). *See also* Bernard S. Black, *The Value of Institutional Investor Monitoring: The Empirical Evidence*, 39 UCLA L. Rev. 895, 900 (1992) (asserting that boards with a majority of independent directors make better acquisition decisions, citing an unpublished study by John Byrd and Kent Hickman).

[81] Paul MacAvoy, et al., *ALI Proposals for Increased Control of the Corporation by the Board of Directors*, in *Statement of the Business Roundtable* on the American Law Institute's Proposed "Principles of Corporate Governance and Structure: Restatement and Recommendations" C-1 (Feb. 1983).

[82] April Klein, *Firm Performance and Board Committee Structure*, 41 J.L. & Econ. 275 (1998).

[83] Sanjai Bhagat & Bernard Black, *The Uncertain Relationship Between Board Composition and Firm Performance*, 54 Bus. Law. 921, 922 (1999).

[84] Dan R. Dalton et al., *Meta-Analytic Reviews of Board Composition, Leadership Structure, and Financial Performance*, 19 Strategic Mgmt. J. 269 (1998).

[85] Eric M. Fogel & Andrew M. Geier, *Strangers in the House: Rethinking Sarbanes-Oxley and the Independent Board of Directors*, 32 Del. J. Corp. L. 33, 35 (2007).

[86] *Id.* at 52.

Another survey further complicated the empirical landscape by effectively splitting the baby. John Wagner and his coauthors' meta-analysis of 63 correlations found a U-shaped curve. While increasing the number of outsiders on the board was positively associated with higher firm performance, increasing the number of insiders on the board had the same effect. A second meta-analysis confirmed that greater board homogeneity was positively associated with higher firm performance, which is not what standard theory would predict.[87]

If independent directors are not effective monitors of senior management, why might that be the case? One obvious answer is that shirking is an endemic problem. Monitoring the performance of the firm's officers and employees is hard, time-consuming work. Moreover, most outside directors have full-time employment elsewhere, which commands the bulk of their attention and provides the bulk of their pecuniary and psychic income. Independent directors therefore may prefer leisure or working on their primary vocation to monitoring management. A 1911 British decision, describing the selection of a rubber corporation's board, provides an amusing anecdote illustrating the problem:

> The directors of the company, Sir Arthur Aylmer Bart., Henry William Tugwell, Edward Barber and Edward Henry Hancock were all induced to become directors by Harboard or persons acting with him in the promotion of the company. Sir Arthur Aylmer was absolutely ignorant of business. He only consented to act because he was told the office would give him a little pleasant employment without his incurring any responsibility. H.W. Tugwell was partner in a firm of bankers in a good position in Bath; he was seventy-five years of age and very deaf; he was induced to join the board by representations made to him in January, 1906. Barber was a rubber broker and was told that all he would have to do would be to give an opinion as to the value of rubber when it arrived in England. Hancock was a man of business who said he was induced to join by seeing the names of Tugwell and Barber, whom he considered good men.[88]

---

[87] John A. Wagner et al., *Board Composition and Organizational Performance: Two Studies of Insider/Outsider Effects*, 35 J. Mgmt. Stud. 655 (1998).
[88] *In re Brazilian Rubber Plantations & Estates Ltd.*, [1911] 1 Ch. 425.

Hence, as Adam Smith observed three centuries ago:

> The directors . . . being the managers rather of other people's money
> than of their own, it cannot well be expected, that they should watch
> over it with the same anxious vigilance with which the partners in
> a private co-partnery frequently watch over their own. Like the
> stewards of a rich man, they are apt to consider attention to small
> matters as not for their master's honour, and very easily give them-
> selves a dispensation from having it. Negligence and profusion,
> therefore, must always prevail, more or less, in the management of
> the affairs of such a company.[89]

Other factors impede an independent director from monitoring management, even if he wishes to do so. Board meetings meet more often and for
longer periods today, but meetings generally still are few and short.[90]
Moreover, outside directors still are generally dependent upon management for information.

Worse yet, nominally independent directors may be effectively
controlled by the insiders. It long was common practice, for example, for
a corporation's outside directors to include lawyers and bankers (of both
the investment and commercial varieties) who were concurrently providing services to the corporation or might have wished to provide services
subsequently. The new, tougher definitions of independence imposed by
the stock exchanges eliminated the worst of these abuses. Yet, there are
still loopholes. University faculty or administrators, for example, may be
beholden to insiders who control corporate donations to their home
institutions.

Even if the independent directors are not actually biased in favor of
the insiders, they often are predisposed to favor them. Most of the learning on this phenomenon, known as structural bias, has arisen in connection with the use of special litigation committees (SLCs) to terminate
shareholder derivative litigation against officers or directors. Outside
directors tend to be corporate officers or retirees who share the same
views and values as the insiders.[91] A sense of "there but for the grace of

---

[89] Adam Smith, *The Wealth of Nations* 700 (Modern Library ed. 1937).
[90] Telman, *supra* note 1, at 860.
[91] *See* Joy v. North, 692 F.2d 880, 888 (2d Cir. 1982); George W. Dent, Jr., *The Power of Directors to Terminate Shareholder Litigation: The Death of the Derivative Suit*, 75 Nw. U. L. Rev. 96, 111–13 (1980).

God go I" therefore is said to be a likely response to litigation against fellow directors.[92]

Query, however, whether the derivative litigation context is really all that special. All outside directors—not just those who serve on SLCs—are nominated by the incumbent board members and passively elected by the shareholders, which supposedly biases the selection process toward directors whose cooperation and support the incumbents can count on. As such, if purportedly independent directors are likely to favor their fellow directors when the latter are sued, they are equally likely to do so in any conflict of interest situation. Consider, for example, the hostile take-over context. According to a survey taken during the "merger mania" days of the 1980s, over 50 percent of responding companies believed they were possible takeover targets, 45 percent had been the subject of takeover rumors, and 36 percent had experienced unusual or unexplained trading activity.[93] Where a nominally independent director's principal occupation is serving as an officer of another corporation, the "there but for the grace of God go I" syndrome again rears its head. Despite his being an outsider, fears for his own firm may often render an independent director sympathetic to insiders' job security concerns when a hostile takeover threatens the firm.[94]

To be sure, the potential for shirking and bias easily can be overstated. Not all directors are biased—actually or structurally—and the annals of corporate law are replete with instances in which seemingly biased directors nevertheless did the right thing. Better still, as we have seen, independent directors have affirmative incentives to actively monitor management and to discipline poor managers. If the company fails on the independent directors' watch, for example, their reputation and thus their future employability are likely to suffer.

As such, we might expect majority independent boards to have their greatest impact during crisis situations. A study by Tod Perry and Anil Shivdasani supports that possibility. They examined the relationship

---

[92] See, e.g., Zapata Corp. v. Maldonado, 430 A.2d 779, 787 (Del. 1981).

[93] S. Rep. No. 265, 100th Cong., 1st Sess. 79 (1987) (additional views of Sens. Sasser, Sanford & Chaffee).

[94] See Dynamics Corp. v. CTS Corp., 794 F.2d 250, 256 (7th Cir. 1986) ("No one likes to be fired, whether he is just a director or also an officer. The so-called outsiders moreover are often friends of the insiders."), rev'd on other grounds, 481 U.S. 69 (1987); see generally Michael P. Dooley & E. Norman Veasey, The Role of the Board in Derivative Litigation: Delaware Law and the Current ALI Proposals Compared, 44 Bus. Law. 503, 534 (1989) ("the structural bias argument has no logical terminus").

between board composition and restructuring activities in a sample of 94 firms that had experienced a material decline in performance. Corporations with a majority independent board proved to be more likely to initiate asset restructurings and employee layoffs than firms without a majority of outside directors. They further found that corporations with majority independent boards experienced subsequent improvements in operating performance after a restructuring.[95]

All of which leads to a logical question; namely, would an insider-dominated board be effective in carrying out the board's monitoring role? Eugene Fama contends that lower level managers commonly monitor more senior managers.[96] Such upstream monitoring, however, does not take full advantage of specialization. Fama and Michael Jensen elsewhere point out that one response to agency costs is to separate "decision management"—initiating and implementing decisions—from "decision control"—ratifying and monitoring decisions.[97] As we've seen, such separation is a defining characteristic of the central office typical of M-form corporations. In particular, the central office's key decision makers—the board of directors and top management—specialize in decision control. Because low- and mid-level managers specialize in decision management, expecting them to monitor more senior managers thus asks them to perform a task for which they are poorly suited.

A different critique of Fama's hypothesis is suggested by evidence on the subject of meeting behavior garnered from research on group decision making. In mixed-status groups, higher-status members talk more than lower-status members. Managers, for example, talk more than subordinates in business meetings.[98] Such disparities result in higher-status group members being more inclined to propound initiatives and having greater influence over the group's ultimate decision.

One function of the board of directors thus is providing a set of status equals for top managers.[99] As such, corporate law's insistence on

---

[95] Tod Perry & Anil Shivdasani, *Do Boards Affect Performance? Evidence from Corporate Restructuring,* 78 J. Bus. 1403 (2005).

[96] Eugene Fama, *Agency Problems and the Theory of the Firm,* 88 J. Pol. Econ. 288, 293 (1980).

[97] Eugene F. Fama and Michael C. Jensen, *Separation of Ownership and Control,* 26 J.L. & Econ. 301, 315 (1983).

[98] Sara Kiesler & Lee Sproul, *Group Decision Making and Communication Technology,* 52 Org. Beh. & Human Decision Processes 96 (1992).

[99] Robert J. Haft, *The Effect of Insider Trading Rules on the Internal Efficiency of the Large Corporation,* 80 Mich. L. Rev. 1051, 1061 (1982) (describing the board as "a peer group—a collegial body of equals, with the chief executive as the prima inter pares).

the superiority of the board to management makes sense even with respect to insider-dominated boards. To the extent law shapes social norms, admittedly a contested proposition, corporate law may empower the board to constrain top management more effectively by creating a de jure status relationship favoring the board. Interestingly, note that the status effect of board membership may be especially important with respect to insider-dominated boards. Because subordinate managers have ample opportunity to monitor the CEO's effectiveness but are constrained by status relationships from acting on their knowledge, board membership might empower them to act.

Finally, although monitoring is an important board function, one easily can overstate the argument that there is something problematic about board protection of insider interests. Oliver Williamson in fact suggests that one of the board's functions is to "safeguard the contractual relation between the firm and its management."[100] Insider board representation may be necessary to carry out that function. Many adverse firm outcomes are beyond management's control. If the board is limited to monitoring management, and especially if it is limited to objective measures of performance, however, the board may be unable to differentiate between acts of God, bad luck, ineptitude, and self-dealing. Insiders' greater knowledge and firm-specific human capital would help them make such distinctions. Under such conditions, a variety of adverse outcomes may result. Risk-averse managers may demand a higher return, for example. Alternatively, managers may reduce the extent of their investments in firm-specific human capital, so as to minimize non-diversifiable employment risk.

Insider representation on the board, in turn, will encourage learned trust between insiders and outsiders. Insider representation on the board thus provides the board with a credible source of information necessary to accurate subjective assessment of managerial performance. If the CEO is the only insider on the board, the CEO will have significant information advantages over other board members. Inclusion of additional insiders may tend to offset that information asymmetry by providing outsiders with access to status-empowered alternative sources of information. In addition, however, insider representation also serves as a bond between the firm and the top management team. Insider directors presumably will

---

[100]   Oliver E. Williamson, *The Economic Institutions of Capitalism* 298 (1985).

look out for their own interests and those of their fellow managers. Board representation thus offers some protection against dismissal for adverse outcomes outside management's control.

At this point in our review of the debate, the reader may be thinking of Harry Truman's famous plea for a "one-handed economist." Jeffrey Gordon, however, recently capped an exhaustive review of the literature by advancing a plausible explanation for the ambiguous nature of the evidence:

> The strongest explanation is the diminishing marginal returns hypothesis: most of the empirical evidence assesses incremental changes in board independence in firms where there is already substantial independence and after the cultural entrenchment of norms of independent director behavior. But ... the most important effects of the move to independent directors, particularly over the long term, are systematic rather than firm specific and thus are unlikely to show up in cross-sectional studies. One systematic effect, the lock-in of shareholder value as virtually the exclusive corporate objective, could have benefits for early adopters, but other effects, such as the facilitation of accurate financial disclosure and corporate law compliance, have principally external effects.[101]

Even so, the takeaway lesson remains that one size does not fit all, which should not be surprising. On one side of the equation, firms do not have uniform needs for managerial accountability mechanisms. The need for accountability is determined by the likelihood of shirking, which in turn is determined by management's tastes, which in turn is determined by each firm's unique culture, traditions, and competitive environment. We all know managers whose preferences include hard, faithful work. Firms where that sort of manager dominates the corporate culture have less need for outside accountability mechanisms.

On the other side of the equation, firms have a wide range of accountability mechanisms from which to choose. Independent directors are not the sole mechanism by which management's performance is monitored. Rather, as we have seen, a variety of forces work together to encourage boards to function effectively and/or to constrain shirking by managers: the capital and product markets within which the firm functions;

---

[101]   Gordon, *supra* note 8, at 1505–6 (footnote omitted).

the internal and external markets for managerial services; the market for corporate control; incentive compensation systems; auditing by outside accountants; and many others. The importance of the independent directors' monitoring role in a given firm depends in large measure on the extent to which these other forces are allowed to function. For example, managers of a firm with strong takeover defenses are less subject to the constraining influence of the market for corporate control than are those of a firm with no takeover defenses. The former needs a strong independent board more than the latter does.

The critical mass of independent directors needed to provide optimal levels of accountability also will vary depending upon the types of outsiders chosen. Strong, active independent directors with little tolerance for negligence or culpable conduct do exist. A board having a few such directors is more likely to act as a faithful monitor than is a board having many nominally independent directors who shirk their monitoring obligations.

The Bottom Line: Are Boards Becoming More Effective?

At the end of the day, director primacy is a theory about what boards do, not about who sits on them. Performance is what matters, not composition. Accepting Gordon's argument as well taken, the trend toward supermajority independent boards may well be a particularly important factor in uplifting corporate governance performance. As we have seen, moreover, there are other factors—reputation, fear of liability, best practices, and so on—that incent both insiders and outsiders to behave as Platonic masters.

The trouble is that the boardroom has been aptly called "an empirical black box."[102] Research on boards therefore tends to be dominated by efforts to link various structural or demographic characteristics to financial performance or other metrics, such as CEO turnover. Although we've seen evidence from such studies supporting the claims of director primacy, our analysis of the debate over the merits of director independence illustrates that the data from such studies sometimes prove inconclusive.

---

[102] David O'Donnell & Philip O'Regan, *Exploring Critical Dialogue in the Boardroom: Getting Inside the Empirical Black Box of Board Dynamics* (March 2006), available at http://papers.ssrn.com/sol3/papers.cfm?abstract_id=900967.

Having said that, there is a substantial body of evidence that boards of directors are becoming far more effective than were their predecessors, even though there remains room for improvement. Studies of post-SOX boards of directors find that average board size has increased, presumably because companies are adding more independent directors rather than replacing incumbent insiders. Conversely, the average number of companies on whose boards a director sits has gone down, presumably because boards and committees meet more often and have to process more information. The amount of time required for board service has especially gone up for members of audit committees, who have a host of new duties. Overall, "[t]he average commitment of a director of a U.S. listed company increased from 13 hours a month in 2001 to 19 hours in 2003 (and then fell to 18 hours in 2004)."[103]

Additional evidence is provided by Michael Useem and Andy Zelleke's survey of governance practices. They found that boards of directors increasingly view delegation of authority to management as properly the subject of careful and self-conscious decision making. The surveyed board members acknowledged that they do not run the company on a day-by-day basis, but rather are seeking to provide stronger oversight and supervision. Increasingly, boards are establishing written protocols to allocate decision-making rights between the board and management, although the protocols vary widely, ranging from detailed and comprehensive to skeletal and limited in scope. Useem and Zelleke conclude that executives still set much of the board's decision-making agenda. At the same time, they found that boards are increasingly asserting their sovereignty in recent years and that a norm is emerging among managers that, at the very least, they must be mindful of what information boards want to hear and what decisions directors believe the board should make.[104]

As the Useem and Zelleke study indicates, a critical test of director primacy is board access to information. Indirect evidence that independent directors now have good access to information is provided by a study of their trading results. The authors found that independent directors earn substantial positive abnormal returns when trading in their corporation's stock. Even more interestingly, the difference between their results and those of the same firm's executive officers is relatively small, although

---

[103] Robert F. Felton, *A New Era in Corporate Governance*, McKinsey Q., 2004 No.2, 28, 60.
[104] Michael Useem & Andy Zelleke, *Oversight and Delegation in Corporate Governance: Deciding What the Board Should Decide*, 14 Corp. Gov.: An Int'l Rev. 2 (2006).

it widens in firms with weaker governance regimes.[105] It seems reasonable to infer from this evidence that outsiders now have pretty good access to material information about firm performance; indeed, that their access to such information is comparable to that of executive officers.

The bottom line is that modern boards of directors typically are smaller than their antecedents, meet somewhat more often, are more independent from management, own more stock, and have somewhat better access to information. Are there still supine boards? Yes. But is real world practice closer to the director primacy model than it was in earlier periods? Yes.

---

[105] Enrichetta Ravina & Paola Sapienza, *What Do Independent Directors Know? Evidence from Their Trading* (December 2006), available at http://ssrn.com/abstract=928246.

CHAPTER 5

The Future of Corporate Governance: Director or

Shareholder Primacy

Although managerialism remains director primacy's principal competitor as a descriptive model, it no longer has much traction with either academics or policy makers as a normative theory of corporate governance. Instead, shareholder primacy is the dominant normative model at present. As Chancellor Allen famously claimed, "the shareholder franchise is the ideological underpinning upon which the legitimacy of directorial power rests."[1]

Some such understanding of shareholder voting rights presumably motivates the many recent efforts to extend the shareholder franchise. The major stock exchanges, for example, have implemented new listing standards expanding the number of corporate compensation plans that must be approved by shareholders.[2] As of this writing, the SEC is still at least nominally considering a proposal to permit shareholders, under limited circumstances, to nominate directors and have their nominees listed in the company's proxy statement and on its proxy card.[3] A number of states have amended their corporation code to allow majority voting—rather

---

[1] Blasius Indus., Inc. v. Atlas Corp., 564 A.2d 651, 659 (Del. Ch. 1988).

[2] New York Stock Exchange, Listed Company Manual § 3.12.

[3] Security Holder Director Nominations, Exchange Act Release No. 48,626 (October 14, 2003).

than the traditional plurality vote—in the election of directors, which has prompted some investors to use SEC Rule 14a-8 to propose amendments to corporate bylaws requiring a majority vote in the election of directors.

This chapter will argue that director primacy—not shareholder primacy—ought to be the future of corporate governance. Specifically, it argues that shareholder primacy is flawed both as a positive and as a normative account of corporate governance. Accordingly, efforts to extend the shareholder franchise are fundamentally misguided. In public corporations of the sort with which we are concerned, shareholder voting has very little to do with corporate decision making. To the contrary, as we have seen, the separation of ownership and control observed in such firms is inherent in the basic structure of the law of corporate governance.

The statutory framework thus poses two puzzles. First, why do shareholders—and only shareholders—get the vote? We addressed that question in Chapter 1. Second, why are shareholder voting rights so limited? Answering that question is the task of this chapter, as is making the argument that shareholder rights should remain limited.

Shareholders Are Rationally Apathetic

A rational shareholder will expend the effort to make an informed decision only if the expected benefits of doing so outweigh its costs. Given the length and complexity of proxy statements, especially in a proxy contest where the shareholder is receiving multiple communications from the contending parties, the opportunity cost entailed in reading the proxy statements before voting is quite high and very apparent. Shareholders also probably do not expect to discover grounds for opposing management from the proxy statements. Finally, most shareholders' holdings are too small to have any significant effect on the vote's outcome. Accordingly, shareholders can be expected to assign a relatively low value to the expected benefits of careful consideration.

Shareholders thus traditionally proved to be rationally apathetic. For the average shareholder, the necessary investment of time and effort in making informed voting decisions simply was not worthwhile. Instead, shareholders traditionally adopted the aforementioned Wall Street Rule; namely, it's easier to switch than fight. To the extent the shareholders were satisfied, they voted for management. Disgruntled shareholders sold their shares. As a result, shareholders were likely to vote for management even where that was not the decision an informed shareholder would reach.

Does the assumption of shareholder apathy continue to hold, however, given the rise of institutional investors? Since the early 1990s, various commentators have argued that institutional investor corporate governance activism was becoming an important constraint on agency costs in the corporation.[4] Institutional investors, they argue, approach corporate governance quite differently from individual investors. Because institutions typically own larger blocks than individuals, and have an incentive to develop specialized expertise in making and monitoring investments, the former should play a far more active role in corporate governance than dispersed shareholders. Institutional investors' greater access to information, coupled with their concentrated voting power, should enable them to more actively monitor the firm's performance and to make changes in the board's composition when performance lagged. Corporations with large blocks of stock held by institutional investors thus might reunite ownership of the residual claim and ultimate control of the enterprise. As a result, concentrated ownership in the hands of institutional investors might lead to a reduction in shirking and, hence, a reduction in agency costs.

Institutional Passivity

In the early 1990s, it seemed likely that shareholder activism might eventually become an important factor in corporate governance. Institutional investors increasingly dominated U.S. equity securities markets. They also began to play a somewhat more active role in corporate governance than they had in earlier periods: taking their voting rights more seriously and using the proxy system to defend their interests. They began voting against takeover defenses proposed by management and in favor of shareholder proposals recommending removal of existing defenses. Many institutions also no longer routinely voted to reelect incumbent directors. Less visibly, institutions influenced business policy and board composition through negotiations with management. But while there seemed little

---

[4]   See, e.g., Mark J. Roe, *Strong Managers, Weak Owners: The Political Roots of American Corporate Finance* (1994); Bernard S. Black, *Shareholder Passivity Reexamined*, 89 Mich. L. Rev. 520 (1990).

doubt that institutional investor activism could have effects at the margins, the question remained whether the impact would be more than merely marginal.

By the end of the 1990s, the answer seemed to be no. A comprehensive 1998 survey found relatively little evidence that shareholder activism mattered.[5] Even the most active institutional investors spent only trifling amounts on corporate governance activism. Institutions devoted little effort to monitoring management; to the contrary, they typically disclaimed the ability or desire to decide company-specific policy questions. They rarely conducted proxy solicitations or put forward shareholder proposals. They did not seek to elect representatives to boards of directors. They rarely coordinated their activities. Most importantly, the review found "no strong evidence of a correlation between firm performance and percentage of shares owned by institutions."[6]

A more recent literature review analyzed empirical studies measuring "short-term stock market reactions to announcement of shareholder initiatives, longer-term stock market and operating performance, outcomes of votes on shareholder proposals, and changes in corporate strategy and investment decisions in response to activism."[7] According to the review, event studies of shareholder proposals and announcements of other forms of shareholder activism generally found no statistically significant abnormal returns to shareholders, although some studies of various subsamples did find significant returns. The review also reports that results of long-term performance studies have been "mixed," but virtually all such studies find no statistically significant changes in operating performance.[8]

Today, although conventional wisdom is to the contrary, institutional investor activism in fact remains rare. It is principally the province of union and state and local public employee pension funds. But while these investors' activities generate considerable press attention, they can hardly be said to have reunited ownership and control. Indeed, the extent to which even public pension funds engage in shareholder activism varies widely. Much public pension fund activism, moreover, takes the form of

[5]   Bernard S. Black, *Shareholder Activism and Corporate Governance in the United States*, in *The New Palgrave Dictionary of Economics and the Law* 459 (1998).
[6]   *Id.* at 462.
[7]   Stuart L. Gillian & Laura T. Starks, *The Evolution of Shareholder Activism in the United States* 18 (undated), available at http://ssrn.com/abstract=959670.
[8]   *Id.* at 26–27.

securities fraud litigation rather than corporate governance activities. Most funds have demonstrated little interest in such core governance activities as nominating directors or making shareholder proposals. [9]

To be sure, activism by hedge and private equity funds often is identified as an important exception to the general rule of shareholder apathy. A recent study by Robin Greenwood confirms the growing impact of such funds:

> [B]etween 1994 and 2006, the number of public firms targeted for poor performance by hedge funds grew more than 10-fold.
>
> More importantly, hedge funds may be up to the task of monitoring management—a number of recent academic papers have found that hedge funds generate returns of over 5 percent on announcement of their involvement, suggesting that investors believe these funds will increase the value of the firms they target.[10]

But do these funds generate value by effecting governance or operational change? Greenwood argues that hedge fund managers generally are poorly suited to making operational business decisions and, with their short-term focus, are unlikely "to devote time and energy to a task delivering long-term value. After all, there are no guarantees that the effort will pay off, or that other shareholders would recognize the increase in value by paying a higher price per share."

Instead, hedge funds profit mainly through transactions in corporate control, rather than corporate governance activism. Private equity funds like KKR long have been active acquirers. In the 1980s, for example, KKR was the famously prevailing barbarian at the gate in the fight over RJR Nabisco.[11] More recently, however, private equity acquisitions have simply exploded. The dollar value of announced private equity deals went from less than $50 billion in the first quarter of 2003 to $400 billion in the second quarter of 2007.[12] A mid-2007 credit crunch put the brakes on private equity deals, but long-term fundamentals continue to favor an active role for private equity in the market for corporate control.

---

[9] Stephen J. Choi & Jill E. Fisch, *On Beyond CalPERS: Survey Evidence on the Developing Role of Public Pension Funds in Corporate Governance* (2007), available at http://ssrn.com/abstract=1010330.

[10] Robin Greenwood, *The Hedge Fund as Activist*, HBR Working Knowledge, Aug. 22, 2007.

[11] Bryan Burrough & John Helyar, *Barbarians at the Gate: The Fall of RJR Nabisco* (1990).

[12] Grace Wong, *Buyout Firms: Pain Today, Gain Tomorrow*, CNNMoney.com. Sept. 27, 2007.

In other cases, the private equity firm seeks not to acquire the target company, but rather to put it into play so as to profit on its stake when someone else buys the target. If the target is successfully put into play, the stock price runs up, attracting arbitragers and other short-term speculators who then put intense pressure on management to cut a deal. The private equity firm that started the ball rolling can then sell its shares at a substantial premium. In some cases, private equity holding shares in the target also may actively intervene in a pending deal by refusing to support the deal or threatening litigation unless the price and/or other important terms are improved.[13]

Conversely, where the private equity firm holds shares in a potential acquirer, it may seek to prevent the deal from happening at all. A successful bidder typically pays a premium of 30 to 50 percent, sometimes even higher, over the pre-bid market price of the target's stock. Consequently, target shareholders demonstrably gain substantially—on the order of hundreds of billions of dollars—from takeovers.[14] In contrast, studies of acquiring company stock performance report results ranging from no statistically significant stock price effect to statistically significant losses.[15] By some estimates, bidders overpay in as many as half of all takeovers. Being aware of this risk, private equity holders have sometimes tried to block the acquirer from going forward.[16]

Greenwood argues that a preference for control rather than governance activism makes sense because "hedge funds are better at identifying undervalued companies, locating potential acquirers for them, and removing opposition to a takeover."[17] His hypothesis was confirmed by his study of over 1,000 cases of hedge fund activism, which found that "targets of investor activism earn high returns only for the subset of events in which the activist successfully persuades the target to merge or get acquired." As a result, neither hedge nor private equity funds seem

[13] See, e.g., Marcel Kahan & Edward B. Rock, Hedge Funds in Corporate Governance and Corporate Control, 155 U. Penn. L. Rev. 1021, 1037–39 (2007) (citing examples).

[14] See, e.g., Bernard S. Black & Joseph A. Grundfest, Shareholder Gains from Takeovers and Restructurings Between 1981 and 1986, J. Applied Corp. Fin., Spring 1988, at 5; Gregg A. Jarrell et al., The Market for Corporate Control: The Empirical Evidence Since 1980, 2 J. Econ. Persp. 49 (1988); Michael C. Jensen & Richard S. Ruback, The Market for Corporate Control: The Scientific Evidence, 11 J. Fin Econ. 5 (1983).

[15] See, e.g., Julian Franks et al., The Postmerger Share-Price Performance of Acquiring Firms, 29 J. Fin. Econ. 81 (1991).

[16] Kahan & Rock, supra note 13, at 1034–37 (citing examples).

[17] Greenwood, supra note 10.

plausible candidates for being the ultimate solution to the principal-agent problem inherent in the public corporate form. Instead, they merely offer an alternative form: the private company.

Why Are Institutions Passive?

One should not be surprised that most institutions appear to be just as apathetic as individual shareholders. In the first place, there are significant legal barriers to shareholder activism. As we've seen, for example, in corporation law, shareholder control rights in fact are so weak that they scarcely qualify as part of corporate governance. As we also saw, corporation law's direct restrictions on shareholder power are supplemented by a host of other rules that indirectly prevent shareholders from exercising significant influence over corporate decision making.

Even in the absence of such legal barriers, however, the economic realities would continue to disfavor shareholder activism. Because institutional investors generally are profit maximizers, they will not engage in an activity whose costs exceed its benefits. Even ardent proponents of institutional investor activism therefore concede that institutions are unlikely to be involved in day-to-day corporate matters. Instead, they are likely to step in only where there are serious long-term problems. On the benefit side of the equation, corporate governance activism is unattractive because in many cases activism is unlikely to be availing. In some cases, intervention will come too late. In others, the problem may prove intractable, as where technological changes undercut the firm's competitive position.

Turning to the cost side of the equation, because it is impossible to predict ex ante which corporations are likely to experience such problems, activist institutions will be obliged to monitor all of their portfolio firms. Because corporate disclosures rarely give one a full picture of the corporation's prospects, moreover, additional and more costly monitoring mechanisms must be established.

In any case, monitoring costs are just the price of entry for activist institutions. Once they identify a problem firm, steps must be taken to address the problem. In some cases, it may suffice for the activist institution to propose some change in the rules of the game, but less tractable problems will necessitate more extreme remedial measures, such as removal of the incumbent board of directors.

In public corporations with dispersed ownership of the sort under debate here, such measures necessarily require the support of other shareholders, which makes a shareholder insurrection against inefficient but entrenched managers a costly and difficult undertaking. Putting together a winning coalition will require, among other things, ready mechanisms for communicating with other investors. As noted, however, SEC rules on proxy solicitations, stock ownership disclosure, and controlling shareholder liabilities have long impeded communication and collective action, and continue to do so despite the 1992 SEC rule amendments that somewhat lowered the barriers to collective action.

Even where gains might arise from activism, only a portion of the gains would accrue to the activist institutions, for the reasons discussed above. As a result, free riding is highly likely. In a very real sense, the gains resulting from institutional activism are a species of public goods. They are costly to produce, but because other shareholders cannot be excluded from taking a pro rata share, they are subject to a form of nonrivalrous consumption. As with any other public good, the temptation arises for shareholders to free ride on the efforts of those who produce the good.

Granted, if stock continues to concentrate in the hands of large institutional investors, there will be marginal increases in the gains to be had from activism and a marginal decrease in its costs. A substantial increase in activism seems unlikely to result, however. Most institutional investors compete to attract either the savings of small investors or the patronage of large sponsors, such as corporate pension plans. In this competition, the winners generally are those with the best relative performance rates, which makes institutions highly cost-conscious. Given that activism will only rarely produce gains, and that when such gains occur they will be dispensed upon both the active and the passive, it makes little sense for cost-conscious money managers to incur the expense entailed in shareholder activism. Instead, they will remain passive in hopes of free riding on someone else's activism. As in other free riding situations, because everyone is subject to and likely to yield to this temptation, the probability is that the good in question—here shareholder activism—will be underproduced.

In addition, corporate managers are well-positioned to buy off most institutional investors that attempt to act as monitors. Bank trust departments are an important class of institutional investors, but are unlikely to emerge as activists because their parent banks often have or anticipate commercial lending relationships with the firms they will purportedly monitor. Similarly, insurers "as purveyors of insurance products, pension plans, and other financial services to corporations, have reason to mute their corporate governance activities and be bought off."[18] Mutual fund families whose business includes managing private pension funds for corporations are subject to the same concern.

This leaves us with union and state and local pension funds, which in fact generally have been the most active institutions with respect to corporate governance issues.[19] Unfortunately for the proponents of institutional investor activism, as we'll see below, these are precisely the institutions most likely to use their position to self-deal—i.e., to take a non-pro rata share of the firms assets and earnings—or to otherwise reap private benefits not shared with other investors.

Vehicles for Shareholder Activism

In the preceding section, we examined the general barriers to shareholder activism. In the sections that follow, we examine specific vehicles for shareholder activism. Shareholders have a number of ways of making demands on the boards of directors and managers of their portfolio companies. Some are provided by legal rules, such as the ability to conduct proxy contests and to put certain proposals on the ballot. Others are extra-legal, such as the shaming of boards and managers perceived as poor performers. Ultimately, of course, most depend on the fact that shareholders—and only shareholders—possess the corporate franchise. As we'll see, most also have proven ineffective.

Exit

Selling one's shares is the simplest form of shareholder activism. It also can be quite effective, as "empirical studies provide evidence that the act of selling shares can have disciplinary effects on companies that lead to changes in governance. For example, the probabilities of CEOs being fired and replaced by executives from outside the firm are higher after large sell-offs by institutional investors."[20]

---

[18] Roe, *supra* note 4, at 62.

[19] *See* Randall S. Thomas & Kenneth J. Martin, *Should Labor Be Allowed to Make Shareholder Proposals?*, 73 Wash. L. Rev. 41, 51–52 (1998).

[20] Gillian & Starks, *supra* note 7, at 5–6.

Proxy Contests

Shareholders normally vote only at meetings, called (logically enough) shareholder meetings. All statutes require that there be at least one shareholder meeting a year (called, logically enough, the annual meeting of shareholders). In addition, all statutes have some provision for so-called special meetings—i.e., meetings held between annual meetings, typically to consider some extraordinary matter. In either case, most shareholders will not attend the meeting in person. Instead, most shareholders vote by proxy.

In the usual case, only the incumbent board of directors solicits proxies and the board's recommendations almost always receive overwhelming support from the shareholders. Occasionally, however, a shareholder (often called an insurgent) may solicit proxies in opposition to the board-nominated slate (a so-called election contest). Alternatively, the insurgent may solicit proxies in opposition to some proposal made by the board (a so-called issue contest). In either case, the process is doubled. Both sides independently prepare proxy cards and proxy statements that are separately sent to the shareholders.

Henry Manne famously described proxy contests as "the most expensive, the most uncertain, and the least used of the various techniques" for acquiring corporate control.[21] A would-be insurgent's obstacles are legion. Various state statutes permit corporations to adopt measures—so-called shark repellents—making it more difficult for an insurgent to gain control of the board of directors via a proxy contest. Among the more important of these are classified boards, the elimination of cumulative voting, and dual class stock plans. Other impediments include management's informational advantages and investor perceptions that proxy insurgents are not serious contenders for control.

The critical obstacle, however, typically is money. Proxy contests are enormously expensive. Any serious contest requires the services of lawyers, accountants, financial advisers, printers, and proxy solicitors. Even incidental costs, such as mailing expenses, mount up very quickly when one must communicate (usually several times) with the thousands of shareholders in the typical public corporation.

---

[21] Henry G. Manne, *Mergers and the Market for Corporate Control*, 73 J. Pol. Econ. 110, 114 (1965).

In theory, incumbent directors do not have unbridled access to the corporate treasury. In practice, however, incumbents rarely pay their own expenses. Under state law, the board of directors may use corporate funds to pay for expenses incurred in opposing the insurgent, provided the amounts are reasonable and the contest involves policy questions rather than just a "purely personal power struggle."[22] Only the most poorly advised of incumbents find it difficult to meet this standard. The board merely needs have its lawyers parse the insurgent's proxy materials for policy questions on which they differ.

In contrast, insurgents have no right to reimbursement out of corporate funds. Rather, an insurgent will be reimbursed only if an appropriate resolution is approved by a majority of both the board of directors and the shareholders.[23] If the incumbents prevail, of course, they are unlikely to look kindly on an insurgent's request for reimbursement of expenses.

The rules on reimbursement of expenses take on considerable importance when coupled with the rules on standing in proxy litigation. In *J. I. Case Co. v. Borak*,[24] the U.S. Supreme Court held that proxy claims under § 14(a) are both direct and derivative in nature. Consequently, *Borak* gives management standing to sue the insurgent in the corporation's name.[25]

As a practical matter, the incumbent board thus has another weapon with which to fend off insurgent shareholders. If the Supreme Court had treated proxy litigation as direct in nature, only shareholders would have standing to sue for violations of the proxy rules. Although the board still could bring suit against the insurgent, it would have to do so in the directors' individual capacities as shareholders. As such, they could not use firm resources to finance the litigation. Because the firm is permitted to sue in its own name for violations of the proxy rules, however, the board can use the firm's deep pockets to pay for legal expenses incurred in such suits. In contrast, because of the rules on reimbursement of expenses, the insurgent's litigation costs come out of its own pocket.

Given the rules governing expenses, the proxy contest thus is highly unattractive as a vehicle for shareholder activism. Instead, most proxy

---

[22] Rosenfeld v. Fairchild Engine & Airplane Corp., 128 N.E.2d 291 (1955), reh'g denied, 130 N.E.2d 610 (1955).

[23] Steinberg v. Adams, 90 F. Supp. 604 (S.D.N.Y. 1950); Grodetsky v. McCrory Corp., 267 N.Y.S.2d 356 (Sup. Ct. 1966).

[24] 377 U.S. 426 (1964).

[25] Studebaker Corp. v. Gittlin, 360 F.2d 692 (2d Cir. 1966).

contests occur in conjunction with an effort by a prospective buyer to obtain control of the target corporation. In fact, empirical studies indicate that only proxy contests that trigger a liquidation or sale of the company increase shareholder value,[26] suggesting that the proxy contest is more properly viewed as a tool in the market for corporate control rather than as a vehicle for shareholder activism.

Withholding One's Votes in Director Elections

One of the curiosities of the corporate electoral system is that it does not actually provide for a straight up or down—for or against—vote for directors. Instead, one either grants authority to the proxy agent to vote for the specified candidates or one withholds authority for the agent to do so.[27] Withholding one's support does not have the same effect as a vote against the candidate. Delaware General Corporation Law § 216(3) formerly provided, for example, that "Directors shall be elected by a plurality of the votes of the shares present in person or represented by proxy at the meeting and entitled to vote on the election of directors." The Comments to Model Business Corporation Act § 7.28(a), which also used a "plurality" standard, explain that: "A 'plurality' means that the individuals with the largest number of votes are elected as directors up to the maximum number of directors to be chosen at the election."

In the 2004 shareholder revolt at The Walt Disney Company, for example, the board of directors had eleven vacancies to be filled and there were exactly eleven candidates. Under the plurality standard, so long as the holder of at least one share granted the proxy agents authority to vote for, say, CEO Michael Eisner, Eisner would have been reelected even if a majority had withheld authority for their shares to be voted for him. In effect, withholding authority amounts to abstaining.

The Disney episode is instructive because the campaign had a central organizing figure—Roy Disney—with a private motivation for challenging the incumbents. Disney management later persuaded Roy Disney to drop his various lawsuits against the board and sign a five year standstill

---

[26] Lynn A. Stout*The Mythical Benefits of Shareholder Control*, Regulation, Spr. 2007, at 42, 45.

[27] Under SEC Rule 14a-4(b), the company must give shareholders three options on the proxy card: vote for all of the nominees for director, withhold support for all of them, and withhold support from specified directors by striking out their names.

agreement pursuant to which he would not run an insurgent slate of directors in return for being named a Director Emeritus and consultant to the company, which nicely illustrates how a company can buy off the requisite central coordinator when that party has a private agenda.[28]

Nonetheless, although the insurgent shareholders failed either to unseat Eisner or even to deny him a majority, their efforts triggered considerable interest in changing the traditional plurality standard. In 2006, Delaware amended the statutory provisions on director election to accommodate majority voting. Section 141(b) of the Delaware General Corporation Law was amended by adding the following sentence: "A resignation [of a director] is effective when the resignation is delivered unless the resignation specifies a later effective date or an effective date determined upon the happening of an event or events. A resignation which is conditioned upon the director failing to receive a specified vote for reelection as a director may provide that it is irrevocable." This amendment was designed to validate bylaws that had been voluntarily adopted by a number of companies, most notably Pfizer, pursuant to which directors who received a majority of withhold "votes" are required to submit their resignation to the board.

Section 216 was amended by adding the following sentence: "A bylaw amendment adopted by stockholders which specifies the votes that shall be necessary for the election of directors shall not be further amended or repealed by the board of directors." This amendment validates bylaw provisions requiring that a director receive a majority vote in order to be elected. As of late 2006, more than 250 companies—including 31 percent of Fortune 500 firms—had adopted some form of majority voting bylaw.[29]

Critics of majority voting schemes contend that failed elections can have a destabilizing effect on the corporation. Selecting and vetting a director candidate is a long and expensive process, which has become even more complicated by the new stock exchange listing standards defining

---

[28] *Roy Disney, Gold Agree to Drop Suits*, Corp. Gov. Rep. (BNA), August 1, 2005, at 86. In contrast, in 2004, when CalPERS struck out on its own, withholding its shares from being voted to elect directors at no less than 2,700 companies, including Coca-Cola director and legendary investor Warren Buffet, the project went nowhere. *See* Dale Kasler, *Governor's Plan Could Erode CalPERS Clout*, Sac. Bee, Feb. 28, 2005, available on Westlaw at 2/28/05 SACRAMENTOBEE A1.

[29] William J. Sjostrom, Jr. & Young Sang Kim, *Majority Voting for the Election of Directors* (Feb. 24, 2007), available at http://papers.ssrn.com/sol3/papers.cfm?abstract_id=962784.

director independence. Suppose, however, that the shareholders voted out the only qualified financial expert sitting on the audit committee. The corporation immediately would be in violation of its obligations under those standards.

Critics also complain that qualified individuals will be deterred from service. The enhanced liability and increased workload imposed by Sarbanes-Oxley and related regulatory and legal developments has made it much harder for firms to recruit qualified outside directors. The risk of being singled out by shareholders for a "no" vote presumably will make board service even less attractive, especially in light of the concern board members demonstrate for their reputations.

Finally, critics claim that, at least as it is being implemented so far, majority voting is "little more than smoke and mirrors." William Sjostrom and Young Sang Kim conducted an event study of firms adopting some form of majority vote bylaw. They found no statistically significant market reaction to the adoption.[30] The implication is that the campaign for majority voting has created little shareholder value.

Shareholder Proposals

Under SEC Rule 14a-8, a shareholder-proponent who has owned at least 1 percent or $2,000 (whichever is less) of a public corporation's voting securities for at least one year, may submit a proposal and supporting statement—collectively not to exceed 500 words—for inclusion in the company's proxy statement and on its card. Absent Rule 14a-8, there would be no vehicle for shareholders to put proposals on the firm's proxy statement. Shareholders' only practicable alternative would be to conduct a proxy contest in favor of whatever proposal they wished to put forward. The chief advantage of the shareholder proposal rule, from the perspective of the proponent, thus is that it is cheap. The proponent need not pay any of the printing and mailing costs, all of which must be paid by the corporation, or otherwise comply with the expensive panoply of regulatory requirements.

Shareholder proposals traditionally were used mainly by social activists. Prior to the end of apartheid in South Africa, for example, many

---

[30] William K. Sjostrom, Jr. & Young Sang Kim, *Majority Voting for the Election of Directors* (Working Paper Series, 2007), available at http:// ssrn.com/abstract=962784.

proposals favored divestment from South Africa. The rule is still widely used by social activists, but the rule also is increasingly being used by institutional investors to press matters more closely related to corporate governance. In recent years, such proposals have addressed such topics as repealing takeover defenses, confidential proxy voting, regulating executive compensation, and the like.

In 2006, for example, a group of Bally Total Fitness shareholders put forward a proposal under Rule 14a-8 to amend Bally's corporate bylaws to allow shareholders the right to remove the company's Chief Executive Officer and President by the affirmative vote of a majority of the company's outstanding stock, to prevent the board of directors from acting unilaterally to amend the new bylaw provision, and to remove the incumbent CEO Paul Toback from office. In the same proxy season, shareholders at over 60 companies offered bylaw amendments that would require directors to be elected by a majority of shareholder votes rather than the present plurality system.

Activists relying on Rule 14a-8 face a number of obstacles. The rule contains several procedural rules, such as deadlines for submission, that are rigorously enforced. More important, there are a number of substantive grounds on which a proposal may be excluded from the proxy statement. Where the corporation's board or management believes that the proposal violates one of those exclusions, either may request SEC authorization to omit the proposal from the proxy statement.

Two of the substantive grounds for excluding a proposal are especially significant for shareholder activists. First, SEC Rule 14a-8(i)(1) provides that a shareholder proposal must be a proper subject of action for security holders under the law of the state of incorporation. Under state law, all corporate powers shall be exercised by or under the authority of the board.[31] Consequently, state corporate law commits most powers of initiation to the board of directors. The shareholders may not initiate corporate actions; they may only approve or disapprove of corporate actions placed before them for a vote. The SEC's explanatory note to Rule 14a-8(i)(1) recognizes this aspect of state law by explaining that mandatory proposals may be improper. The note goes on, however, to explain the SEC's belief that a shareholder proposal generally is proper if phrased as a request or recommendation to the board. As a result, most proposals

---

[31] *See, e.g.,* DGCL § 141(a).

are phrased in precatory language that will not bind the board of directors even if the proposal receives a majority vote of the shareholders.[32] Rule 14a-8(i)(1) thus leaves shareholder proposals mostly toothless as a tool for activists.

Shareholder amendments to the bylaws may constitute an exception to the general rule that proposals cannot mandate board action. The corporation's initial bylaws are adopted by the incorporator or the initial directors at the corporation's organizational meeting. At early common law, only shareholders had the power to amend the bylaws. Many states thereafter adopted statutes allowing shareholders to delegate the power to amend the bylaws to the board of directors. Delaware General Corporation Law (DGCL) § 109(a) typifies this approach. It provides that only shareholders have the power to amend bylaws, unless the articles of incorporation expressly confer that power on the board of directors. An article provision authorizing the board to amend the bylaws, moreover, does not divest the shareholders of their residual power to amend the bylaws.

DGCL § 109(b) imposes an important limitation on the otherwise sweeping scope of permissible bylaws:

> The bylaws may contain any provision, not inconsistent with law or with the certificate of incorporation, relating to the business of the corporation, the conduct of its affairs, and its rights or powers or the rights or powers of its stockholders, directors, officers or employees.

A bylaw that relates only to a specific business decision probably is invalid under § 109(b), as an improper intrusion on the board's exclusive power to make ordinary business decisions. Broader, more fundamental bylaws, especially ones that impose constraints rather than order the board to take action, however, pose a more difficult set of problems. If valid under state law, a mandatory shareholder proposal to adopt such a bylaw presumably could not be excluded under Rule 14a-8(i)(1). The legality of such bylaws under state corporate law is sharply contested, however.

A critical issue here is whether shareholder-adopted bylaws may limit the board of directors' discretionary power to manage the corporation. There is an odd circularity in the Delaware code with respect to this issue.

---

[32] If a precatory proposal passes, the board is not obligated to implement it. Indeed, a board decision not to do so should be protected by the business judgment rule. On the other hand, the risk of adverse publicity and poor shareholder relations may encourage a board to implement an approved precatory proposal even where the board opposes the proposal on the merits.

On the one hand, DGCL § 141(a) provides that "[t]he business and affairs of every corporation organized under this chapter shall be managed by or under the direction of a board of directors." A bylaw that restricts the board's managerial authority thus seems to run afoul of DGCL § 109(b)'s prohibition of bylaws that are "inconsistent with law." On the other hand, DGCL § 141(a) also provides that the board's management powers are plenary "except as may be otherwise provided in this chapter." Does an otherwise valid bylaw adopted pursuant to § 109 squeeze through that loophole?

In *Teamsters v. Fleming Companies*,[33] the Oklahoma Supreme Court upheld a bylaw limiting the board of directors' power to adopt a poison pill. The bylaw provided:

> The Corporation shall not adopt or maintain a poison pill, shareholder rights plan, rights agreement or any other form of 'poison pill' which is designed to or has the effect of making acquisition of large holdings of the Corporation's shares of stock more difficult or expensive . . . unless such plan is first approved by a majority shareholder vote. The Company shall redeem any such rights now in effect.

The board argued that shareholders could not adopt a bylaw imposing such mandatory limitations on the board's discretion. The court rejected that argument. Absent a contrary provision in the articles of incorporation, shareholders therefore may use the bylaws to limit the board's managerial discretion.

Although the relevant Oklahoma and Delaware statutes are quite similar, there are suggestions that Delaware would reach a different result. The Delaware Supreme Court has opined that:

> One of the most basic tenets of Delaware corporate law is that the board of directors has the ultimate responsibility for managing the business and affairs of a corporation. Section 141(a) requires that any limitation on the board's authority be set out in the certificate of incorporation.[34]

Note that, read literally, this dictum clearly precludes the result reached in *Fleming*.

---

[33] International Broth. of Teamsters General Fund v. Fleming Companies, Inc., 975 P.2d 907 (Okla. 1999).
[34] Quickturn Design Systems, Inc. v. Shapiro, 721 A.2d 1281, 1291 (Del. 1998).

Whether Delaware courts will follow through on that reading of the statute remains unclear. In *General DataComm Industries, Inc. v. State of Wisconsin Investment Board*,[35] Vice Chancellor Strine observed:

[W]hile stockholders have unquestioned power to adopt bylaws covering a broad range of subjects, it is also well established in corporate law that stockholders may not directly manage the business and affairs of the corporation, at least without specific authorization either by statute or in the certificate or articles of incorporation. There is an obvious zone of conflict between these precepts: in at least some respects, attempts by stockholders to adopt bylaws limiting or influencing director authority inevitably offend the notion of management by the board of directors. However, neither the courts, the legislators, the SEC, nor legal scholars have clearly articulated the means of resolving this conflict and determining whether a stockholder-adopted bylaw provision that constrains director managerial authority is legally effective.[36]

Until this conflict is authoritatively resolved, the utility of mandatory bylaw amendments as a vehicle for shareholder activism remains uncertain.

The second broad basis under Rule 14a-8 for excluding a shareholder proposal is stated in Rule 14a-8(i)(8), which provides that a proposal may be excluded if it "relates to an election for membership on the company's board of directors or analogous governing body." Clearly, this rule would allow exclusion of a shareholder proposal nominating a specific individual for election to the board. But what if the proposal relates to changing the corporation's bylaws or articles of incorporation governing director elections?

The issue came to a head when American Federation of State, County & Municipal Employees (AFSCME) submitted to American International Group, Inc. (AIG), a proposal for inclusion in AIG's 2005 annual meeting proxy statement. If passed, the proposal would have amended AIG's bylaws to provide a mechanism for shareholders meeting certain minimum qualifications to nominate candidates for the board of directors that the company would be obliged to include on the proxy card and in the proxy statement. In *AFSCME v. AIG*,[37] the SEC took the position as amicus

---

[35] 731 A.2d 818 (Del. Ch. 1999).
[36] *Id.* at 821 n.2
[37] 462 F.3d 121 (2nd Cir. 2006).

that the proposal properly could be excluded pursuant to Rule 14a-8(i)(8). The Second Circuit, however, held that the rule allows exclusion only of proposals "dealing with an identified board seat in an upcoming election."

On July 25, 2007, the SEC took the unusual step of issuing two contradictory proposals for rulemaking in response to the *AFSCME* decision. If adopted, the so-called Status Quo proposal would constitute an authoritative agency interpretation of the rule under which all shareholder-proposed bylaws concerning director nominations may be excluded. In contrast, if the so-called Access Proposal is adopted, it would amend Rule 14a-8(i)(8) to authorize inclusion of a proposal amending the corporation's bylaws to create a mechanism for shareholders to nominate board candidates if the proposal is submitted by a shareholder (or group of shareholders) that has continuously held more than 5 percent of the company's securities for at least one year and has filed a Schedule 13G containing all required information.

Communication

Some institutional investors prefer quiet, private negotiations with portfolio corporation management. They resort to more adversarial activism techniques, if at all, only if negotiations fail. A well-known study of TIAA-CREF's corporate governance activities, for example, found that between 1992 and 1996 TIAA-CREF was able to reach negotiated agreements with management on governance issues over 95 percent of the time.[38] The study found statistically significant negative abnormal returns when targeted companies agreed to adopt TIAA-CREF's board diversity proposals. Significantly significant positive abnormal returns were found when firms adopted restrictions on the use of blank check preferred stock. Adoption of TIAA-CREF's confidential voting proposals had no statistically significant effects.

Shaming by activists is the opposite approach. As we have seen, gaining some institutional investors have sought to shame directors whose performance the institutions regard as faulty.

---

[38] Willard T. Carleton et al., *The Influence of Institutions on Corporate Governance Through Negotiations: Evidence from TIAA-CREF*, 53 J. Fin. 1335 (1998).

Litigation

The Private Securities Litigation Reform Act of 1995 (PSLRA) included a
so-called lead plaintiff provision designed to counteract the dominance
of lawyers over such suits. The district judge is charged with selecting a
representative plaintiff having a financial stake large enough to encourage
the plaintiff to monitor the conduct of its counsel, as well as the time and
skills to do so effectively. The motivating premise was that monitoring by
such investors would help to ensure that both the bringing and resolving
of securities suits would be done in the interest of investors, rather than
of the lawyers who traditionally had been the de facto party in interest in
these cases. In particular, the provisions were designed to encourage institutional investors to step forward as lead plaintiffs.

Initially, passage of the PSLRA did not significantly change the rate at
which institutional investors served as lead plaintiffs in securities class
actions, but the widely publicized success of three public pension funds as
lead plaintiffs in the Cendant securities fraud litigation is credited with
having encouraged institutions to come forward. By 2006, institutions
served as lead plaintiff in 50 percent of settled securities suits.[39] Importantly,
however, not all classes of institutional investors are equally active. Instead,
union and state and local employee pension funds have been far more
active in litigation than private institutional investors such as insurers,
bank trust departments, or mutual funds.[40]

The viability of litigation as an activism vehicle recently received a
potentially devastating body blow in a Massachusetts Federal District
Court decision. Robert Monks and John Higgins sought to act as lead
plaintiffs in a securities case against Stone & Webster, Inc. Monks is one
of the most prominent shareholder activists. The judge took that factor
into account in denying Monks and Higgins lead plaintiff status:

> Both Higgins and Monks are "shareholder activists" and, as such,
> subject to unique defenses. Specifically, defendants aver, Higgins
> and Monks purchased shares of S&W to "engag[e] in activist strate-
> gies [and] overcome existing corporate governance problems to
> enhance shareholder value." In particular, defendants argue that

---

[39] Cornerstone Research, *Securities Class Action Case Settlements 2006: Review and Analysis*, available at http://securities.stanford.edu/clearinghouse_research.html
[40] *See* Arden Dale, *Pensions Join Class-Action Suits at Faster Pace, Lending Clout*, Wall Street Journal, Jan. 14, 2004.

Higgins and Monks purchased shares of S&W on the theory that the company was poorly managed and that the stock price would likely decline; therefore, they could not have relied on any alleged misstatements. They point to, inter alia, the following facts: (1) Higgins and Monks "had numerous communications with S&W directors and management"; (2) Monks had two friends "[who] were S&W directors, whom he regarded as sources of inside information"; and (3) Monks "published several books . . . which undermine any suggestion by plaintiffs' counsel that Monks[or] Higgins relied on any alleged misstatements by Defendants."

While their status as "shareholder activists" does not, ipso facto, disqualify Higgins and Monks from serving as class representatives, in this case, the record suggests that they may be subject to unique defenses and therefore do not satisfy the "typicality" requirement. Accordingly, I decline to name them class representatives.[41]

The reliance point is particularly interesting. In a misrepresentation case like this one, the fraud on the market (FOTM) theory often permits a presumption of reliance. But that presumption is rebuttable. Although defendants rarely seek to rebut the FOTM presumption with respect to the entire class, because doing so would require a plaintiff-by-plaintiff series of actions, it has become a common way of arguing that proposed lead plaintiffs are not typical of the class and therefore should not be allowed to serve as such. Here, the court draws a logical inference. Higgins and Monks bought into the company precisely to shake things up. They thought the company was on the decline and wanted to bring their activist tools to bear. Logically, they could not have relied on the alleged misrepresentations. They would have bought stock anyway. (Note, by the way, that they therefore also would lose on transaction causation.)

If followed elsewhere, this opinion would be a body blow to the activist community. Indeed, it prompted Robert Monks to observe that:

Over many years of active involvement in the governance of American corporations, I have come to the conclusion . . . that shareholder rights are, in fact, a nullity. It has often been observed that the only meaningful role for an American shareholder is as a plaintiff, particularly in class-action litigation. There is, therefore, profound

---

[41] In re Stone & Webster, No. 00-10874-RWZ, slip op. (D. Mass. Sept. 7, 2007).

irony in the fact that someone characterized as an "activist share-holder" would, by virtue of that designation, be foreclosed from representing a class in securities-fraud suits. The logical and linguistic torture of being excluded from the class—made all the more difficult by the fact that it was gratuitous, given that the court permitted another plaintiff to serve as class representative—simply because I am a "shareholder activist," subject only to the assurance that this status is not an ipso facto disqualifier from serving as a representative, is less painful than the realization that, in the year 2007 in the Commonwealth of Massachusetts, one is literally powerless to have an impact in cases of acknowledged corporate fraud.[42]

Proposals for Expanding the Shareholder Franchise

Seemingly recognizing that current vehicles for activism are problematic, at least from their perspective, proponents of shareholder activism have put forward an ever-growing array of proposals for empowering share-holders. In general, the objects of proposed reforms can be divided into three basic categories: the director nomination process; the mechanics of voting; and expanding the substance of what shareholders may decide by vote.

Reforming the Director Nomination Process

In 2003, the SEC proposed a dramatic shakeup in the process by which corporate directors are elected. The director nomination machinery long has been controlled by the incumbent board of directors. When it is time to elect directors, the incumbent board nominates a slate, which it puts forward on the company's proxy statement. There is no mechanism for a shareholder to put a nominee on the ballot. Instead, a shareholder who wishes to nominate directors is obliged to incur the considerable expense of conducting a proxy contest to elect a slate in opposition to that put

---

[42] Robert A. G. Monks, *Shareholder Rights?*, The Harvard Law School Corporate Governance Blog, October 8, 2007, available at http://blogs.law.harvard.edu/corpgov/ 2007/10/08/shareholder-rights/.

forward by the incumbents. This is the situation the SEC proposed to change.

If adopted, proposed new Rule 14a-11 would permit shareholders, upon the occurrence of certain specified events and subject to various restrictions, to have their nominees placed on the company's proxy statement and ballot. A shareholder-nominated director thus could be elected to the board in a fashion quite similar to the way shareholder-sponsored proposals are now put to a shareholder vote.

As proposed, Rule 14a-11 contemplated a two-step process stretching over two election cycles. Under the rule, a shareholder may place his or her nominee on the corporation's proxy card and statement if one of two triggering events occurs:

1. A shareholder proposal is made under Rule 14a-8 to authorize shareholder nominations, which is then approved by the holders of a majority of the outstanding shares at a meeting of the shareholders; or
2. Shareholders representing at least 35 percent of the votes withhold authority on their proxy cards for their shares to be voted in favor of any director nominated by the incumbent board of directors.

At the next annual meeting of the shareholders at which directors are elected, shareholder nominees would be included in the company's proxy statement and ballot.

Not all shareholders would be entitled to make use of the nomination process, however. Only shareholders satisfying four criteria would have access to the company's proxy materials; namely, a shareholder or group of shareholders who: (1) beneficially own more than 5 percent of the company's voting stock and have held the requisite number of shares continuously for at least two years as of the date of the nomination; (2) state an intent to continue owning the requisite number of securities through the date of the relevant shareholders meeting; (3) are eligible to report their holdings on Schedule 13G rather than Schedule 13D; and (4) have filed a Schedule 13G before their nomination is submitted to the corporation. Because the eligibility requirements for use of Schedule 13G include a disclaimer of intent to seek control of the corporation, the proposed Rule 14a-11 presumably would not become a tool for corporate acquisitions.

As of this writing, proposed Rule 14a-11 neither has been adopted nor withdrawn; instead, it remains in administrative limbo. At many companies, however, shareholders have sought to use Rule 14a-8 to put forward mandatory bylaw amendments that would have much the same effect as the SEC proposal.

As proposed, shareholder access to the nomination process made little sense. The impact of a shareholder right to elect board members on the effectiveness of the board's decision-making processes will be analogous to that of cumulative voting. Granted, some firms might benefit from the presence of skeptical outsider viewpoints. It is well accepted, however, that cumulative voting tends to promote adversarial relations between the majority and the minority representative. The likelihood that cumulative voting results in interpersonal conflict rather than cognitive conflict thus leaves one doubtful as to whether firms actually benefit from minority representation. There will be a reduction in the trust-based relationships that cause horizontal monitoring within the board to provide effective constraints on agency costs. There also likely will be an increase in the use of pre-meeting caucuses and a reduction in information flows to the board.

Proposals to Reform the Mechanics of the Voting Process

Majority voting and confidential voting are longstanding demands of shareholder activists. As we saw above, in most states, majority voting is now available as an option. Because plurality voting remains the statutory default, however, action must be taken on a firm-by-firm basis.

At one time, confidential voting was the first principle listed among the "core corporate governance policies" of the Council of Institutional Investors. Proponents of confidential voting claim that shareholders with conflicts of interest—such as a mutual fund family that offers 401(k) plans to corporate employees—feel constrained to vote with management. If management cannot determine how such shareholders voted, the conflict of interest is abrogated. An empirical study by Roberta Romano, however, found that adoption of confidential voting procedures had no significant impact on voting outcomes. Romano also found that the stock value of firms adopting confidential voting was not significantly affected thereby.[43]

---

[43] Roberta Romano, *Does Confidential Voting Matter?*, 32 J. Legal Stud. 465 (2003).

Many firms have adopted majority voting on a voluntary basis, with the board putting forward appropriate amendments to the articles of incorporation or bylaws. In contrast, firms have generally resisted confidential voting. Where the incumbent board of directors opposes switching from plurality to majority voting or adopting confidential voting, shareholder proponents of doing so will have to rely on Rule 14a-8 to put forward appropriate mandatory bylaw amendments.

Expanding the Substance of Shareholder Voting Rights

In 2007, the House of Representatives passed a bill by Chairman of the House Financial Services Committee Barney Franks that would amend the federal Securities Exchange Act of 1934 to provide shareholders with an advisory vote on executive compensation. A similar bill was introduced in the Senate by Barack Obama, but stalled.

Bebchuk and Fried have proposed allowing shareholders to initiate changes in the corporation's state of incorporation or to amend the articles of incorporation.[44] Bebchuk separately has proposed allowing shareholders, as part of their power to make rules-of-the-game decisions, to adopt charter provisions that would give them power to intervene in some specific business decisions.[45]

Should the Shareholder Franchise Be Expanded?

Let us assume that legal reforms such as those just reviewed in fact could promote institutional investor activism. Would such reforms be desirable? The answer to that question begins with a review of current problems in shareholder voting that undermine the legitimacy of the franchise. I then argue that shareholders have a revealed preference for director primacy. Finally, I argue that the separation of ownership and control has a strong theoretical justification.

---

[44] Lucian Bebchuk & Jesse Fried, *Pay Without Performance: The Unfulfilled Promise of Executive Compensation* 212 (2004).
[45] Lucian Ayre Bebchuk, *The Case for Increasing Shareholder Power*, 118 Harv. L. Rev. 833 (2005).

Pathologies of Voting

If the shareholder franchise really is the "ideological underpinning upon which the legitimacy of directorial power rests,"[46] and shareholder activism is to be encouraged, the first prerequisite for such a regime would be a system of shareholder voting in which one has confidence. In fact, however, the shareholder franchise is rife with serious pathologies. "First, there are pathologies caused by the sheer complexity of the system. Second, there are pathologies caused by a misalignment of the property concepts implicit in the beneficial-owner-as-shareholder paradigm and the property rules that, in fact, govern the voting of shares held by nominees. Third, there are pathologies caused by a misalignment between voting rights and economic interests."[47]

In the first category fall such problems as the fact that, because the system of share ownership is so complex, the beneficial owners of the shares often do not receive the proxy materials. In other cases, votes are cast but not counted. Finally, it is often difficult to verify that votes were properly cast.

The second and third categories are the more troubling ones for our purposes. As a simple example, consider the case of a shareholder who owns one share of stock that he has sold short. The shareholder retains the voting right associated with that share, but now has a direct economic interest adverse to that of other shareholders, since he will profit only if the stock falls. Such a shareholder will be tempted to vote against value-increasing proposals and to vote for value-decreasing ones.[48] The Mylan Laboratories case discussed below is a prime example of this phenomenon in the real world.

A more complex example arises out of the burgeoning market for securities lending. In order to avoid rules on naked short sales, many institutional investors participate in the borrowing and lending of shares. In theory, when shares are lent, the borrower is entitled to vote the shares. In practice, however, the complexity of lending programs means that lenders are often unaware that the shares in question are on loan. Over-voting, in which the same shares are voted twice, is a not uncommon result.

---

[46] Blasius Indus., Inc. v. Atlas Corp., 564 A.2d 651, 659 (Del. Ch. 1988).
[47] Marcel Kahan & Edward B. Rock, *The Hanging Chads of Corporate Voting* (2007), available at http://ssrn.com/abstract=1007065.
[48] Shaun Martin & Frank Partnoy, *Encumbered Shares*, 2005 U. Ill. L. Rev. 775.

These sorts of pathologies are particularly troubling because exploiting them is one of the major profit strategies of most hedge funds.[49] Even were that not the case, however, the infirmities of the shareholder franchise call into serious question the merits of shareholder activism. If we cannot have confidence in the fairness and accuracy of the process of shareholder voting, the case for further shareholder empowerment rests on a foundation of sand.

The Revealed Preferences of Shareholders

Because investors can identify and demand corporate governance terms that serve their interests, it is possible to draw instructive conclusions from observed investor behavior. As Lynn Stout thus observes, "shareholders display a revealed preference for rules that promote director primacy at early stages of a firm's development."[50] It is well established, for example, that the combination of a poison pill and a staggered board of directors is a particularly effective way of preventing shareholders from holding the board of directors to account through the market for corporate control.[51] Yet, almost 60 percent of public corporations now have staggered boards.[52] Even more strikingly, among firms going public, the incidence of staggered boards has increased dramatically (from 34 percent in 1990 to over 70 percent in 2001).[53] Finally, activist shareholders have made little headway in efforts to "de-stagger" the board.[54] If what investors

---

[49] Kahan & Rock, *supra* note 13, at 1070–83.

[50] Lynn A. Stout, *Bad and Not-so-Bad Arguments for Shareholder Primacy*, 73 S. Cal. L. Rev. 1189, 1206 (2002).

[51] Lucian Arye Bebchuk et al., *The Powerful Antitakeover Force of Staggered Boards: Theory, Evidence, and Policy*, 54 Stan. L. Rev. 887, 931 (2002) (combining a staggered board and a poison pill almost doubled the chances of a target corporation remaining independent).

[52] Bebchuk et al., *supra* note 51, at 895. Another published estimate puts the figure even higher, at more than 70 percent of U.S. public corporations. Robin Sidel, *Staggered Terms for Board Members Are Said to Erode Shareholder Value, Not Enhance It*, Wall Street Journal, Apr. 1, 2002, at C2.

[53] Bebchuk et al., *supra* note 51, at 889.

[54] *Id.* at 900. Bebchuk elsewhere argues that shareholder attitudes cannot be inferred from the IPO data, offering as a counterfactual the declining number of attempts by established corporations to amend their articles to allow for a staggered board. Lucian Arye Bebchuk, *The Case Against Board Veto in Corporate Takeovers*, 69 U. Chi. L. Rev. 973, 1017 (2002). As noted, in his article with Coates and Subramanian, Bebchuk showed that almost 60 percent of public corporations now have staggered boards, but he gave no data on the remaining 40 percent. Bebchuk et al., *supra* note 51, at 895. Perhaps the

do matters more than what they say, IPO investors are voting for director primacy with their wallets.

Why Not Shareholder Democracy?

Why might shareholders prefer director to shareholder primacy?[55] First, empowered shareholders may use their newly granted powers to pursue private agendas at odds with those of the firm's shareholders as a whole. Second, shareholder empowerment threatens the foundation of modern corporate governance; namely, the separation of ownership and control.

The Risk of Private Rent Seeking

The interests of large and small investors often differ. For example, large holders with substantial decision-making influence will be tempted to use their position to self-deal; i.e., to take a non-pro rata share of the firms assets and earnings. As management becomes more beholden to the interests of such large shareholders, moreover, management may become less concerned with the welfare of smaller investors.

With respect to union and public pension fund sponsorship of shareholder proposals under existing law, for example, Roberta Romano observes that:

> It is quite probable that private benefits accrue to some investors from sponsoring at least some shareholder proposals. The disparity in identity of sponsors—the predominance of public and union funds, which, in contrast to private sector funds, are not in competition

---

remaining public corporations lacking a staggered board do not need one as a takeover defense, because they have other strong takeover defenses in place (such as the existence of a friendly controlling shareholder or dual class stock). Consequently, contrary to Bebchuk's claim, the declining number of management-initiated staggered board proposals may be attributable to factors other than shareholder opposition to director primacy.

[55] Even if we assume that shareholder control has agency cost-reducing benefits, those benefits may come at too high a social cost. There is evidence, for example, that bank control of the securities markets has harmed Japanese and German economies by impeding the development of new businesses. *See generally* Bernard S. Black & Ronald J. Gilson, *Venture Capital and the Structure of Capital Markets: Banks Versus Stock Markets*, 47 J. Fin. Econ. 243 (1998); Curtis J. Milhaupt, *The Market for Innovation in the United States and Japan: Venture Capital and the Comparative Corporate Governance Debate*, 91 Nw. U. L. Rev. 865 (1997). Increased institutionalization of the capital markets thus might impede the active venture capital market that helps drive the U.S. economy.

for investor dollars—is strongly suggestive of their presence. Examples of potential benefits which would be disproportionately of interest to proposal sponsors are progress on labor rights desired by union fund managers and enhanced political reputations for public pension fund managers, as well as advancements in personal employment. . . . Because such career concerns—enhancement of political reputations or subsequent employment opportunities—do not provide a commensurate benefit to private fund managers, we do not find them engaging in investor activism.[56]

This is not just academic speculation. The pension fund of the union representing Safeway workers, for example, used its position as a Safeway shareholder in an attempt to oust directors who had stood up to the union in collective bargaining negotiations.[57] Nor is this an isolated example. Union pension funds tried to remove directors or top managers, or otherwise affect corporate policy, at over 200 corporations in 2004 alone.[58] Union pension funds reportedly have also tried using shareholder proposals to obtain employee benefits they couldn't get through bargaining.[59]

Public employee pension funds are vulnerable to being used as a vehicle for advancing political/social goals of the fund trustees that are unrelated to shareholder interests generally. Activism by CalPERS during the run up to the 2006 California gubernatorial election, for example, reportedly was "fueled partly by the political ambitions of Phil Angelides, California's state treasurer and a CalPERS board member," who ran for governor of California in 2006.[60] In effect, Angelides used the retirement savings of California's public employees to further his own political ends.

---

[56] Roberta Romano, *Less Is More: Making Shareholder Activism a Valued Mechanism of Corporate Governance*, 18 Yale J. Reg. 174, 231–32 (2001). None of this is to deny, of course, that union and state and local pension funds also often have interests that converge with those of investors generally. *See* Stewart J. Schwab & Randall S. Thomas, *Realigning Corporate Governance: Shareholder Activism by Labor Unions*, 96 Mich. L. Rev. 1020, 1079–80 (1998).

[57] Iman Anabtawi, *Some Skepticism About Increasing Shareholder Power*, UCLA L. Rev. 561 (2006).

[58] Stephen M. Bainbridge, *Flanigan on Union Pension Fund Activism*, available at http://www.professorbainbridge.com/2004/04/flanigan_on_uni.html.

[59] *Id.*

[60] Stephen M. Bainbridge, *Pension Funds Play Politics*, Tech Central Station, April 21, 2004, available at http://www.techcentralstation.com/042104G.html.

As Stout explains, however, the problem extends beyond union and public pension funds:

> [B]y making it easier for large shareholders in public firms to threaten directors, a more effective shareholder franchise might increase the risk of inter-shareholder "rent-seeking" in public companies.
>
> According to Iman Anabtawi, shareholders in public firms have conflicts of interest that can give rise to opportunistic behavior. An especially troubling situation involves the investor who takes a position in a stock and uses his voting power to push for business strategies that increase the value of another security the investor also holds. Hedge fund Perry Capital, for example, recently acquired a block of Mylan Laboratories common stock while simultaneously entering a derivatives contract with a brokerage firm that allowed Perry to keep the Mylan votes while hedging away its economic interest in the stock. Perry then used its position as a large Mylan shareholder to pressure Mylan's board to acquire another company, King Pharmaceuticals, at a hefty premium over market price. Why would Perry want Mylan to overpay for King? Because Perry also held a large block of King stock—and had not hedged away its economic interest in King.
>
> The case of Perry Capital illustrates the danger inherent in changing the rules of corporate law in a way that gives opportunistic shareholders in public companies greater leverage over boards.[61]

Bebchuk dismisses such concerns as unwarranted, claiming that "a shareholder-initiated proposal for a change that would likely be value-decreasing would be highly unlikely to obtain majority support" and that a shareholder therefore could not use such a proposal to "blackmail management."[62] In other work, however, Bebchuk has claimed that because members of the board of directors own such a small percentage of the stock of the company they will agree to value-reducing executive pay packages because the private benefits they reap from remaining in control exceed the lost value of their stock.[63] I'm skeptical of the merits of that argument, but if it is true of executive compensation, wouldn't it also be

---

[61] Stout, *supra* note 26, at 44.
[62] Bebchuk, *supra* note 45, at 885.
[63] Bebchuk & Fried, *supra* note 44, at 34–35.

true of value-decreasing shareholder proposals? Indeed, he claims that empowering shareholders will produce "benefits in large part by influencing management's behavior rather than by leading to actual interventions."[64]

Granted, Bebchuk seemingly anticipates this argument by suggesting that these indirect benefits accrue only when managers expect a proposal to pass a shareholder vote.[65] Accordingly, he argues that the majority vote rule ensures that managers will not be subject to blackmail by a rent-seeking proposal advanced by an institution seeking private benefits because management knows such a proposal will not pass. There are several reasons, however, to believe that Bebchuk overestimates the extent to which the majority vote requirement insulates the board and management from being blackmailed.

In the first place, people who are risk-averse by definition will seek to avoid a loss even if the event in question has a positive expected value. As Bebchuk puts it here, managers "prefer not to lose votes" and, as he has put it elsewhere, "managers are risk-averse."[66] Accordingly, managers may still give in to blackmail even where an objective analysis suggests the proposal has little chance of passage.

Second, there are several situations in which a rent-seeking proposal plausibly could threaten to achieve majority support. The rent-seeking institution might propose a value-increasing change, for example, which it will agree to drop in exchange for some private benefit.[67] Bebchuk concedes this possibility, but also dismisses it on grounds that "a blackmail argument can be made not only against increasing shareholders' power, but also against maintaining the power that shareholders currently have," which no one proposes reducing on this account.[68] It's not clear, however, why the absence of proposals to further disempower shareholders necessarily provides a case for granting them extensive new powers. His argument also seems inconsistent with his claim elsewhere in the article that it is "not the case" that the "shareholder veto can ensure [that] decisions

---

[64] Bebchuk, *supra* note 45, at 878.
[65] *Id.*
[66] Lucian Arye Bebchuk, *Federalism and the Corporation: The Desirable Limits on State Competition in Corporate Law*, 105 Harv. L. Rev. 1435, 1464 n.102 (1992).
[67] *See* Schwab & Thomas, *supra* note 56, at 1029 (describing a case in which the Teamsters "seemed to use shareholder pressure," including to a proposal that the board of directors redeem the company's poison pill, to "further traditional organizing and collective bargaining goals").
[68] Bebchuk, *supra* note 45, at 885.

regarding basic governance arrangements will be made in the interests of shareholders."[69]

Alternatively, an institution seeking private benefits could bundle a value-increasing proposal and a value-decreasing proposal in hopes of increasing the prospects of passage.[70] The institution also might offer side payments to other institutions.[71] In lieu of side payments, the institution might seek to assemble a coalition of other institutions that would also receive private benefits, which is perhaps the most likely scenario in which an investor coalition would coalesce.

Accordingly, the majority vote requirement is an inadequate constraint on rent seeking by union and public pension funds (or other institutional investors, such as hedge funds, for that matter). To be sure, as with any other agency cost, the risk that management will be willing to pay private benefits to an institutional investor is a necessary consequence of vesting discretionary authority in the board and the officers. It does not compel the conclusion that we ought to limit the board's power. It does, however, suggest that we ought not give investors even greater leverage to extract such benefits by further empowering them.[72]

---

[69] *Id.* at 862.

[70] Note that Bebchuk accuses management of using precisely this technique to adopt proposals it favors. Bebchuk, *supra* note 45, at 864–65.

[71] Anabtawi, *supra* note 57.

[72] The analysis to this point suggests that the costs of institutional investor activism likely outweigh any benefits such activism may confer with respect to redressing the principal-agent problem. Even if one assumes that the cost-benefit analysis comes out the other way around, however, it should be noted that institutional investor activism does not solve the principal-agent problem but rather merely changes its locus.
The vast majority of large institutional investors manage the pooled savings of small individual investors. From a governance perspective, there is little to distinguish such institutions from corporations. The holders of investment company shares, for example, have no more control over the election of company trustees than they do over the election of corporate directors. Accordingly, fund shareholders exhibit the same rational apathy as corporate shareholders. Kathryn McGrath, a former SEC mutual fund regulator, observes: "A lot of shareholders take ye olde proxy and throw it in the trash." Karen Blumental, *Fidelity Sets Vote on Scope of Investments*, Wall Street Journal, Dec. 8, 1994, at C1, C18. The proxy system thus "costs shareholders money for rights they don't seem interested in exercising." *Id.* Indeed, "Ms. McGrath concedes that she herself often tosses a proxy for a personal investment onto a 'to-do pile' where 'I don't get around to reading it, or when I do, the deadline has passed.'" *Id.* Nor do the holders of such shares have any greater access to information about their holdings, or any greater ability to monitor those who manage their holdings, than do corporate shareholders. Worse yet, although an individual investor can always abide by the Wall Street Rule with respect to corporate stock, he cannot do so with respect to such investments as an involuntary, contributory pension plan.

The Case for Preserving the Board of Directors' Authority

Let us make the heroic assumption, however, that holders of large stock blocks are entirely selfless. Shareholder activism would still be undesirable even if the separation of ownership and control mandated by U.S. law had substantial efficiency benefits. As we have seen, vesting decision-making authority in a centralized entity distinct from the shareholders—i.e., the board—is what makes the large public corporation feasible. The core argument against the control claims of shareholder primacy thus should be readily apparent. Put simply, large-scale shareholder involvement in corporate decision making would disrupt the very mechanism that makes the Berle-Means corporation practicable; namely, the centralization of essentially non-reviewable decision-making authority in the board of directors.

As we have also seen, a complete theory of the firm requires one to balance the virtues of discretion against the need to require that discretion be used responsibly. We have emphasized that neither the power of fiat nor accountability for misuses of that power can be ignored. Both are core values that are essential to the survival of a business organization. Unfortunately, however, we've also seen that the power to hold to account differs only in degree and not in kind from the power to decide and, accordingly, one cannot have more of one without also having less of the other.

The principal argument against shareholder activism thus follows inexorably from the analysis in the preceding chapters. The chief economic virtue of the public corporation is not that it permits the aggregation of large capital pools, but rather that it provides a hierarchical decision-making structure well-suited to the problem of operating a large business enterprise with numerous employees, managers, shareholders, creditors, and other inputs. In such a firm, someone must be in charge: "Under conditions of widely dispersed information and the need for speed in decisions, authoritative control at the tactical level is essential

---

For beneficiaries of union and state and local government employee pension funds, the problem is particularly pronounced. As we have seen, those who manage such funds may often put their personal or political agendas ahead of the interests of the fund's beneficiaries. Accordingly, it is not particularly surprising that pension funds subject to direct political control tend to have poor financial results. Roberta Romano, *Public Pension Fund Activism in Corporate Governance Reconsidered*, 93 Colum. L. Rev. 795, 825 (1993).

for success."[73] While some argue that shareholder activism "differs, at least in form, from completely *shifting* authority from managers to" investors,[74] it is in fact a difference in form only. Shareholder activism necessarily contemplates that institutions will review management decisions, step in when management performance falters, and exercise voting control to effect a change in policy or personnel. For the reasons identified above, giving investors this power of review differs little from giving them the power to make management decisions in the first place. Even though investors probably would not micromanage portfolio corporations, vesting them with the power to review board decisions inevitably shifts some portion of the board's authority to them. This remains true even if only major decisions of A are reviewed by B.

If the foregoing analysis has explanatory power, it might fairly be asked, why do we observe any restrictions on the powers of corporate takeovers or any prospect for them to be ousted in a takeover or proxy contest? Put another way, why do we observe any right for shareholders to vote?

In the purest form of an authority-based decision-making structure, all decisions in fact would be made by a single, central body—here, the board of directors. If authority were corporate law's sole value, shareholders thus in fact likely would have no voice in corporate decision making. As we have seen, however, authority is not corporate law's only value, because we need some mechanism for ensuring director accountability with respect to the shareholders' contractual right requiring the directors to use shareholder wealth maximization as their principal decision-making norm. Like many intra-corporate contracts, the shareholder wealth maximization norm does not lend itself to judicial enforcement except in especially provocative situations. Instead, it is enforced indirectly through a complex and varied set of extrajudicial accountability mechanisms, of which shareholder voting is just one.

Recall that, to "maintain the value of authority," however, accountability mechanisms generally should "take the form of what is termed 'management by exception,' in which authority and its decisions are reviewed only when performance is sufficiently degraded from expectations."[75]

---

[73] *Id.* at 69.

[74] Mark J. Roe, *Strong Managers, Weak Owners: The Political Roots of American Corporate Finance* 184 (1994) (emphasis in original).

[75] Kenneth J. Arrow, *The Limits of Organization* 78 (1974).

Like all accountability mechanisms, shareholder voting thus must be constrained in order to preserve the value of authority.

Properly understood, shareholder voting thus is not an integral aspect of the corporate decision-making structure, but rather an accountability device of last resort to be used sparingly, at best. Indeed, as Robert Clark observes, the proper way in which shareholder voting rights are used to hold corporate directors and officers accountable is not through the exercise of individual voting decisions but rather collectively in the context of a takeover.[76] Because shares are freely transferable, a bidder who believes the firm is being run poorly can profit by offering to buy a controlling block of stock at a premium over market and subsequently displacing the incumbent managers, which presumably will result in an increase in firm value exceeding the premium the bidder paid for control. Hence, just as one might predict based on Arrow's analysis, shareholder voting properly comes into play as an accountability only "when [management] performance is sufficiently degraded from expectations" to make a takeover fight worth waging.

In sum, given the significant virtues of discretion, one ought not lightly interfere with management or the board's decision-making authority in the name of accountability. Indeed, the claim should be put even more strongly: Preservation of managerial discretion should always be default presumption. Because the separation of ownership and control mandated by U.S. corporate law has precisely that effect, by constraining shareholders both from reviewing most board decisions and substituting their judgment for that of the board, director primacy has a strong justification.

---

[76] Robert C. Clark, *Corporation Law* 95 (1986).

INDEX